EDITING

R. Thomas Berner

Pennsylvania State University
School of Journalism

Holt, Rinehart and Winston
New York   Chicago   San Francisco   Philadelphia
Montreal   Toronto   London   Sydney
Tokyo   Mexico City   Rio de Janeiro   Madrid

To the late Gordon K. Pfeil,
my first mentor in
journalism and the person
who introduced me to
Caslon type.

Library of Congress Cataloging in Publication Data
Berner, R. Thomas.
    Editing.

    Includes index.
    1. Journalism—Editing. I. Title.
PN4778.B4   070.4′1   82-915

ISBN 0-03-057469-2   AACR2

Copyright © 1982 by CBS College Publishing
Address correspondence to:
383 Madison Avenue
New York, N.Y. 10017

CBS COLLEGE PUBLISHING
Holt, Rinehart and Winston
The Dryden Press
Saunders College Publishing

ii

Preface

These are exciting times in journalism. In less than a decade, the last newspaper I worked for went from publishing with a method invented nearly a century ago to one almost unheard of in 1970—the video display terminal and related printing equipment. The people who guided me in my early days of journalism lived and died with one method. Beginners in journalism today face the prospect of converting not only from one printing method to another but from one mass delivery system to one of tailor-made products delivered via satellite over a video screen in the home.

How quickly that will happen on a mass scale remains to be seen, but this book anticipates the revolution still to come in journalism. The concepts laid down in this book anticipate still developing technology that is sure to change journalism as we know it today.

But the thrust of the book remains the concepts and principles that make up the whole of good editing and design. A computer will assuredly make the job easier, but a human will have to know what the job is. A computer will tell a headline writer that a headline is short or long, but the same computer cannot judge whether the headline fulfills its main purpose—telling the story. A computer will collapse the laborious chore of designing and building a newspaper page into a brief one-person operation, but it cannot decide which design will attract readers or which content best serves those same readers. The values behind those jobs surface throughout this book, but they have been combined with the technology to ensure the book's readers that the equipment does not make the job, but that the quality of the job comes from the person using the equipment.

The use of finely engineered and computerized equipment may frighten people educated in the arts and humanities as they find themselves seemingly engaged more in formatting stories than editing them. If that becomes a problem, some newspapers will undoubtedly create a new position in the newsroom, that of editorial systems manager. The manager would give all stories a final look to ensure they are correctly formatted.

Technologically, this book might be out of date by the time it is published. When I began this book, pagination systems seemed a decade away. Now I'm not so sure. They may be in mass use tomorrow. But whether a newspaper editor designs a page on a computer or a blank piece of paper, the concepts remain the same. Thus, the readers of this book may be startled by the dichotomy—the computerized approach to editing and the pencil approach to design. But the readers should understand that a computer and a pencil are the same, albeit at different levels. They are both tools. The creative source they both need to function well is a human brain.

In addition to confronting the technology, journalists must also consider other ramifications. Already publishers and journalists have argued over additional compensation for stories used in a printed newspaper and a companion electronic newspaper. For the moment, the solution seems the same as the one in force at newspapers that charge anyone for reprint rights—share the money with the writer. The issue might go much deeper, though, and I can imagine—as farfetched as it might sound today—the reporter writing only those stories that offer the most financial return. Will the First Amendment or the marketplace win out? Stay tuned.

A memorandum soliciting applicants for the editing internship program of The Newspaper Fund Inc. begins: "The need for newspaper copy editors is greater than ever." Truth to tell, the need for copy editors in any medium is greater than ever. Copy editing positions are no longer graveyards for worn-out journalists; college graduates are learning they can step from the classroom to the copy desk without paying any dues in the reporting trenches.

One of the wonderful things about copy editing skills is their transferability. If a person can create a clear sentence in a newspaper, that same person can do the same for a television or radio station, for a magazine or for an advertising agency. Each medium may have different technology and different goals (inform, entertain, sell), but each must first communicate, and words play a large part in the transaction. The message is all important and it is the copy editor who sees to it that the message is clear to others.

Even though the emphasis in this book is on newspaper copy editing, the reader should understand that the skills and concepts explained within are applicable in many jobs. Some of my former students do not work for newspapers, but they still edit for a living and they're quite happy. A good background in journalism prepares a person for a spectrum of opportunities uncommon to many other disciplines.

I've tried to write a book that is both comprehensive and brief, a contradiction that has resulted in little history and few details in some areas. I have not written a history of type or of printing. Both are interesting, but not central to this book's purpose.

In Chapter 10 I talk about research results without specifying which study and when. My goal was not to detail every readership survey that has been done, but to show that readership surveys are a useful tool for editors. I synthesized the results of many readership surveys. One of the problems in detailing the many surveys is that often they contradict each other. In one, readers say they favor sports news; in another, sports news ranks low. According to a colleague and friend, Professor John S. Nichols, who read Chapter 10 in manuscript, until the people who design readership surveys write perfect questions, no editor should stake the newspaper's future on the results of one survey. Perhaps that is the major point a reader should derive from Chapter 10.

In other places throughout I discuss concepts as well as skills. Copy editing is an art not a science, and what the beginner needs is the conceptual framework as well as an understanding of the basics. I have long argued with students who want courses in sports reporting, consumer reporting and court reporting that reporting is reporting is reporting and that once learned conceptually can be applied to any subject. The same is true of editing.

Occasionally I use the word "sophisticated" to refer to an advanced newspaper computer system, one that can perform a variety of work more primitive and inexpensive systems cannot. Wilson L. Barto, the city editor of *The Trentonian* in Trenton, New Jersey, puts "sophisticated" into context with this anecdote:

In the early 1970s the publisher and editor of the *Trenton Times*, James Kerney, was listening to a salesman make his pitch to get the *Times* to purchase the computer system he was selling. Several times the salesman referred to his system as "sophisticated" and each time Kerney followed with "complicated." The exchange continued until the exasperated publisher finally said: "Young man, I'm sophisticated; that's complicated."

You have been warned.

Many people helped write this book. Some are credited throughout, their contributions acknowledged in photo or illustration credits or citations within the text. One such cited person deserves special acknowledgement. That is Don Black of the Salem, Oregon, *Statesman-Journal.* Don and I first met as photographer and city editor in the late 1960s and forged a professional and personal relationship that has not waned through the years or despite the miles now separating us. It is Don who taught me to see photojournalistically, and I think I have finally made the first grade. If this book's chapter on photojournalism makes the photographer's mission clear to "word" people, that is a credit to Don. If the chapter does not succeed, blame me.

Two others contributed immensely, sometimes in ways not always easy to categorize. One is H. Eugene Goodwin, with whom I share the pleasure of teaching copy editing and newspaper design. He is an open-minded colleague who has tolerated my experimentation even when he knew it was doomed. The other is Gerry Lynn Hamilton, whom I had the pleasure of sharing a copy desk with many years ago. Today Gerry is the adviser to the student daily at Penn State where he has overseen the installation of a VDT system (on which I wrote this book). He helped me with many aspects of the book but especially with the electronic ones.

Jerry Schwartz and Mike Shanahan, both reporters for the Associated Press, provided insights not even a former city editor has. They helped me appreciate how the wire services operate and dispelled a few myths that were about to see print.

Professor Nichols not only helped me understand the strengths and weaknesses of readership surveys but through his speciality of international mass communication and his belief that we live in a world of interdependent nations he has positively influenced my attitude toward international news.

Some other people in journalism education who helped me are the following professors who read this book when it was an uncertain manuscript: Ralph L. Holsinger, School of Journalism, Indiana University; Richard R. Cole, School of Journalism, University of North Carolina—Chapel Hill; Thomas Simonet, Department of Journalism, Rider College; Edward D. Yates, College of Journalism, University of Florida. I appreciate their comments and I hope they recognize their valuable contributions throughout.

But despite the help, all errors are mine.

R. Thomas Berner
January 1982

Contents

CHAPTER FIVE   Language Skills for the Desk   89

CHAPTER SIX   Headlines   107

CHAPTER ONE

The Electronic Newsroom

Evolution and Revolution

Once upon a time an editor in a medium-sized newspaper, needing to get a story set in type, arose from her desk and walked 35 feet to a room inhabited by large, noisy machines that printers used to set type. She handed the copy to the foreman of the room (called "the shop") who in turn assigned the story to one of his typesetter operators. At five flawed lines a minute, the operator slowly set the story in type. The operator produced the story in 22 minutes. It contained typographical errors that had to be fixed later—providing a proofreader caught them.

The next day the newspaper finished its changeover to electronic editing and typesetting equipment, putting the Linotype (as the typesetting equipment was popularly known) and its operator out of work and completing a revolution that began at the close of World War II. The editor now edits stories on a television screen attached to a typewriter-like keyboard (see Figure 1.1). She writes the headline on the same screen, and then, by pushing a certain key on the keyboard of her video display terminal, she orders the story and headline set in type (at 1,000 lines a minute), and in seconds, the story and headline appear machine-error free and ready to be pasted onto a make-up grid.

Countless anecdotes could be served up to demonstrate how rapidly the mechanical tasks of publishing a newspaper have changed since the

Figure 1.1 A video display terminal used in newspapers for writing and editing. The cursor appears near the lower right-hand side of the screen in this photograph. (R. Thomas Berner photograph)

dawn of the computer age, but all would come down to one word—speed. Suddenly (or so it seems) it doesn't take as long to produce a newspaper. A reporter still takes a certain amount of time to write a story and an editor still takes a certain amount of time to edit the story, write a headline for it and position it on the page, but even those processes have been subtly speeded up by electronic editing equipment. Meanwhile, the gain in speed from the editor's desk to finished type must be measured by the speed of light. A laborious mechanical process has yielded to the electronic age.

A computer can do anything it's programmed to do. Reuters reports that some Benedictine monks in Belgium have programmed a computer with the Bible in five languages. Reuters correspondent Paul Eedle called it "an ambitious project to make high technology serve God."

In the secular world, reporters for the Providence, Rhode Island, *Journal-Bulletin* relied on portable electronic equipment to cover the visit of Pope John Paul II to Boston in 1979. In the pre-electronic age, reporters had to write their stories on portable typewriters clumsily perched on their knees or dictate a story over a telephone. The *Journal-Bulletin* reporters of the electronic era carried portable video display terminals on which they wrote their stories and then sent them the 50 miles from Boston to Providence over telephone lines to waiting editors' video display terminals in mere minutes. The gain in time between old and new allowed the reporters to get their stories to Providence in time for the first edition.

Although less dramatic, *Journal-Bulletin* reporters and photographers readily kept in touch with each other over walkie-talkies. In another time, reporters would have used inconvenient telephones or, worse still, remained out of touch with each other in a classic right-hand-not-knowing-what-the-left-hand-is-doing case. The same technology that produced video display terminals and their junior traveling units also made walkie-talkies smaller and better.

A year before the pope's visit a small plane crashed into a jetliner over San Diego little more than an hour before the first-edition deadline for the San Diego *Evening Tribune*. More than 40 staff members went to work immediately and put together a Pulitzer prize-winning package that delayed the first edition for only 10 minutes. The editor had expected a delay three or four times longer. The editor credited the *Tribune's* electronic system for making the process so fast. He credited the people on his staff for winning the Pulitzer prize.

Portable video display terminals show up everywhere, although they first proved their mettle in sporting events. *Philadelphia Inquirer* sports columnist Bill Lyon has only two hours after a Saturday afternoon college football game in Central Pennsylvania to file a game story and a column to make the edition the *Inquirer* wants to sell in Central Pennsylvania. The edition gets trucked to Central Pennsylvania in four hours; Lyon's story and column—written on a portable video display terminal—travel a similar distance in minutes.

The aforementioned *Tribune* has placed portable terminals in its bureaus around San Diego County as well as providing them to sportswriters and police and court reporters. No more running back to any office to write a story, no more tangling with traffic, no more dictating over a telephone. A reporter with a portable terminal is a traveling bureau that can move around a beat unfettered by the need to get back to an office to write. A telephone provides the link from the portable bureau to the main office and its computer. Newsrooms will never be the same.

In essence, the introduction of VDTs (as video display terminals are called) has turned the typesetting duties performed by printers over to reporters and editors. That has meant fewer printers at a newspaper but more editors who find themselves as the only check on a story. (Printers were reliable back-up editors.) Because the computer will have typeset whatever the editor allows on the screen, editors function as proofreaders, another position disappearing from newsrooms. The greater responsibility should translate into higher wages since the reporters and editors are now performing other tasks. The higher wages, unfortunately, haven't always come with the increased responsibilities.

The storage capacity of a computer (see Figure 1.2) provides newspapers with a variety of opportunities to publish a more personal and local newspaper. Newspapers have long published zoned editions, but now that the newspapers are freed of the pokiness of the Linotype age, they can divide their product into more zones—from parts of a county to neighborhoods. Obviously, a page or a section devoted to one neighborhood will carry more detailed news than would the same section devoted to a larger area. It's not impractical to store a lot of information on a

Figure 1.2 The workhorse of any modern newspaper is a computer to which video display terminals and printing equipment are connected. (R. Thomas Berner photograph)

computer with its almost infinite storage space. The speed of the equipment, of course, contributes significantly to the growth in zoned editions because it has made them easier to produce quickly.

The storage capacity of a computer allows a newspaper editor to use a story in one zoned edition, withhold it from a second, but reuse it in a third with a different headline and in a different format (such as a different type size and width). Doing the same thing in the past would have taken more time than it was worth. One college daily stores its local stories for reuse in a weekly newspaper sold by mail to alumni. Even the mailing lists are kept in a computer—in zip code order.

Another tremendous advantage of the storage capacity is the library service it can offer a newspaper. Forget the bound editions of the paper or the yellowing and dog-eared clips in a file; the modern reporter researches an issue by getting information from the electronic library, which is available through the keyboard of the reporter's VDT. Depending on the sophistication of the system, the reporter can find information through various means. One of the best allows the reporter to command the computer to produce all stories mentioning, say, "rezoning" within the past year. In that way, the reporter gets to read stories from other beats and obtains a broader picture. Less sophisticated systems require more searching time but are nevertheless faster than a reporter turning page after page of old newspapers. The computer not only speeds up the search time, it does the searching too.

The library function goes beyond the newsroom, for it turns the newspaper into a holder of information that can be sold and resold to anyone who wants it. Newspapers, in other words, are extending their short shelf life by increasing the availability and accessibility of their content. The daily newspaper of old satisfied readers for a short time and then became wrapping for fish or covering for the bottom of a bird cage.

That still happens in the electronic age, but the information on the printed page can now be stored for later "accessing" (to use a computer age word) for a fee.

Chief among the first to recognize the long-range potential of usually short-range news material is *The New York Times*, which created The New York Times Information Service Inc. That service allows subscribers to retrieve information from a computer storage base. The users of such a service are not only other newspapers but corporations and libraries that want the information easily available but do not have the time or space to gather and store it themselves.

In addition, The Associated Press joined with the *Times* to produce the Associated Press Political Databank, used by subscribers in 1980 to keep up with the presidential campaign. Daily the AP updated the stored information to provide subscribers with current facts on the candidates, issues, strategies and changes. The service also provided background information. All of the information went to subscribers on high-speed wires, making it available in seconds. Thus, a political writer with a portable terminal in Neola, Kansas, could receive current and detailed information on the presidential race merely by coupling the portable terminal to a telephone (easily done) and dialing the correct telephone number and talking to the computer. Other news services and newspapers have followed suit.

The implications go far beyond the corporation, library or newspaper needing information. Given that many individuals in the United States have personal computers and terminals, what is to stop a college professor in Laramie, Wyoming, from purchasing access to an information computer at *The New York Times* or the University of North Carolina and retrieving information on rural poverty? Nothing. The technology already allows for that. As costs go down, more people will buy home computers. The expense after that will be for the supplier's computer time and the user's long-distance telephone calls or satellite time.

Some newspaper watchers suggest that what has just been described foreshadows the death of the printed page. Why buy a newspaper that is susceptible to late delivery, to getting blown off your porch on a windy day, or to getting soaked while the carrier delivers during a rainstorm when your newspaper can appear story by story on a television screen? Perhaps newspapers will disappear. Other people contend that the average reader will not want to spend time sitting at a computer terminal to select and read that day's news. After all, if the average reader gives a newspaper no more than 20 minutes, why would a video substitute fare better? Theoretically, it should fare worse. The beauty of the newspaper as we know it is that it provides news pre-selected by editors who try to publish what they believe readers want. They separate the wheat from the chaff—to use a newsroom metaphor. A video "newspaper," on the other hand, would offer everything, and the reader/viewer would have to select what to read and what to ignore. In other words, the modern newspaper also does 90 percent of the reader's work.

Secondly, because of the way a modern newspaper is designed, the reader knows some stories are more important than others and will ignore some stories because of their small headline size or low placement on a page. The video screen treats coups and tea parties alike typographically; not much to distinguish one from the other.

These problems can be overcome, but that still leaves the one enduring quality of a newspaper—the printed page. The emphasis on literacy has ennobled the printed page. It contains detailed information in black and white; it is there tonight, tomorrow and next year. It can be consulted. It can be kept on a shelf; it can be stored in a family album. An account of someone's wedding looks better in a newspaper, clustered as it is among other wedding stories, than it would as a single item on a computer printout. A family album of computer printouts lacks the command presence of the printed page.

Someday, of course, we may buy all of our books via a computer terminal, and we may do all of our shopping the same way. And, alas, we may receive our news that way too. But for the moment, it boggles the mind to envision someone sitting at great length in front of any screen in order to obtain the kind of depth information a newspaper provides.

Photographers have also benefitted from the electronic changes. The wire services have the ability to improve the quality of a photograph through computer enhancement, a process that speeds cropping and enlarging, makes those procedures more precise and removes them from the confines of a darkroom to a television screen. Computer-enhanced photographs are nothing new; they are a product of a space age that propelled camera-bearing satellites to the ends of the universe. Those spacecraft transmitted to earth photographs of the distant planets; the weak images were fed through a computer, which turned them into photographs.

Still developing is the camera that sends the photographic image to a computer via the telephone or satellite, thus allowing the editor in the main office to select the photographs. Missing from the process are film and the chemicals needed for processing. Electronic photography eliminates time-consuming mechanical processes from the photographic procedure and offers more time for a human brain to use creativity in taking and processing photographs.

The computer does the work for the human, but the human decides what work has to be done. One newspaper has programmed its computer to quickly figure batting averages, at a great savings in time for the sports department. Another newspaper's computer alphabetizes long lists of sports scores, allowing readers to find their favorite team whether it won or lost. If Nebraska loses to Florida State, 21–10, the score will be found under *Nebraska 10, Florida State 21* and under *Florida State 21, Nebraska 10.* For casual fans who might have forgotten whom their favorite team played over the weekend, finding the score is easy.

The right computer married to the right printer can create just about anything. Computing batting averages and alphabetizing a weekend's worth of scores from athletic events are first-grade functions compared to the advanced graphic elements a good system can produce through human input. A graphic journalist needing a three-dimensional map showing population distribution in the United States no longer spends laborious hours over a drawing pad; the journalist can speedily and simply draw the map on a VDT screen the way automobile engineers, for example, design automobiles on a computer. Such a system provides the newsroom with opportunities to tell stories more graphically even when up against a very tight deadline (See Figure 1.3). Putting together a breaking story of words, photographs and other graphics has become practical because of the computer.

The computer also has non-news functions. Advertising departments are able to file classified ads on a computer, make up ads on a video display terminal and run credit checks on customers. One newspaper has programmed a floppy disc table-model computer to offer five options for paper size based on the number of advertisements sold for

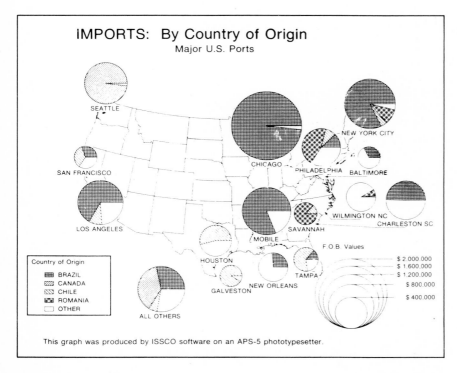

Figure 1.3 Once the values were given to a computer, this graph showing imports to the United States by country of origin was generated in a few minutes. (Courtesy of Roger F. Fidler, corporate design consultant, Knight-Ridder Newspapers Inc.)

that day. The computer also tells the users how much printing costs will increase if that day's newspaper size is increased. Hours of calculation are done instantaneously, leaving it then up to the editor and business manager to pick the appropriate paper size. In the circulation department, the manager keeps a close watch on all newspaper routes through a computer file that has replaced clumsy card indexes. The computer revolution has bypassed no department in the newspaper.

Tools to an End

The usual cry raised against technological change is that it dehumanizes any system. "Machines are replacing people," the doom sayers warn; "people don't count any more." The truth is, the electronic changes in newspapers have hurt some people, primarily printers who have lost their jobs to machines that do the printers' work better, faster, cheaper and without going on strike. Many publishers, however, did not fire printers made antiquated by computers, but instead trained them for other work or offered them large financial settlements to retire.

By the same token, some in the newsroom and the darkroom complain that the computer hinders their creativity and replaces their thought process. That is nonsense. For example, when manufacturers developed cameras that automatically determine lens speed and aperture size, good photographers realized that the camera's so-called brain was not replacing their brain but was taking over mechanical functions. Photographers still control the creative aspect of the photograph—its substance and content.

The newsroom computer has not changed the fact that humans must gather, write, edit, evaluate and package news for other humans. The editor who pushes a button on a VDT and removes a word from a story is no different from the editor in a non-electronic newsroom who does the same thing with a pencil—only slower. The brain determines redundancy, not the computer.

No computer can decide if a story is libelous. Only a person—someone able to ask, "How would I feel if this story were about me?"—can sense the nuances of a story that might wrongly harm someone for life. A computer can enhance any photograph, but it cannot evaluate the photograph for creativity or news value. A computer cannot judge a photograph in terms of taste or ethics. A human can.

A computer is a tool that is as good as the user—and no better. The electronic gadgetry in a newsroom is not mere wizardry installed by the publisher as a tax write-off; the equipment serves the people in the newsroom. Studies have shown, for example, that after VDTs are installed, the speed of writing and editing drops and the quality of editing diminishes—until everyone becomes accustomed to the new system and then speed and quality rise above the pre-electronic high. The editor who spends what seems like hours cutting apart and pasting back together misorganized stories has to appreciate a system that allows the same process carried off in seconds—and without the smell and mess of rubber cement.

If a neophyte needs any additional preparation for using a VDT, it is typing, and only because a VDT keyboard is more sensitive to human touch. Fingers trained to type on an electric typewriter glide through the transition from typewriter to VDT because the sensitivities of both keyboards are about the same.

True, a neophyte must learn something new when turning away from a pencil and gluepot to a video display terminal. But the creators of good electronic equipment designed their products with people in mind and the electronic commands on a VDT keyboard are similar to those of a manual newsroom. Reporters and editors who realize that the electronic equipment serves them will exploit it to the fullest and get the most out of it. Those who approach the equipment with a servile attitude will not enjoy or make the most of it.

The VDT

While it would be an oversimplification to say a VDT is nothing more than a typewriter keyboard married to a television set and linked to a computer and and (in some cases) a typesetter, that description suffices for the layperson not intent on learning the technical aspects of the system. In fact, users do not have to know the technology of a VDT system to use and appreciate it. Users, however, must know what they want to do and then be able to explain their goals to the newspaper's computer expert, often someone who programs the newsroom and business computers and is responsible for maintenance and upkeep.

VDTs are not perfect. For one, they are expensive, although as more and more newspapers install them, the cost will decline. In fact, those newspapers that are slow in adopting VDT systems will benefit from the pioneers because the costs will have gone down through mass demand and the resulting mass production.

Terminals have raised more serious concerns. Foremost, there is the health question. The issue of whether or not radiation from VDTs causes severe eye problems such as cataracts may never be resolved to everyone's satisfaction, but the fact remains that some users perceive that they suffer health problems and that alone represents a barrier for manufacturers and publishers to ethically overcome. VDTs do emit radiation, according to the National Institute for Occupation Safety & Health, but not at levels hazardous to humans.

To a lesser extent, improperly lighted rooms that house VDTs can create glare that tires eyes and causes fatigue. Strenuous copy editing of any kind can result in eye fatigue if a room is not properly lighted, but it appears that a VDT needs a more diffused light than would be tolerable in a pre-electronic newsroom. Polarizing filters that can be simply installed have been developed to help increase contrast and reduce eye fatigue.

Whatever, users should have their eyes checked regularly and should rest if their eyes tire. The health benefits are obvious, but the advice also carries a practical message—tired eyes don't do a good job of editing.

A poorly planned system can frustrate a user. Such frustration usually arises when an editor strikes a key and the computer takes 10 or more seconds to execute the command. The delay signals an overtaxed computer that needs to be upgraded. An editor who experiences a brief delay may execute the command a second time because the editor believes the system is not working. Some VDT systems, however, will execute any given command in time, meaning a command given twice will (if possible) be annoyingly executed twice.

VDT systems have advantages beyond speed and savings. They come in all sizes. They're big enough to serve the *New York Daily News*, one of the largest circulation newspapers in the country, and the Fairmont *Sentinel*, a small Minnesota daily that purchased a low-cost yet easily updated and maintained system. And just because a system is small doesn't mean it doesn't do the job; it means only that it does the job on a smaller scale.

Another advantage is the portable VDT, which, as noted, creates mobile bureaus. If portable VDTs cause any problem, it is that they range in weight from 12 to 26 pounds, which can tire any arm carrying one from one airline to another at a metropolitan airport. They are small enough, though, to fit under an airplane seat. Such sensitive equipment does not belong in the baggage hold.

The VDT can serve as a note file for reporters who, before writing a story, transcribe their shorthand notes into longhand. Since each reporter can be given a queue or workspace in the computer, the notes won't get mixed with someone else's. By the same token, reporters and editors do not write anything personal for VDT storage because it is unprofessional, because what is written might accidentally show up in print, because the personal work takes up storage space the computer needs for working data, and because no one has a guarantee that what is written won't be located by someone else. Some systems offer private files and invisible sign-on passwords, but they don't provide absolute privacy. Anyone who uses a VDT system long enough begins to understand how it works and can divine passwords and other secrets.

Finally, the VDT has usefulness in advertising and news page design. Manufacturers have developed VDT equipment that allows advertising personnel to write an advertisement and then design it around all graphics planned for the ad (see Figure 1.4). In seconds, the operator can adjust the type arrangement of the entire advertisement. Such an operation done by hand takes much longer.

Some of the equipment allows a user to create an advertisement no larger than a standard quarter page. Innovative users, however, have discovered that through a production camera they can increase—without loss of quality—the size of their original work.

Each VDT system is different and where one system's command to call up a story might be **OPEN** another's could be **FETCH.** But the principles behind the different words are the same, and new users should remember that as they learn a system. Reduced to newsroom needs, a VDT system is merely the typical newsroom—but with electronic circuits instead of pencils and paper.

Figure 1.4 Advertisements can be formed on a video display terminal designed for the task. All that cannot be done on such terminals—yet—is the creation of graphic elements. They are added later. (R. Thomas Berner photograph)

Using the Terminals

VDT keyboards are similar to a typewriter's but contain more keys (see Figure 1.5). The additional keys are command functions and are often colored differently from the keys used for writing a story. The command functions include a key that when pressed will delete an entire paragraph; another key will delete a word; still another will rid the screen of a single letter. They are variously labeled **PARA DEL** or **DEL PARA, SENT DEL** and **CHAR DEL.** To ensure that someone does not accidentally delete, say, a paragraph, those keys usually need to be pressed twice before the computer fulfills the command. When pressed once, the key causes the section marked for deletion to blink as a precaution to the user. Other systems underline the word or phrases marked for deletion.

Very important keys on any VDT are the ones that move the cursor, a blinking rectangular light that pinpoints a spot the editor wants to work on (see Figure 1.1). The cursor must be on a character before an editor can delete that character. Similarly, the cursor must be aligned with a story code before an editor can summon that story to the screen. The cursor, thus, is essential. An editor can move a cursor up, down, left or right. If the cursor is at the bottom of the screen and the editor wants to move it to the top, the editor strikes the **HOME** key and the cursor instantaneously moves to the top. **SKIP TO START** will take the cursor to the beginning of the story.

Another very essential key is **CONTROL** or **COMMAND** or **SUPERSHIFT.** Such a key turns a standard key into an extra command, depending on how the computer is programmed. Any repetitive information (such as a header) can be programmed into a computer and called up time and time again with, say, **CONTROL I** or any other key so designated. On large systems the computer automatically affixes header in-

Figure 1.5 The keyboard of a video display terminal contains the standard keys found on a typewriter in addition to special command keys (left, right and top of keyboard). (R. Thomas Berner photograph)

formation to a story. The computer will not execute some commands unless they are given with the control key. The command to **KILL** is an example; it requires two fingers to operate—one on **CONTROL** and one on **KILL.** That way a story is not accidentally bumped off. A back-up against the accidental death of a story is the **COPY** key, which when pressed will make a copy of a designated story.

In order to use a terminal, a reporter or editor must first sign on to his or her own work space in the computer. To ensure some privacy, the reporter has a secret password that when typed on the keyboard does not appear on the screen. The secrecy thwarts anyone from getting into a file and destroying its contents. Once signed on, the reporter must give the story a slug. The slug can be the reporter's initials and a number. The number represents the number of stories the reporter has written that day. KLB-2 represents KLB's second story. If in creating the slug, KLB typed 2 for the third story, the computer would correct the error. The computer corrects duplicate slugs based on sequential numbering.

A reporter in the pre-VDT days of a large newspaper would notice around the newsroom the many editors who contribute to putting out the paper. For example, the paper might have a city editor, an obituary editor, national, foreign, news, sports, financial, features, editorial page editor and so on. On smaller papers, where one editor might perform the functions of several, that editor would have wire baskets or hooks to store the variety of copy. VDT systems satisfy either approach because a computer can be programmed to have many queues or files that equate to the many editors or wire baskets just mentioned. Such a system meshes with wire service copy, which arrives coded for a particular desk and automatically goes to a particular file.

In signing on, a reporter does not work in the file of the editor for whom the reporter is writing the story. Instead, the reporter writes in a file called **WORK** or **SCRATCH PAD** or whatever the computer programmer has named it. Reporters with their own file to work in don't tie up other files, which would interfere with the editors putting out the newspaper.

The reporter then writes the story. Newcomers discover that they don't have to worry about returning the carriage because a VDT has no carriage. Instead, the letters continue to a following line as the reporter types. The reporter does not have to insert end-of-line hyphens; the computer will insert those when driving the typesetter. The reporter does not have to worry about hitting a tab key to indent for a new paragraph. A key variously marked **END PARA** or **PARA,** when pressed, automatically moves the cursor to the next line—with the correct indentation.

The mechanics of writing the story are easy. The reporter who rejects one or two leads does not have to worry about ripping out paper and starting over. The reporter keeps on writing and electronically erases the scribblings with the touch of a button or two. No more ripped paper that has been pulled too fast from the typewriter by an excited beginner. And no more paper cluttered around a wastepaper basket—the usual evidence of a reporter who started a story many times. When finished, the reporter checks the story the way any reporter would. Neophytes find themselves removing **xxxxxx** from their copy because they've become accustomed to **x-ing** out words when using a typewriter. **CHAR DEL** rids copy of typographical errors; you cannot **x** out on a VDT. Somewhere in the story the reporter has written:

The prsident saic that . . .

To correct **prsident,** the reporter strikes a command key labeled **INSERT** or **INSERT CHAR,** then places the cursor on top of **s** and types **e.** It will appear between **r** and **s.** If the reporter remains in the insert mode to fix the next error, however, the result will be **saidc,** in which case the reporter will need to **CHAR DEL.** The reporter could get out of the insert mode so that when the **d** key is struck it rubs out the **c.**

The reporter also discovers a sentence that needs rewriting. In this case, the insert mode functions best so that the old sentence and its information remain on the screen until the reporter is satisfied with the rewrite. **SENT DEL** will remove the old sentence from the story.

At no time during the writing of the story does the reporter worry about the computer "crashing" (failing) and causing the loss of the story on the screen. The reporter is working with a sophisticated system that automatically duplicates stories sentence by sentence (the process is called "mirror writing"). If the system crashes, the reporter will find the story filed away in a back-up queue. In less sophiscated systems, the reporter would have to **CLOSE** and **OPEN** periodically to ensure that the story was stored. Although annoying, the effort can be worthwhile during, for example, lightning storms when computers are especially vulnerable.

An imaginative VDT user exploits the system and makes it do more than its designers anticipated. No system contains the command **PHRASE DELETE** for how would a computer know which phrase? But the exploitive user can define the phrase by making it a sentence, simply done by inserting periods at both ends of the phrase. Once the phrase is a "sentence," **SENT DEL** will chase it from the screen. For short phrases, though, **CHAR DEL** is faster.

The story completed, the reporter does not rise from the screen and carry the story to an editor but instead electronically sends it to the editor's file. In some systems the reporter strikes the **ASGN** key (for "assign") and the story goes to the appropriate editor. In other systems **DONE** performs the mission. The story leaves the work file and enters the editor's in seconds. In this case, the reporter sent the story first to the news editor, who checked it for facts and organization and added a message for the chief of the copy desk before assigning it to the latter's file. The chief of the copy desk does some preliminary work, such as giving the story a more comprehensive slug than KLB-2. **FATAL/FIRE** will serve for this example.

Then the copy desk chief sends the story to a copy editing file where all copy editors select their work on a priority system. Since **FATAL/FIRE** is marked for the first edition, a copy editor checking the directory of stories in the file will call it up and edit it quickly. To edit **FATAL/FIRE** the editor must move it "up" the screen. For that function, called scrolling, the VDT contains a key labeled **ROLL UP** or **SCROLL UP** and for the reverse function, **ROLL DOWN** or **SCROLL DOWN**. The command can move a story along a line at a time or in a continuum, depending on the editor's needs.

The copy editor will move the story along a line at a time, but when the copy desk chief takes one last look at the work before sending it to production, he or she will skip through the story a "page" at a time. A "page" equals about 20 lines.

During editing the editor finds late in the story a paragraph that belongs higher up. The editor uses the electronic equivalent of scissors and glue, a series of command keys that define the paragraph to be moved, and then move it to the new location in seconds. The editor also discovers that the reporter has misspelled a name throughout the story. With few exceptions, most systems allow the editor to fix the word once and then tell the computer to fix it all other times. Some computers will correct any misspelled word—except homonyms—without an editor first designating them as misspelled. A computer does not know if the reporter meant **main** or **mane** in a "horse's mane," but it has been programmed to caution a copy editor that a word might be misspelled. The word in doubt blinks.

Also during editing, the editor realizes that a related story exists and the editor wants to compare the two to avoid duplication. Split-screen capability—limited to a few terminals because it is expensive—allows the editor to call up both stories for side-by-side comparison, to shift blocks of type between two displayed stories and to combine displayed stories (see Figure 1.6). The editor can shift blocks of type between stores or combine them much easier than when the system allows the display of only one story at a time.

Among other things, the copy editor has been told to reduce the story's length by four inches. To make sure the story meets the desired length, the copy editor presses a key marked **H&J** (for hyphenate and justify). After **H&J**, the story's new length appears at the top of the screen. The copy editor takes one last glance to make sure the computer raised no questions about hyphenations. If the computer has doubt, it inserts a message—**CHECK HYPHENATION**—at the questionable spot.

Done editing, the editor writes a headline, first telling the computer what size the headline will be. After writing the headline, the editor

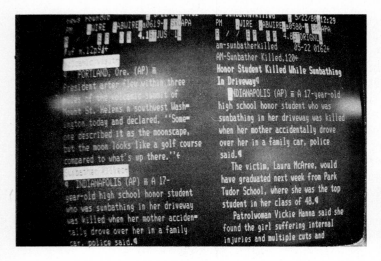

Figure 1.6 Split-screen capability allows an editor to display two stories and to combine them as needed. (R. Thomas Berner photograph)

presses the **HEADFIT** key and the terminal shows if the headline fits. If the headline is too long, the terminal will tell the editor.

Satisfied with the story and headline, the editor sends them to the typesetter machine, which produces both immediately. The story took the reporter one hour to write and the editor a half-hour to edit. A computer-driven typesetter, printing with a cathode ray tube beam, produces the story in 9-point type and the headline in 36 point within seconds. If the story contains errors, they were made by the reporter or the editor; the computer does not make mistakes.

Pagination

Computer systems designed to allow editors to lay out pages owe their existence to the advertising department needs. In 1975 two researchers at the Massachusetts Institute of Technology developed a computer program that told the advertising make-up people where to place each ad without burying the ads or without placing them on the same or facing page with a competitor. Furthermore, the computer program told the person making up the ad dummy where to place advertisements with coupons so that they were not back to back. After all, if people want to clip both coupons, they don't want one on the back of another.

From that concept have come still-developing pagination systems planned around editors designing pages. The early models satisfied advertising make-up needs and produced the basis for a complete page make-up program and equipment. One drawback to early-1980 pagination systems was the inability of any to process graphics or photographs. Thus, the make-up editor had to rely on someone else to place graphics and photographs. However, computerized darkrooms will one day wed computerized pagination systems to overcome that drawback.

The "cruder" pagination systems present the user with a dummy sheet on a VDT screen. Stories are set in place with a cursor but the user does not see the actual stories. All that appears on the screen is the story slugs. The user trims all stories as needed and, once completed, signals the computer to print out the page with everything (except graphics and photographs) in place.

More advanced models actually display the type on a screen, thus allowing an editor to edit the story at the same terminal used for design (Figure 1.7). To get around the graphics deficiency, such equipment allows a user to define the graphics shape so type can flow around it. Later, the graphics and photographs are added to the page.

The system that would no doubt suit editors the most would be one that would allow editing, photographic manipulation, and story and graphic placement all on the same terminal or unit. Then the editor would retain control over all aspects and phases of designing a page. The editor could make last-minute decisions to change leading (the space between lines), for example, and not delay production of the paper since a finished page would still appear in minutes, if not seconds. The delay in

Figure 1.7 An editor uses a pagination terminal to edit and design a page. Graphic elements appear as Xs. (Photograph by Ted Kawalerski. All rights reserved/Courtesy of Gannett Co. Inc.)

getting such a pagination system into the marketplace stems from the uncertainty of editors about what they want and how much publishers are willing to invest. Furthermore, no manufacturer will invest in developing a pagination system if it satisfies only a handful of customers. However, the need for producing a newspaper as economically as possible and keeping it competitive with other media will clear up the uncertainties—probably by the end of the 1980s.

The Sky's the Limit

One of the major competitors facing newspapers is not television or radio but the changing technology that can put a low-cost two-way computer terminal in every home, allowing a person to summon forth news, advertisements and any other information at the touch of a couple of buttons on a keyboard. Who would need a newspaper?

Aware of the competition, news organizations have moved into the field of electronic home delivery. For example, people with terminals at home can receive from United Press International a world news report. Newspapers can join the system and make their files available to a central computer, allowing anyone with a computer and a telephone to receive information about any community whose newspaper provides information for accessing. The newspaper receives a royalty every time someone uses its information. Such a program, because it extends the shelf life and value of news, has attracted the interest of publishers who are creating their own systems.

Selected member newspapers of The Associated Press and a computer company have experimented by offering information to home computers at $5 an hour. The users call up news, sports, business and features provided by the newspapers and AP. In essence, the person with a home computer obtains information that might normally appear in the local newspaper, except the home computer operator has a wider base to draw from. No editor filters out the AP report.

Another potential newspaper competitor turns television screens into displayers of text and graphics, which in and of its own is not new. But what happens next is: The viewer can "talk" to the television screen and purchase information or products without leaving the home. The people providing the two-way capability often own cable television systems and already have a link to many homes.

Newspapers appear threatened by the new technology because the users of any of the preceding systems can attach inexpensive printers to their computers and television sets and receive information in printed form. (The user could also simply store the information on disks and use it as desired later.) That allows the subscriber to save the information for later use. Most observers of the newspaper scene feel that for the short run, newspapers will have to change but that they won't go out of style. Long-range predictions are fuzzy. The technology exists to allow newspapers to exploit home delivery systems by creating a system that would deliver the newspaper electronically—in the same broadsheet or tabloid size that it already comes in on the front doorstep. If newspapers can create a low-cost system (cost is the major problem), they can overcome circulation problems and compete with the many video marvels around them.

The next century looks interesting for newspapers. A person wanting to know where newspapers are headed would be advised to look to the skies. Up there satellites are taking over the distribution of news (and entertainment) as they beam information from one land base to another. The wire services already send their reports to some newspapers equipped with a dish antenna that focuses on satellites parked more than 22,300 miles above the Equator. Any wire service subscriber can receive a wire report from a neighboring antenna via telephone lines. Thus, the news media of one city need only one dish antenna. (see Figure 1.8). By the middle of the 1980s, the dish antenna will also appear atop the homes of those subscribing to a nationwide satellite service that will directly broadcast three channels of commercial-free television programming. While not born out of necessity, the service is expected to provide

Figure 1.8 Wire service stories arrive at the *Sentinel Star* in Orlando, Florida via this dish antenna. (*Sentinel Star* photograph by David Cotton)

programming not normally offered to consumers in addition to providing programming for those who lack access to cable television.

The two major wire services, meanwhile, had to go into space to deliver their reports because of the increasing high costs and unreliability of earthly telephone lines. The AP has projected an annual reduction of $3.6 million in delivery costs. One satellite cannot monopolize the skies the way one company has monopolized telephone service; satellites don't require rate hearings. Besides, landlines are about 10 times as expensive as satellite transmission. Similarly, snowstorms and rainstorms don't wipe out satellite transmissions the way they knock down telephone lines. A satellite in space is easier to maintain than a telephone line on earth (see Figure 1.9). The wire services had no choice.

Back on earth, newspapers went to the air to beat traffic jams and to speed production. At least four metropolitan newspapers—the *Detroit Free Press*, the *Detroit News*, *Chicago Tribune*, *Washington Post* and *The New York Times*—built printing plants some distance from their downtown offices. To get finished pages to those printing plants the four send

Figure 1.9 Wire service news travels from one earth site to another via Western Union's Westar communications satellite "parked" in geostationary orbit 22,300 miles in space. (Artist's rendition provided by Western Union)

their pages via laser beams over microwave systems—above the traffic. The *Detroit News* beams to a satellite plant 100 miles from the city. The *News* built the plant to improve its distribution throughout Michigan.

The newspaper known for pioneering that technology is the *Wall Street Journal*, which transmits its pages via satellite to 13 printing plants around the United States. In effect, the *Journal* has become a national paper, for it can be written, edited and printed on the same day everywhere in the United States. *The New York Times*, which abandoned a functioning West Coast edition as too costly, started a Middle West edition because the *Times* can now transmit via satellite to a printing plant in Chicago. Before, the *Journal* and the *Times* relied heavily on slow-moving trucks and expensive airplanes. *Time* magazine has replaced jet travel with satellite delivery to speed full color pages from New Jersey to the Netherlands or to the West Coast and on to Hong Kong. In those countries *Time* prints its zoned foreign editions.

The ultimate use of satellite delivery rests with how easy it will be to persuade individuals to buy their own antennae to receive television programs, Hollywood movies, stock market reports, advertising—and their local newspaper in addition to one metropolitan newspaper. The only thing for newsstands to do then will be to sell candy bars.

Suggested Reading

Goodbye Gutenberg The Newspaper Revolution of the 1980's, Anthony Smith, The Oxford University Press, 1980.

CHAPTER TWO

News Evaluation

What Makes News

No newspaper can possibly publish every story it receives through local sources and over the wires, so it falls to editors to decide which stories will see print and which will not. The choice, some days, is easy; other days it is hard. After all, a newspaper uses perhaps no more than 10 percent of all the wire news it receives; the editor decides which 10 percent along with what local news and how long it all will be.

Editors make judgments with their readers in mind. But on top of that, the editors also decide what is newsworthy and what is not based on some ideas that have been around newsrooms for a long time. The old saw about news goes like this: If a dog bites a man, that's not news; if a man bites a dog, that's news. Following that formula didn't make the person an editor, just a cataloguer.

Similarly, newspapers of old placed a lot of emphasis on crime, which resulted in an unending, unrelated series of stories about, for example, house burglaries without giving a reporter time to dig deeper into the matter to survey the entire scene, to tell the reader about the crime wave and how to avoid it. When you consider how cheap it is to hire someone to merely copy down the police report daily and spit it back at readers, you can understand why the police station became such a great source of news. The analogy today is the newspaper or television station that devotes a great amount of space, time or footage to automobile accidents. Such information is easily and cheaply obtained—and, thus, some consider it newsworthy.

In more sophisticated operations, editors of all news media realize that news today is something else. When the associate publisher of a newspaper approached the managing editor and asked him why he was publishing a story about the CIA's attempt to raise a Soviet submarine from the sea, the editor stammered: "It's a great story; it's news." But the executive replied: "You're just telling them our secrets. What makes it news?" The editor could not respond. To him the story's newsworthiness was so obvious that even a child should have seen it.

The associate publisher, through, had raised a good question. He wanted to know what in the editor's mind made news and the editor flunked the test. But such an adventure by the CIA *is* news because of the unusual and unexpected nature of the event. How many have read spy stories in which various missions are undertaken to learn the secrets of the other side? Here was an attempt—in the deep sea no less—by one nation to steal another's submarine. Quite a feat if the mission had worked, for you do not just blissfully steal another's submarine, especially a sunken one.

What was the news in the Pentagon Papers case of 1971? After all, the papers revealed history—not current war policy. No secrets there. What the papers really revealed was a government of deceit, and by providing that insight into the government, the papers also provided the citizens of the country with a better opportunity to govern or at least generated a more watchful attitude on the part of the governed toward the government. After all, someone had abused their consent. Their news outlets told them that.

But when editors across the country read either story—and many more like them—they did not run through their minds the many points raised here. Such abstractions do not arise in the publishing of a news report. Instead, an editor examines a story and decides whether or not to publish or broadcast it because . . . because it is news.

News can sometimes defy compartmentalization—the man-bites-dog formula that says news is black and white; either it is news or it isn't. Just when scholars believe they have figured out what is news, the "rules" change. Still, some categories stand out.

To be newsworthy, a story must have interest to many of the readers of the newspaper. That can be tricky. Take *The New York Daily News* and *The New York Times*. The murder of someone in New York City might be a big story in the *News* but get barely a mention in the *Times*. But if some official in a program to eradicate honeybees from Texas dies of a bee sting, the *Times* might consider the article worth the lead of its National page and worthy of a reference line on Page One. The *News* wouldn't use the story. The people who read the *Times* know that generally the *Times* is not interested in local news unless it relates to a larger pattern or is national or international in scope. The federal bailing out of New York City was newsworthy to the *New York Times* because of its implications for all old cities as much as because New York City is the home of the *Times*. The same problem in Detroit or Cleveland or Chicago would merit coverage by the *Times*—but not by the *News.*

Other news categories include closeness, such as the death of a local person in a local accident or in an accident some place else. The dentist who cut down one of only four white ash trees in a small community so he could put in a driveway to his office parking lot was not only news in that community, he was Page One news for three days running. The dentist had offended the community by violating the tree ordinance. Impact on readers determines a story's newsworthiness, which is why government receives a lot of coverage. The lack of impact is also newsworthy. A bad winter storm that floods Los Angeles and does nothing to San Francisco is newsworthy in both communities—for different reasons. Farmers in Illinois will read with interest about the problems of farmers in Nebraska—two states away—because Illinois farmers are trying to learn if the problem is headed their way and if a solution exists.

News carries with it that implied "Did you hear about this?" News, to paraphrase the legendary editor Charles A. Dana, makes people talk. But, a modern editor hastens to add, "news does not necessarily make people act."

Timeliness often determines news. An event that happened last week may lack newsworthiness but an event that is 2-years-old could be worth Page One. When *The New York Times*, for example, discovered an unpublicized Canadian trial that found that an oil company had once inflated prices, the *Times* ran the story on its front page *even through the issue had been resolved two years before*. It was news because the issue of price gouging during an energy crisis was a current event which the 2-year-old trial shed some light on. Similarly, confirmation of massive earthquakes in China is newsworthy even when the confirmation occurs years after the event. Any society that operates under a closed-door policy invites the curious to snoop around when that door is opened a crack.

Scientific discoveries—even the hint of some—rate coverage because of the way these discoveries may affect the lives of readers. Any seeming step toward the cure of cancer is sure to generate headlines and magazine cover stories even if the researchers taking the step affirm that it is but a small one. The hint is newsworthy.

Archeological events, especially those that give clarity to the present, are newsworthy. But whether they do or not, revealing secrets of ancient civilizations appeals to the curiosity of many. When Pope John Paul II toured the United States in 1979, he attracted one of the largest press followings in history. The visit of a pope is newsworthy in itself, but this visit, to quote one journalist, also enabled the news media to use the visit as an opportunity to study Catholicism in the United States.

State and local news still rank as the major focal points in newspapers followed by (in any order depending on the newspaper) crime, education, cultural events, health, social problems, obituaries, labor, environment, sports, disasters, tragedies, politics, business and fashion. On any given day, of course, the editors of different newspapers will rank the events differently and what might be worth Page One in one newspaper could rate no more than the bottom of the first break (or section) page. By the same token, the editors may have so much Page One-worthy news that they create a second front page to accommodate it (see Figure 2.1).

The use of international news varies frequently depending on how much the international event affects people in the United States or by how much of an investment a newspaper may have made in covering foreign events. The civil war in Vietnam would have meant nothing to U.S. readers until Congress debated whether or not President Eisenhower should send troops to replace the defeated French. Eisenhower didn't and Vietnam remained relatively unnewsworthy for another decade.

Any newspaper with television and/or radio competition finds itself doing well when it plays up state and local news—both areas not well covered by the other two media. With a state capital bureau and back-up from their wire services, newspapers can daily present state news packages that include reports on how local legislators vote. The electronic media can present some of that, but not in the convenient unperishable form of a newspaper. The newspaper that puts its strength into local coverage increases readership and fullfills an obligation to that readership. That in no way means national and international events should be ignored. Too often an international crisis springs on newspaper readers because the newspaper has not published stories about the events leading to the crisis. The newspaper has failed to keep its readers informed, which is one of the functions of newspapers. International news is more than stories on coups and earthquakes.

Editors who daily evaluate stories (see Figure 2.2) for publication or broadcast realize that the spot or breaking news that was once the staple of many news organizations no longer serves the total reader. Editors realize that what makes news is often the story behind the event, the trend, be it a crime wave or a back-to-basics movement in education. Editors now look for stories that tell about people and what makes them act. Editors want stories that tell how people think. The social questions mean a lot to the editors making news judgments. Editors want to know how stories will affect readers, involve readers, attract readers. Does the story say something important and does it say it well? What's in the story for the reader? None of those categories defends gimmicks that attempt to trick readers into the paper; good editors know that news long on tricks but short on substance detracts from the overall news product.

Editors too realize that news can be more than bad or sensational-

Figure 2.2 The story conference gives editors from the different departments of a newspaper the opportunity to discuss the day's news and how it will be displayed throughout the paper. Wayne Sargent, editor of *The Sun* in San Bernardino, California listens as an editor proposes a story for Page One. (R. Thomas Berner photograph)

istic or saber rattling. They know that behind every story people exist and that the readers want to know about the people in the story as well as the story itself. This attempt to put stories in people terms does not obviate an editor's job to publish the news nor does it change the substance of news, just the approach. The evolving process of defining news continues today; it's that tension of evolution that makes news evaluation more than just a cataloguer's job.

Hard vs. Soft

One of the major changes in the content of some newspapers in the 1970s was a new emphasis on so-called "soft" news. Soft news sometimes showed up as a feature story on what to wear when sledding or as a gossipy tract on show business people. Hard news became soft news in the hands of skilled writers who put feature rather than hard leads on stories, who deferred time elements and put the emphasis on people. Typically, sportswriters excelled in this field because they had been doing it longer (although not necessarily better).

Some newspapers went overboard in the soft news field and turned their front-page content over to magazine-style stories. The readers, though, did not want to be puffed to death; they still wanted to know what happened in the world and they didn't want to have to hunt through a collection of stories on rock stars and recipes to find that. The newspapers had put too much soft news on their front pages at the expense of hard or had put too much soft throughout their pages at the expense of hard. Editors forgot that *The National Observer*, which distinguished itself with what many would consider a soft approach to news, died in the late 1970s just as many newspapers were joining the soft news parade. Some editors missed the message.

Real soft news is serious. It provides readers with an extra dimension for their lives. Soft news is not a piece of puff but shows up as a depth look at credit policies at local banks, an analysis of cancer research, a look at the housing market. A good soft news story tells itself in human terms. The news is called soft only because what the reporter writes about did not occur within the 24-hour cycle that used to determine news. Thus, the story could just as easily have been used on Tuesday as Thursday.

Lacking a hard news bent should not detract from the value of any story. The reader has to know what city council did last night, of course, but reporters—under assignment from editors—should be examining the action for its long-term implications, and when those implications are found, editors should be as willing to display the story on Page One. The soft approach to news does not mean an absence of substance, and editors who make news story selections must understand that.

Brief vs. Long

A major criticism of newspapers is that too many stories continue from the front page to another page in the same section, or worse still, to another section. Sometimes the continuation results from poor design, but more frequently it results from poor planning.

Obviously, an editor cannot know in advance how long a story will be and the reporter who covers a news event sometimes can only estimate how long the resulting story will run. But both, through a more careful overall scheme, can package news better to make reading it easier on the reader. Some of what they can do is discussed in Chapter 7, Design. But for this discussion, editors should set limits on story length and then encourage reporters to break up long stories into sidebars or related stories. This approach enables editors to package their products better.

Although that solution means packaging differently, it also suggests that readers do not need all of a story, only parts of it, and that individual readers will need different parts. Thus, editors and reporters must present the entire story but in a form that allows the readers to pick and choose among the variety of information.

Reporters can still be allowed to write long stories after which editors can cut them apart and repackage them, but that consumes valuable time, both in the writing and in the editing. Better to establish a clear policy that encourages reporters to discuss story length in advance of writing so editors can make decisions early in the cycle. Editors and reporters should remember that newspapers are quickly read and that unnecessarily long stories impede readers who want to get in and get out.

The Want To Know vs. The Need To Know

Readers can be a notoriously fickle bunch and can throw curve balls to editors attempting to learn what readers want in their newspaper. The 1970s preoccupation with soft news at some newspapers went over the brink and brought out readers complaining that their newspapers lacked news.

By the same token, those same readers seemed to complain about an overemphasis on some government reporting. Those who complained should not be faulted, but their editors need guidance on how to better present the news. The reader who asks, "Why am I reading this? I don't need to know it," reflects poor presentation on the part of the newspaper. Often the reader does need to know the information but has not been told that. Government stories especially can appear either as mundane outlays of words or as a gaggle of officials trading barbs and the reader will be none the wiser to the story's value (if any). A college newspaper published a story about the questionable use of funds by a branch of the student government and readers complained that the paper was "crucifying" the student leaders. The newspaper's stories failed to say: "The money in question came from student fees. The cost of this venture came from your pocket."

Too frequently decisions are made that affect people, but they never realize it until it is too late because the newspaper failed to make the issue clear. Any time an editor reads a story and asks, "Why does the reader want to know this?" the editor has placed the burden of proof on the newspaper. Such stories need more polish so the reader can see the obvious impact. Don't give the readers something whose value to them is not clear.

Over-Reliance on Wire Service Budgets

Daily the wire services provide clients with a list of what the wire editors consider the top stories of the day. The lists are called budgets, digests or directories. The stories listed have usually received more reporter attention and are longer than the average wire story. Because of that, some editors place great stock in the wire services' judgment and determine the content of their newspapers by the wire services. But what the wire services are providing is an advisory service, not a newspaper content service, and their editors are making decisions far removed from the local community where the editor lives.

Wire service budgets and directories reflect a big city, East Coast mentality that does not apply in Austin, Texas or Butte, Montana, or Bend, Oregon. The wire service editors who say a major snowstorm in the East Coast is a top story are not aware of what is happening in small communities across the country and are trying to supersede that local judgment. Editors should take the wire service list of stories as suggestions and build their paper around local needs and local interests.

A Member of the Community

The best newspapers are more than newsprint filled by advertisements, press releases, wire service stories and event reporting. The best newspapers cover their communities with a critical but a loving eye. In some cases, they dig deeply to see how or if the community works. The implications of such reporting are not lost on readers who see the newspaper as working for them. Community concern in a newspaper makes the reader say: "The paper's on my side."

Newspapers have shown this involvement in many ways and will continue to show it as new ideas bear fruit across the nation. *The Los*

Angeles Times started an obituary page to report the deaths of local people who may not have been famous but who led interesting lives. In Lansdale, Pennsylvania, the *Reporter* publishes an elementary level newspaper with specific lessons enclosed for grades kindergarten through fourth. For adults, the *Jacksonville* (Florida) *Journal* publishes an advertising-free tabloid newspaper providing parents with suggestions on helping their children learn (see Figure 2.3). School teachers prepare the stories. In Harrisonburg, Virginia, the *Daily News Record* scientifically polled its readers to learn how they felt about the newspaper's coverage of a controversial brewery that had been proposed for the area. The newspaper also asked how readers felt about the brewery, a question no government agency had thought to ask the community.

Like some other newspapers around the country, the *Louisville Times* and *Courier-Journal* began zoning news and advertising sections to provide better neighborhood coverage in their county. Each section contains detailed local news of interest only to a particular part of the county. Similarly, the Long Beach, California, *Independent Press-Telegram* created a section called "neighbors" in which it features the more personal news many newspapers overlook, such as Scout news and school honors.

Figure 2.3 Contributing to the community, the *Jacksonville* (Florida) *Journal* provides parents with a tabloid containing advice on how to help children learn. (Copyright 1980 by Florida Publishing Company and the University of North Florida Foundation)

Jacksonville Journal, Monday, March 10, 1980

How to help your child learn

One section of town that newspapers have been accused of overlooking is the section where the poor live. In Monroe, Louisana, the *Monroe Morning World* published a depth look at the community's housing in a 12-page special section (see Figure 2.4). The newspaper learned that almost 40 percent of the community's housing was substandard and that the community's building code was not enforced. The research took three months. Nine months later the *World* followed up its study to see if anything had been done (see Figure 2.5). After stirring the pot, the cook also has to taste the soup.

One ambitious in-depth look at the community occurred in Fort

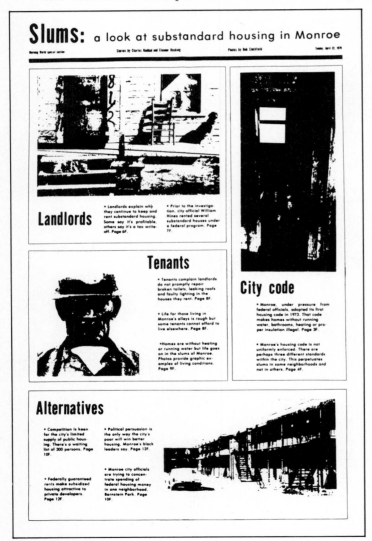

Figure 2.4 Newspapers must be willing to tackle difficult issues and not shy away from stories that may upset some members of the community. One such effort by the *Monroe* (Louisiana) *Morning World* produced this in-depth look at substandard housing.

Figure 2.5 After the *Monroe Morning World* stirred the community with its report on substandard housing, it followed up on the story to see what action public officials had taken.

Myers, Florida, where the *News-Press* published a report on that city's black community. The report included not only criticism of government leaders but of the newspaper itself for failing to cover the community (see Figure 2.6). Generally, the newspaper "covered" minorities but the coverage lacked a commitment to their needs as people and had, instead, treated them as just another reader to sell a newspaper to. The *News-Press'* nine-part series, which included editorials, ran for a week, but it involved eight months of work. It was conceived to go beyond the myths and stereotypes of the community to find out what influenced the lives of the people.

Still another ambitious depth report came from the *Columbia* (Missouri) *Daily Tribune,* which examined in a 24-page tabloid (see Figure 2.7) the effects of a tank car spill for 20,000 gallons of chlorinated pehnolic chemicals. Entitled "The Sturgeon spill, more questions than answers," the report admitted it could not answer all of the questions raised, but like a good member of the community the *Tribune* was willing to lay out those questions. The town of Sturgeon at the time of the crisis numbered 800 people yet the *Tribune* dispatched two reporters and a photographer on the assignment. A year later the paper conducted a follow-up and learned that the problem had not been solved.

Figure 2.6 Pointing the finger of blame is a function newspapers carry out with more credibility when they also examine their role in an issue. That's what the *News-Press* of Fort Myers, Florida, did when it examined the plight of the city's black community.

Figure 2.7 Even though the community examined numbered no more than 800, the *Columbia* (Missouri) *Daily Tribune* devoted a 24-page tabloid to the town of Sturgeon to see what had happened since a tank car spill of chlorinated phenolic chemicals.

Less spectacular but still as community minded is the consumer page of *Today* of Cocoa, Florida, (Figure 2.8) and similar efforts that provide critical information for consumer use. The consumer page that serves up puffballs when it could be throwing hardballs doesn't rate a place in the community. But the page that names names—even at the risk of losing advertising—puts its honor on the reader's side.

These varied examples show one of the strengths of great newspapers—their ability to cover their areas with concern and sensitivity, to praise as well as criticize, to expose as well as propose, to admit doubt as well as show the way. Such newspapers lead with their strength—the local story—and show readers that the newspapers are working in the readers' best interests, not the publisher's or the advertisers' or the local politicians'. The newspaper does not do it because it will make a lot of money (the people in Monroe and Fort Myers were not wealthy and the people in Sturgeon were too few to have an impact on the papers' treasuries), but because a good newspaper displays its community consciousness for all to see all of the time.

Figure 2.8 A consumer page published with the readers' interests instead of the advertisers' in mind is another community-minded service newspapers can provide. This page comes from *Today* of Cocoa, Florida.

A First Amendment Obligation

Editors who complain about closed-door meetings but never send a reporter to attempt to get through the closed door do not discharge their First Amendment obligation; instead, they duck it. Such editors no doubt write editorials bemoaning the public's lack of access to government and suggest that someone should do something about it. Sadly, the editors never suggest that they should do anything.

All news media, of course, should never presume to serve as the public's surrogate, although that has happened. Such a self-anointed role highlights inconsistencies when journalists sit in on private meetings and do not report the outcome. Who then is served—the journalist or the public? Obviously, not the public.

The news media must realize, though, that because of their resources they by default serve as the public's representative at public events. Their presence assumes an interest on the part of the public—the missing audience—not the officials conducting the event. Having taken on the surrogate role, the news media must carry through—that is their First Amendment obligation.

The news media must also provide the information each member of a democracy needs to properly discharge his or her role in society. That means the news media must provide more depth, even when there is no heat, and more light where usually only shadows exist. Some editors would complain that such proposals are expensive, but they would be the editors who have for too long filled their newsholes—in print and on the air—with easy-to-get stories that require little (if any) legwork and can be mechanically put together without much thought. The people who do such work receive low pay—and it's no wonder why. The commitment to quality goes beyond one day's news to a feeling that the flow of democracy turns out a continuing obligation to observe and report for everyone. The editors who decided to publish the Pentagon Papers were exercising their First Amendment obligation to the fullest. Seemingly lesser situations arise daily throughout the world of journalism and good editors rise to the challenge.

Suggested Reading

The following books provide insight on news evaluation:

Coups and Earthquakes: Reporting the World for America, Mort Rosenblum, Harper & Row, 1979.

Deciding What's News, Herbert J. Gans, Pantheon Books, 1979.

Media Power Who is Shaping Your Picture of the World, Robert Stein, Houghton Mifflin, 1972.

News From Nowhere: Television and the News, Edward J. Epstein, Random House, Inc., 1973.

The Papers and the Papers: An Account of the Legal and Political Battle over The Pentagon Papers, Sanford J. Ungar, E. P. Dutton, 1972.

CHAPTER THREE
The Editing Function

A Variety of Editors and Their Duties

Given the number of editors any one newspaper might have, an outsider would get the impression of too many bosses and no workers. In newspapers, though, the tendency is to put someone in charge of something and then call that person an editor. Thus, the person who writes play reviews might be called the Arts Editor or the Culture Editor on the basis that the person is a specialist and deserves to be so tagged. And despite the notion that some news executives give subordinates titles rather than pay raises, many newspaper editors perform necessary functions in the day-to-day operation of the paper.

The person responsible for the news and opinion content of a newspaper is the executive editor or editor. Under that person can be found the editor responsible for overseeing the daily operation, the managing editor. Depending on the newspaper's size, the managing editor usually has more contact with reporters than the editor or executive editor, who must also deal with corporate responsibilities and long-range planning.

At some newspapers the person holding the job of editor is the editor of the editorial page only. If the paper is large enough and has an op-ed (for *opposite-editoral*) page, that page has an appropriately titled editor. Top editors have associates and assistants, listed under those titles or called by different titles such as news editor, city editor, metro (for *metropolitan*) editor, national, foreign, sports, feature. Newspapers in non-metropolitan areas often have county editors who are responsible for seeing that news in the less populated areas of the newspaper's circulation area gets covered. Give a newspaper a speciality and an editor will be named to oversee it. A printer once quipped that if he walked into the newsroom at his newspaper and said, "I need an editor out back," everyone in the newsroom would follow him to the shop because everyone held an editorship.

Token editorships aside, more and more women are rightfully filling positions of responsibility in newsrooms of all media as publishers and station managers discover that a person's sex does not correlate with a person's abilities. *The New York Times*, for example, named a woman sports editor in 1978 with no more fanfare than would have accompanied a man getting the promotion. (She later moved to another position, with an equal amount of minimal fanfare). Elsewhere, women fill a variety of responsibile positions, including running bureaus for the wire services. In the Gannett chain, especially, women have moved into the publisher's chair. Sexual discrimination appears on the wane in journalism.

If the top editors of all news media have failed in any field, it is in the skillfull handling of their subordinates. Time and time again journalism school graduates will complain that on their first job "nobody tells me how I'm doing" or "nobody edits my copy." One of the long-standing problems of journalism is that in a field predicated on communication, some of its members cannot talk to each other. No matter what the level, editors must participate in the communication process.

One breakdown occurs in the hiring process in which the news executive fails to clearly explain what the company expects of a person in a job. The result is that after a person is hired or promoted, the executive says, "Oh, by the way, I also want you to do such-and-such," tasks the person has no interest in doing or for which the person is not qualified. Had the executive defined the job clearly, the problem could have been avoided.

The good editor recognizes that the newspaper's success depends on the staff. The good editor hires people who are not only bright but who are brighter than the editor. If editors who are weak writers hired only those people who wrote at the editor's level, the newspaper would surely fail. Editors who hire don't feel threatened by talented people, and, in fact, seek them out.

Once a talented staff is assembled, the good editor primes it for success. No recent journalism graduate can whine about not being told how he or she is doing because the good editor sees that the top editors routinely—albeit sometimes informally—meet with reporters to explain what they're doing wrong—and right. On a daily basis, copy editors ensure high morale by explaining to reporters why stories had to be cut or held. Nobody's left in the dark. By the same token, reporters should talk to editors and not wait for them to initiate every discussion.

The editor continues staff training beyond that first day when the new reporter received a copy of the newspaper style guide and a list of office personnel and their telephone extension numbers. Formal and informal training sessions, including in-house critiques, continue throughout the reporter's career, and at larger newspapers, reporters are sent back to school for updating or to workshops to pick up information on a specialty.

In the training process, the good news executive is looking for managerial talent—those who not only possess qualities of leadership but who also want to lead. Not every person of leadership talent wants the promotion and not every person who wants the promotion should get it. The classic example of poor management is repeated time and time again when a very good reporter is promoted to the copy desk, there to fail because the reporter's interests lie in reporting. If kept too long in the failed position, the reporter suffers the stigma of being a loser and the editor finds it more difficult to solve the problem. Making the copy editor a reporter again appears to be a demotion, even in the reporter's eyes.

When not functioning as executives, the many editors in newspapers perform a variety of duties not always foretold in their titles. The managing editor at a small newspaper might unlock the door in the morning, clear the wire, edit copy, write headlines, lay out Page One, hire and fire staff—and make coffee. In large newspapers, the managing editor ensures that the newsroom budget includes money to buy coffee.

At some newspapers, the city editor—often portrayed as a gruff-talking person whose acid tongue makes reheated coffee taste delicious—has final responsibility for all local copy. The city editor might check each story for content and then assign it an assistant for editing and headline writing or the editor might process the story on the spot.

Other people working with the city editor are the wire editor, who at some newspapers is responsible for the state, national and international news sent by the wire services; the news editor, who might be in charge of dummying Page One; the photo editor, who may be a photographer in charge of the photo department or who may be responsible for the cropping and sizing of all photographs, and the copy editor, who edits and headlines stories under the direction of a chief copy editor or the city editor. Figure 3.1 shows a variety of editors at work at the *South Bend* (Indiana) *Tribune.*

The Newsroom Hierarchy

As just noted, the same title does not always mean the same duties. Larger newspapers, for the most part, are better organized and more tightly structured. The following briefly describes the hierarchy of a composite medium-sized daily (75,000 circulation) that also publishes a Sunday edition.

Figure 3.1 Editors at the *South Bend* (Indiana) *Tribune* occupy a six-sided desk and keep in close touch with each other. (Courtesy, *South Bend Tribune*)

At the top is the managing editor, who sits as an equal with other newspaper department heads, such as the advertising director and the circulation manager. The managing editor answers to the publisher. (On a larger newspaper, an executive editor would fill the role.) The managing editor, while exercising overall control, does not sit on the desk or edit copy. The M.E. (as the person is called) assures overall quality by coordinating the work of the many assistants. The managing editor may not daily coordinate the assistants' work but the assistants know that the managing editor insists they work together and they do so without being told. The best managing editors have organized newsrooms that run smoothly without them.

Working under the managing editor are five assistants, who in some newspapers might carry titles such as chief copy editor, state editor, news editor, wire editor, local or city editor. In this composite daily, these people are assistant managing editors.

The primary concern of the first assistant is the quality of headlines and copy editing. This assistant managing editor not only supervises the universal copy desk (explained presently), but also evaluates the writing in the paper and works with individual reporters who are having writing problems. One of this editor's duties is frequently compiling and writing a critique of the newspaper. (One of the best know critiques is "Winners & Sinners," which the late Theodore M. Bernstein wrote for *The New York Times*.) Our editor is also responsible for evaluating the work of copy editors.

The second assistant managing editor oversees coverage of state news—that is, news that occurs in the state but outside the paper's immediate circulation area. This editor also oversees the newspaper's bureau in the state capital and any other bureaus the paper may have within the state. All correspondents work under this editor, who also oversees the production of the paper's state edition.

The third assistant managing editor coordinates special projects, overseeing, for example, all election coverage. In such a case, this editor would work with the state editor to avoid conflicts, overlaps and duplication and to produce a smooth election package of preview stories and results. The third assistant also oversees the newspaper's special investigative reporting team. The virture of having an editor oversee investigative reporting cannot be played up enough. Some newspapers with investigative reporters forget that the editing of such work needs as much care as the reporting. Some newspapers fail to free an editor to coordinate investigative reporting and the result is that some harried editor with too much to do must take on the additional work of checking the investigative report. Not having been in on the story from the start, the harried editor begins work in the hole. Pressed because daily work awaits, this harried editor rushes through the investigative work and misses holes. A special editor works with the team from the start and avoids those problems.

The fourth assistant managing editor oversees all news received via the wire services. This job is more than just rip, read and route, for this editor must make sure that stories are distributed to the right desks and that updates and corrections get to the right editors. At some dailies this editor is responsible for designing Page One.

The fifth assistant managing editor assigns stories within the newspaper's circulation area. Although the managing editor can generate story ideas, it is this assistant who sees that a reporter gets the assignment and the time to do the assignment.

Subordinate editors on this composite newspaper include graphics (responsible for overall appearance of the paper but does not lay out each page), photo (discussed in Chapter 8), sports, business, lifestyle/leisure. Where appropriate, these editors select which stories go on their pages and then design the pages within the famework established by the graphics editor.

All of these editors meet daily for the story conference at which time they tell what major stories they have and make a pitch to the managing editor for their biggest story to appear on Page One (see Figure 2.2). The managing editor makes the final decision on Page One content.

One other editor oversees the Sunday edition, making sure that the content for the special sections gets in type throughout the week instead of at the last minute. News and sports sections in the Sunday edition fall outside this editor's purview; they are usually the responsibility of the editors mentioned before.

Depending on the newspaper, copy is edited on a universal desk or at individual department desks. In a universal system, all copy is edited by the copy editors at that desk. A universal desk ensures consistency of writing and style much better than individual departments can. In newspapers where individual departments edit their own copy, minor stylistic and editing differences explode into newsroom warfare and the main purpose of the newspaper is forgotten as the lifestyle editor and the business editor feud over, say, the use of last names in second references. As silly as it may sound, such internecine debates can stymie quality work.

The Copy Editor's Duties

Unlike some of the previous editors whose jobs have been immortalized by Hollywood and Broadway, the copy editor remains anonymous. The public image of the intrepid reporter or the barking editor belies the reality of newspapering, for it is the unglamorous copy editor who puts the paper together day in and day out. The fearless investigative reporter can uncover a scandal of national import and the editor can issue directions on how the story is played, but it is the copy editor who polishes the reporter's words and turns the editor's directions into reality. Without the copy editor (or deskperson, as the job-holder is sometimes known), the newspaper would be a ragged resemblance of good intention, and good intention does not sell newspapers.

The copy editor assumed a greater role when newspapers entered the electronic age. Once thought of as the last person who could catch a mistake, the copy editor of old actually enjoyed superb backstopping from printers and proofreaders who were often as skillful as the copy editor. But today those reserves are gone, victims of automation and modernization. The copy editor now bears responsibility once divided among three or four people.

Benefits come from all of that, though. The copy editor is generally better paid than a reporter and at most newspapers no one rises through the ranks without doing some desk work. In fact, newsroom promotions from middle to top level come from the desk, not the reporting staff. Some of this book's content anticipates those promotions.

An advertisement for *The New York Times Manual of Style and Usage* proclaims: "As a writer you're judged by your consistency and accuracy of style and usage." But what it should say is: "As a copy editor you're judged by your ability to catch a writer's inconsistent and inaccurate style and usage." The writer up against a deadline makes mistakes that in more casual circumstances would not get by the writer. Deadline aside, every writer's copy needs an editor's eye to smooth the pace of words and parade of facts for the reader.

The copy editor must know not only how to use language well but also how to fix a writer's story without destroying the writer's style. A copy editor must spot errors lesser mortals would never see, must see the story's unasked questions are answered immediately, must write accurately and with *sparkle* (a favorite word in copy editor job descriptions). The copy editor must select stories with unerring regard for reader interests, must design an attractive page around the selection, see that the tone, style and flavor of the newspaper are maintained, and must write headlines that (again) sparkle.

For that, copy editors, who do not get bylines, take their gratification internally. They are secure in the knowledge that they have helped produce a first-rate product. They know that their sharp eye may have saved the publisher $1 million in libel damages. They are, above all, humble.

The copy editor serves as a professional reader for the good of a very special client—the reader of the newspaper. Even when reading about a favorite subject, the copy editor, despite being well read and knowledgeable, employs ignorance to ensure that the final story is clear to the reader.

The copy editor respects the reporter; in fact, between good copy editors and reporters mutual respect for high standards serves the reader because the copy editors and reporters see themselves as working together. Copy editors engender rapport with reporters. To that end, they do not make changes in copy for the sake of change. "I'd write it differently" is no reason for a copy editor to change a reporter's story. A copy editor remembers that a change can just as easily make a story inaccurate as accurate. Copy editors are not infallible.

Those who aspire to the copy desk should know that unlike other times in journalism, today's newspapers hire copy editors directly out of college instead of making them serve an apprenticeship as a reporter. The copy desk today is not a place where worn-out reporters are tossed. Would-be deskpersons must prove their potential, often by taking a series of tests that show not only the person's ability with the language but also the person's instinct to sense errors. Told to edit a story, one journalism graduate on a job interview asked: "Where's the city directory?" He knew some of the tools of the trade. He went on to pass the tests and get the job. Within four months he was news editor; within two years, managing editor. His assistant, who during college served a Newspaper Fund internship on the desk of *The Boston Globe*, moved on to become a copy editor for *Advertising Age* within a year of graduating from college. The closed door to early advancement has been removed from its hinges.

Copy editors need not feel cut off from writing opportunities either, for while they seldom get a chance to cover hard news, they do have time to produce work hard-pressed reporters don't. Copy editors bent on doing some writing find pleasure in writing editorials, columns, reviews or feature articles for Sunday use.

The copy desk is no place for the indecisive. Copy editors are expected to make quick—and correct—decisions. They must also know how to say "no" firmly when "yes" would be easier. Finally, some practical advice for copy editors. For one, many errors tend to be repetitive and the better copy editors learn that early in their careers. Knowing the typical error created by a certain situation, the copy editor can quickly fix the mistake and spend more time seeking out the atypical.

Secondly, a copy editor should read each story three times. In the first reading, the copy editor merely reads for the sense of the story, doing no editing other than fixing a misspelled word or taking out an extra comma. On the second reading, the copy editor edits. The third time, the copy editor makes sure no mistakes were edited into the story. Figure the minimum time for the process at a minute an inch.

What follows in this chapter and in others is detail on the duties of a copy editor.

Maintain Copy Flow

Although only part of the process that moves a story from reporter to reader, a copy editor is the primary mover behind the story. The copy editor fits into a chain usually started when the city editor orally assigns a story to a reporter. At that point the city editor might record in a video diary whom the story was assigned to and when the reporter is expected to turn in the story.

The reporter, of course, gathers the information and writes the story, sometimes consulting first with the city editor if problems develop. In other cases, the city editor may have to serve as a prod to get the reporter to write the story. That happens not because the reporter is lazy but maybe because the reporter is checking out one last fact. The city editor, given dispassionate distance from the story, can see that the reporter can still write the story and insert the fact later, something that will speed production in the end.

At the time the city editor expects the story, he or she checks the reporter's file to see if the story is done. The city editor may check over the story, although not edit it, then assign it to the chief copy editor who assigns it to a copy editor for editing. Before assigning it, the city editor may decide which page the story will appear on and what size headline the story will get. Those instructions are placed at the beginning of the story.

All copy editors know they can find work in a special file and once finished with one story and its headline, the copy editors automatically check that file to see what other stories remain to be edited. When finished, the copy editor may assign the story to a second file or may return the story to the same file where a second copy editor will retrieve it for a final reading. All copy editors know which stories to read first because the city editor has told them which pages will be set in type early and which pages will go late. If Page 4 is an early page and Page 6 is a late page, copy editors will read all Page 4 copy before proceeding to stories for Page 6. If no other copy exists, Page 6 copy is read. A copy editor doesn't forego editing a story just because it's for a late page or a later edition. Work cleared early in the shift eases the pressure before deadline.

At all times the city editor can learn the status of any story in the system merely by signing into a particular file and checking its directory, which tells how long the story is, its page number, headline size, how many times it has been edited and whether or not it has been sent to production. The story arrives in production two ways—either it is assigned there from one VDT to another or the last copy editor to process the story can, by executing the correct commands, drive an electronic typesetter that will produce the story and its headline in a few seconds. From there, a production employee takes the story to a make-up bank. If the story is assigned from one VDT to another, it is also sent to a special file and the people in production know that stories in that file are ready to be printed. The production people then give the commands that drive the typesetter.

Meet Deadlines

Everyone who has a deadline in a news operation should meet that deadline to help produce an orderly product. Newspapers and newscasts put together at the last minute because someone missed a deadline announce their roughness to the impatient and easily dissatisfied readers and listeners. Although a newspaper's arrival in the home is not as precise as the beginning of a broadcast medium's news program, readers still expect their newspaper to arrive around the same time every day. Given that the reader spends so little time with the product, a later newspaper may mean that day's issue goes unread because the time the reader normally reserved for reading the paper has passed.

Missing deadlines has economic implications. Many people on a newspaper have certain jobs to do at certain times and they report to work at times beneficial to printing and distributing the newspaper. The people who drive the circulation trucks begin work about the time the newsroom is closing. Those people are paid from a certain starting time even if the newspaper isn't off the press. It's not productive to pay people not to work. Eventually, missed deadlines that set set back production result in overtime pay, which in excessive amounts could create financial problems for the publisher. It's incumbent on every employee of the newspaper to work for the economic well-being of the newspaper lest the newspaper fold and jobs are lost.

Frequent overtime is not only hard on corporate profits but also on people's morale. The people who must work overtime grow tired of their jobs and aren't as sharp. As a result, they don't produce a sharp product.

Meeting a deadline is more than turning in all of the assigned work at the deadline. Reporters and editors should strive to avoid peaks and valleys in workloads by working steadily. Copy editors who sit around chatting when work exists create their own pressure when the work piles up. The city editor and copy editors can also avoid peaks and valleys by assigning equitable workloads and by staying on top of the news flow. If some reporters are dealing with late-breaking stories, the desk should advise other reporters on routine stories to get them in sooner.

Most of the time a copy editor works in an almost pressure-free environment. Sure, there's work to be done, but if the pace is steady, the pressure is less. Obviously, though, some work must be done against deadline, which should not be used as an excuse to do poor work. The best copy editors shrug off the maddening pressure, do their finest work, and still meet deadlines.

Deflate Pomposity

A reporter will not always realize that he or she is quoting the gobble-dygook of bureaucrats or the empty sentences of politicians or the big words of academicians. The phrase sounded good at the time and the reporter didn't bother to analyze it. But now the story sits before the copy editor and analysis begins.

Pomposity defies clear-cut rules, but generally it appears in direct quotations which the copy editor should paraphrase into something clear. For example, an academic report says: "First, many respondents indicated the desirability of understanding the relationship between the level of tuition and its impact on enrollment." That means: The report said it was important to understand what a tuition increase did to enrollment. Regretably, the sentence still does not make clear who has to do the understanding.

Politicians are notoriously pompous, often because they want to sound as though they're saying something when they're trying terribly hard not to commit themselves to anything. Thus, this sentence:

> The senator said his proposed new infusion of assistance is needed "to offset the erosion in the value of aid caused by our inflation over the past two years."

Note how the reporter got caught up in the fog of pomposity by using "infusion of assistance." What the sentence means—and the desk should create this through rewriting—is:

> The senator said his proposed aid is needed to offset what inflation has done to the value of aid in the past two years.

A copy editor may also find that many pompous sentences are better deleted than rewritten. But when rewriting is the answer, the copy editor should show the rewrite to the writer to ensure accuracy.

Put Life into Breathless Prose

Newspapers are no longer written for, as an editor once put it, "people who move their lips when they read," but that doesn't excuse this 57-word stiffler:

> One department spokesperson who was asked about the figures that showed Americans had to work longer to eat last year than in 1974, while the average in other countries declined, said that "no doubt inflation rates were higher in the other countries last year" and speculated that wages probably rose higher than food prices in other countries.

The reader who finishes such a sentence is no doubt left breathless. The copy editor who let the sentence into print could have avoided cramping the reader's breathing by creating two sentences, such as:

> One department spokesperson was asked about the figures that showed Americans had to work longer to eat last year than in 1974 while the average in other countries declined. The spokesperson said that "no doubt inflation rates were higher in the other countries last year" and speculated that wages probably rose higher than food prices in other countries.

The resulting two 29-word sentences still make no sense, meaning the copy editor must query the reporter for an explanation. Some long sentences, though, repair easily.

> A government spokesman said the departure had been delayed but would not say why, and unofficial sources said authorities were awaiting assurances from Libya—the eventual destination—that the hijackers would be granted asylum before dispatching the aircraft carrying the hostages.

Broken in two:

> A government spokesman said the departure had been delayed but would not say why. Unofficial sources said authorities were awaiting assurances from Libya—the eventual destination—that the hijackers would be granted asylum before dispatching the aircraft carrying the hostages.

For quick reading, the best sentences are on the average 17 to 20 words long, but a copy editor should not automatically divide every long sentence into shorter ones. A good sentence derives its beauty from the rhythm of the words not the number.

Fill In the Holes

Sitting before a VDT pondering a story, a copy editor puts a story to a test it must pass before getting forwarded to the reader. As the copy editor reads, questions arise. If the story does not provide the answers, back it goes to the reporter.

Some of the questions are obvious. In a story about the suspensions of a police officer for one day without pay, the question is: How much pay did the officer forfeit? Other questions might not be as obvious. The story reporting that city council has lowered property taxes should include an explanation of what the action means to the reader in dollars and cents.

Filling in for the reader, a copy editor examines a story about a legislator calling for a law that would require engaged couples to wait six months before getting married. The story appears complete, but several questions arise in the mind of the copy editor. What is the legislator's marital status? More importantly, what is the constitutionality of such a law? The copy editor returns the story to the reporter to track down the legislator and ask the questions. But if the reporter's not available, then the copy editor should call the legislator and ask. And if the legislator is unavailable, the copy editor should call some legal expert for an opinion because the reader deserves the answer with the question.

Other holes in stories often result from carelessness. An address given only as "Meadow Lane" needs a number with it: Check the telephone book. A story contains a name with "nmi" (no middle initial): Check the city directory or some other source. A suspect's age is missing: Call the police. A direct quotation does not match the speaker's previous stance: Call the source to clarify the quote. Then there's the story announcing that the city is hiring a new public works director; what happened to the former director? Whatever the story's shortcomings, the copy editor sees they are corrected.

Question Facts

It is not unfair to expect copy editors to know when the facts aren't facts. Copy editors are often thought of as trivia experts and knowledgeable in all fields, not just the humanities in which they are usually bred. One legendary editor found an error in a complicated equation done by Albert Einstein.

Sometimes, though, the error is not so clear-cut. What is the fact error in a story saying that a state's Supreme Court ruled that the state police may not reveal a suspect's prior record? The case involved an action taken by the state police but the decision really applied to all police in the state. Realizing that, a copy editor called the wire service that produced the story and shortly after received a correction.

Such fussiness not only gives the reader a better product but also serves historians who frequently rely on newspapers as a starting point for research. A historian can lose precious time chasing a false start provided by a newspaper. Corrections often don't help because they receive less prominent display than the error.

Get the Facts Straight

The suspicious minds that edit newspapers do not know everything, but they know enough to recognize their limitations. Good copy editors are smart enough to know what they don't know.

A story that says a jury ordered testimony stricken from the record should raise the eyebrows of a high school student in a civics class and should move a copy editor to change "jury" to "judge," the only person in a trial with authority to order testimony stricken. The same copy editor knows that referring to the senators who represent the 50 states in Congress as "state senators" confuses them with the senators who convene in state capitols. A senator in Washington is a "U.S. senator." Similarly, the copy editor knows that the headline **Soviet ambassador appointed** suggests someone from the Union of Soviet Socialist Republics, not the U.S. ambassador the story is about.

Eyebrows go up again when a reporter turns in a crime roundup story and writes in one paragraph that someone forged the name of "Irene Zepanski" on a check and three paragraphs later that someone damaged a bicycle owned by "Irene Zepanski." Either it's a lightning-strikes-twice story that needs a new lead or it's a case of reporter carelessness. The copy editor must ask.

In that category of suspicious editing is the story about the columnist who referred to wasps, hornets and yellow jackets as "bugs." Checking with a dictionary and an entomologist, the newspaper's in-house critic learned that wasps belong to the superfamilies *Vespoidea* and *Sphecoidea;* yellow jackets are small wasps and belong to the family *Vespidae;* hornets belong to the genera *Vespa* and *Vespula.* Bugs, on the other hand, belong to the order *Hemiptera,* which is none of the preceding. Unfortunately, the abuse appeared in print because a copy editor decided to make a guess rather than check it. Said the entomologist: "All bugs are insects but not all insects are bugs." He said nothing about copy editors.

Exercise Doubt

It's to every copy editor's advantange to know the frailties of each reporter. One reporter overwrites every story because he sees a Pulitzer Prize at the end of the daily press run; another is too lazy to check names; so-and-so fancies herself an expert and knows more about the subject than her sources (she never makes mistakes; her sources do); another turns in sloppy copy; still another begins every story with a direct quotation despite the general injunction against that practice; finally, another is mischievous. He filed this story:

> City police estimate damage of $150 in an incident of criminal mischief at Memorial Park yesterday.

Police said a 1,750-pound gravestone was reportedly moved from its place over a grave. Memorial Park attendant Caesar Romane said he was asleep at the time it occurred. When he went on his early morning rounds he said he noticed the incident in the "J" section of the cemetery.

A sleepy copy editor forgot the reporter's mischievous nature and didn't realize that the story was turned in on Good Friday. The next day's paper reported that the story was fictitious and had not been intended for publication. Neither the copy editor (who removed a direct quote: "Lo, the stone was rolled away.") nor the reporter was fired—but both should have been.

Less spectacular but every bit as much an error is the story about a man who donated 14 gallons of blood to a bloodmobile during one visit. Eventually the story reveals that the man began contributing blood in 1953 and then the reader realizes that the 14 gallons weren't given in one visit.

There's the story quoting an athletic director as saying he has devised a scheme for crowd control at the local football stadium, a scheme that will eliminate the panic and pressure at the stadium's "portholes." Unfortunately, the word appeared four times. The athletic director knows the difference between windows in a ship (portholes) and entranceways in a stadium (portals), but the reporter and copy editor didn't.

Despite the initial tone of this section, future copy editors should not assume that reporters are nothing but a bunch of error-prone, carefree, pompous egotists who care not one wit for quality. While all humans (copy editors included) have their shortcomings, many reporters are dedicated to their craft and become upset with themselves when they make mistakes and unhappy with copy editors who don't catch the errors. Rapport between reporters and copy editors makes for a better newspaper, and both would be remiss to view the relationship as "us vs. them." Reporters and copy editors are not separate camps; in fact, they cannot function as separate camps.

Don't Trust the Wires

The editors of wire services would agree with the advice that their work not go into any newspaper without being checked by a copy editor at that newspaper. The wire services make mistakes—sometimes attributable to humans working in haste but other times attributable to electronic machines malfunctioning.

The human errors show up in such examples as the story that starts out saying four women had themselves sterilized and then refers to one in an attribution tag as "one of the five women sterilized." Here is another human error that got into print:

The victims, in addition to Mrs. Hopp, were identified as PGW customer relations specialist Edward Brown, 47; Henry Traynor, 38; Gerald Ladzenski, 26; Anthony Kasiewski, 54; Harry F. Smith, 50, and Alfred C. Kahrklinsch, about 62.

The seventh body had not been identified, although PGW officials said customer relations specialist Edward Brown, who was at the scene when the explosion occurred, was missing.

The initial story listed the six names that could be confirmed and then published the speculative paragraph quoting PGW officials. Later, officials confirmed the seventh name and the wire service updated its story by sending a new paragraph listing all of the dead. The instructions with the paragraph said **SUB** (for *substitute*) but the wire service editor forgot to add a line advising copy editors to delete the other paragraph.

In a newspaper without a front-end system, an editor might have sent the substitute paragraph to the shop and hoped someone put it in the story. That would account for the confusing paragraph remaining in the story. But in a newspaper with a front-end system, it matters not that the story has been sent to production because the copy editor can easily retrieve it from a holding file, fix it and check it—and catch the confusing paragraph about the seventh victim. The speed of the front-end system makes it easy to reset entire stories in type.

The machine errors show up only occasionally when a computer allows part of one story to merge with another. The people reading a story about a public utility commission meeting and suddenly coming across a paragraph about a terrorist group will certainly wonder what it all means to their electric bills. What it means to the newspaper is that some copy editor did not read through the entire wire service story. Thus, while all the errors noted here are wire service errors, they become the newspaper's once they appear in print.

A final note: A copy editor should immediately report to the responsible wire service bureau any error in a wire service story so the wire service can issue a correction.

Watch for New Words Made by "Typos"

Many typographical errors leap out at copy editors—when they're reading the newspaper, which is the wrong time. The more serious errors are those that create new words, usually turning an otherwise serious story into a funny one. For example, when Gerald R. Ford was president in the mid-1970s, this headline appeared: **110 refugees hit by Ford poisoning.** The headline writer either was making a political statement or not thinking.

Countless other "typos" (as typographical errors are called) include the infamous "not" of "not guilty" being turned into "now" and the "Taft" of "Taft-Hartley" anti-union fame becoming "Daft" at the hands of a union Linotype operator. Less serious errors include those that refer to "closet friends" (which we could all use) or "closest fiends" (which we don't need). Then there's the bluegrass music columnist whose reference to a "mandolin picker" came out "pecker." With the copy editor now the only backstop between reporter and reader, vigilance to catch errors must be tripled. VDTs don't proofread stories.

Keep Style Consistent

"Style," a beginning copy editor once said, "is like a pica. Every editor works with it, but there's always an aura of mystery over the concept." The editor was complaining because she felt her co-workers did not appreciate the need for a consistent style. "You cannot have as many styles as you have reporters and copy editors," she said. "Style is not just a needless, antiquated detail, but a way of keeping the consistency and thus the credibility of the paper alive." The reader who sees a reference to "110 E. Foster Ave." in one story and to "110 East Foster Avenue" in another must wonder about the reliability of the people reporting the news. The reader affixes that doubt to the newspaper, whose credibility suffers not only on Page One but in every department. A newspaper that lacks credibility speaks with a muted editorial voice.

Protect Against Libel

One restaurant reviewer said a restaurant offered "rock-hard Italian bread, pricey steaks and indifferent cooking" and cost his newspaper $23,000 in libel damages, while another reviewer at another paper said of a different restaurant: "My steak, listed as 10 ounces, seemed smaller. It appeared to have been cooked in a blast furnace, which may have accounted for its scrawny look." The reviewer also said that the prime rib his spouse ordered had "a strange, unpleasant flavor." The restaurant sued and lost. If you were an editor in Florida and you looked to those court decisions to figure what is libelous and what is not, you'd have a hard time deciding. Both decisions were made in Florida.

No editor can be certain what a judge will find libelous and what a judge will say represents truth, qualified privilege, or fair comment and criticism—all defenses against libel. But a copy editor has to have a sense of what libel is. Generally, libel is anything written that besmirches a person's good name. It does not matter if the libel appears in a letter to the editor, an advertisement or a comic strip, the newspaper is responsible for it and can be sued, an expensive proposition even before a court hearing begins. (Radio and television stations are not responsible for libel committed in a live broadcast, but the person speaking the libel is.) In the heat of a good story, a copy editor should remember that waiting 24 hours before printing a charge against someone is better than damning a person to an onslaught of innuendo brought on by an erroneous newspaper story. When a person's reputation is being maligned, proceed cautiously.

Calling someone charged with a murder a "suspected murderer" means the person is a murderer suspected of having murdered again. The safest approach: Say the person has been charged with murder. That's a fact. "Allegedly" won't save the newspaper. A sentence saying someone was "allegedly" involved in a check-forging scheme makes the scheme a fact before a court has found anyone guilty. Thus, even a person "allegedly involved" is tainted by association.

Ascribing any criminal intent to someone invites libel lawyers by the dozens. In a strike, the president of a union was quoted in a newspaper as saying one of his supervisors (and he was named) had sped through a picket line and hit a striker with his car. The story contained no confirmation from the police or the hospital, yet a crime had been claimed (it is illegal to hit someone with a car). Lacking some confirmation from authorities, the newspaper's best bet was to use the item without names and add a sentence saying the newspaper could not confirm the incident. The major point behind that example is that even though the newspaper quoted someone as making the charge, the newspaper can still be sued. So can the person making the charge, of course, but the newspaper has more money.

Libel appears most frequently in crime news, sports stories, restaurant and art reviews (that go beyond the bounds of fair comment and criticism), cartoons (such as caricatures), local government reports and editorials and commentaries (such as satire). All stories, of course, are prone to providing material for a libel suit, and, as Florida restaurant reviewers can attest, a valid defense in one court may not work in another. Saying that someone is a public figure and cannot be libeled offers no hard and fast definition of who a public figure is. The courts continue to offer varying interpretations of what constitutes a public figure. The test a copy editor should try: "How would I feel if this story were about me?" Such caution is unnecessary when people who are obviously public figures are involved. The best example—anyone holding elective office.

Copy editors are not lawyers and should not be the last word when doubt exists about a potentially libelous story. Nevertheless, copy editors can do their best to protect the newspaper by ensuring that all sides of a story are given, that the person presented in a bad light has been given an opportunity to comment, that headline and story agree (in fact, headlines should be muted for they lack the qualified privilege some stories get), that identification of people in a photograph is accurate. Finally, in exceptional cases don't be bashful about consulting a lawyer. Smart publishers keep one on retainer for just such a purpose.

Respect Privacy

The woman in Figure 3.2 complained to the newspaper that published the photograph that it had violated her privacy. Her college lacrosse team had just lost a close match—the final of her collegiate career—and she sought consolation from her father. To many who saw the photograph, it showed no invasion of privacy but a special relationship no

Figure 3.2 A special relationship or invasion of privacy—those were the two reactions to this photograph. (Betsy Overly/*The Daily Collegian*)

words could explain. Legally, the photograph did not invade the woman's privacy because it was taken at a public event and *usually* the courts have held that people do not enjoy a right to privacy at public events. Legality aside, the two interpretations of the photograph show the public is not as willing to concede their privacy as the courts are.

The reporter who interviews a child who just witnessed a fatal shooting has not only invaded the child's privacy but has offered the child a model of insensitivity. The reporter who rings the doorbell of someone whose only child has been missing and asks, "How do you feel about the disappearance of your only child?" deserves the contemptuous stare that serves as a response. If, however, the parents step from their home and conduct a news conference, the right to privacy recedes (although it doesn't go away completely).

A person's privacy seems invaded when that person—as an innocent third party—reports a crime, such as rape, and that person's name appears in print while the name of the victim does not because the newspaper has a policy of not publishing the names of rape victims. Fearful that innocent parties may suffer retaliation, some news media wisely refrain from reporting the names of third parties. After all, the person reporting the crime is not the news.

Other privacy invasions include eavesdropping and publishing or broadcasting stories that intrude on someone's seclusion or that present an excess of publicity on a person's private life. A transsexual who had had a sex-change operation from male to female won a $775,000 libel award after an *Oakland Tribune* columnist called her a male. The plaintiff said the column was a "callous invasion of privacy." A *Tribune* lawyer argued that the transsexual, then president of the student body at a small college, was a public figure, a questionable status at that level. Publishing the criminal record of someone who has paid the debt and lived a crime-free life since may not legally invade that person's privacy but will certainly not win the newspaper any respect in the community. An exception most certainly would include anyone seeking a law enforcement position. The public has a right to know about such a candidate's past because it could have bearing on how the candidate will enforce the law.

Remember Your Audience's Tastes

Community standards sometimes more than the law dictate what a newspaper will publish. In many newspapers four-letter words are taboo simply because editors believe that children will read the newspaper and learn the words. That's not how children learn four-letter words, but seeing them in print can serve as reinforcement that such words are okay.

Sex provides another area where community coyness may determine what a newspaper publishes. Some mental health experts suggest that society has sexual hang-ups, and perhaps the news media that euphemistically publish or broadcast stories on the subject have contributed to the hang-ups.

Unless the newspaper is a sensationalistic tabloid, a newspaper should avoid such tastelessness as the headline on a story about two composers dying two days apart—**Composers dropping like flies**—or the attempt at humor when Ray Kroc, the chairman of the board of McDonald's Corp., announced he had entered an alcoholic treatment center and a columnist wrote: "I guess this means that Ray won't get Krocked anymore." Likewise, the headline on a story about Senator Edward M. Kennedy seems oblivious to the assassinations of two of his brothers. The headline: **Kennedy comes to town to do or die.** On a story about a blind person, an insensitive headline-writer wrote: **Okay to be blind.** The reader takes offense even if none is intended.

Gang Up on Double Entendres

It has been said that if anyone on a newspaper staff needs a dirty mind, it is the copy editor, who must watch for two-faced sentences. One of the double meanings is usually racy—and that's usually the meaning the reader remembers. **Prostitutes appeal to pope** and **Police can't stop gambling** may get by but a reporter who writes about a police officer who "relied on intuitive judgment when he exposed himself to an armed suspect" invites smirks and maybe an angry telephone call or two.

Copy editors must be alert for the reporter who writes "the climax of the meeting arrived with a bang when a spectator's chair broke and the person fell to the floor" because the reporter is obviously trying for the double entendre. The reporter who wrote "Idi Amin is holed up in Libya with his two wives and a concubine" may have missed the subtle double meaning—but then again, so did the newscaster who read the sentence over the air.

Challenge Profanity

Profanity should not be used unless it is part of a direct quotation and then only if necessary to tell the story. People who speak in a continuum of profanities show a mental defect, an inability to select original words. Remove such a person's cursing streak and the copy editor may find nothing was said at all.

One of those necessary times for printing profanity arose when the Watergate tapes of the mid-1970s were released. The profanities showed a mentality impossible to depict without publishing the foul words of a president and his henchmen. The wire services marked the stories so newspapers and readers knew the stories contained profanities. Television newscasters blipped the foul words but as they read a direct quotation, all the words—even the ones not spoken—appeared on the screen. Those were unusual times and called for unusual approaches.

In its entry on "obscenities, profanities, vulgarities," *The Associated Press Stylebook* advises: "In reporting profanity that normally would use the words *damn* or *god*, lowercase *god* and use the following forms: *damn, damn it, goddamn it*. Do not, however, change the offending words to euphemisms. Do not, for example, change *damn it* to *darn it*."

Put Precision into Sentences

Sentences constructed with misused words and phrases quickly fall apart, leaving behind only a rubble of imprecision. The copy editor who allows such contradictions as "about 26.5 percent" or "some 17 people" creates ambiguous situations that becloud a sentence's intent. The reporter who refers to the U.S. House of Representatives as "Congress" and the copy editor who does not fix it both need civics lessons. "Tossle-capped children" may conjure up for the reporter an image of children frolicking in the snow, but the reader sees nothing because "tossle" is not a word. (The writer meant "tassel.")

To say that "Tom O'Hara had both hands amputated at City Hospital" suggests the action of a crazy person. Who knows what kind of action is taking place in this example: "The governor said he spent hours trying to smooth over conflicts but *concluded the constant clashes* were hampering government operations." At first it suggests that the governor ended the clashes but what he really did was "conclude *that* the constant clashes were hampering government operations," which is an entirely different ending.

Given a public not as skilled with the language as journalists are supposed to be, letters to the editor can present challenges for the desk. A letter writer angry that she had missed a deadline for paying a traffic ticket complained about the delay of "receiving a traffic violation in the mail." What she got in the mail was a *"ticket* for a traffic violation," traffic violations being hard to mail. Finally, what of the reporter who wrote that "the controversy erupted last week when the chairperson requested her to respond to published reports about her absences in writing"? How is one absent in writing? The sentence should say: "The controversy erupted last week when the chairperson requested her to respond in writing to published reports about her absences." Those and other examples throughout this book build a case for precise reporting and writing and thorough copy editing.

Be Alert for Duplication

Some stories—especially those on the crime beat—can come from many different sources. One example suffices: A prison inmate is stabbed and his assailant is arraigned before a minor judge who refuses to name the injured prisoner. A story is written. The state police, on the other hand, provide the particulars of the crime and another story is written, although by a different reporter. One of the stories shows up on Page 2, the other on Page 16. Similar problems might arise at a newspaper with two wire services or a regular newswire and, say, a business wire. A story on the same event moves on both wires and appears on a news page and on the business page. The failure here is due to the lack of communication between two editors.

Duplication can also mean the copy distributor was not thinking and failed to exploit the VDT with its split-screen capability (see Chapter 1). Routinely, the desk should question some stories for duplication and when a copy chief suspects duplication, he or she should check. VDTs with split-screen capabilities make the checking and comparison easier. They also offer the desk an opportunity to compare two wire services' versions of the same event.

Do the Math

One of the seldom thought-of basic tools of copy editing is the calculator, which allows a copy editor to easily check a reporter's math. If a story says snow removal costs are up 5 percent over last winter, the copy editor should do the math to make sure. Some newspaper computers have been programmed to calculate percentages, especially in the sports department where batting averages (among others) frequently change.

If the unemployment rate last month was 10 percent and this month's is 5 percent, the decline is 50 percent or 5 percentage points but not 5 percent. On top of that, the 50 percent figure says so much more than the 5 percentage points and is the preferred way to express employment statistics. Only with interest rates does a decline expressed in percentage points mean more to the reader. The desk should be alert for any story in which the insertion of percentages will make the story clearer. Election returns expressed in whole numbers alone are not always as meaningful as when they are accompanied (not substituted) by percentages.

In a mathematical vein of sorts, when a story says five people were arrested, a copy editor should count the names listed. A reporter can easily forget to list a name or two. In general, the desk should check any use of numbers. For example, a news release from a county office included this paragraph:

> According to population figures, Abington Township has taken over the top spot as the most populous municipality in Montgomery County, with a population of 58,624, some 4,200 less than 1970 when the township was the second most populated municipality in the county with 63,625.

The copy editor who automatically checks the math will find a discrepancy of 801. Even if the copy editor must call someone at home at night to clarify the math, the copy editor should not hesitate. The county officer who made the mistake appreciates the backstopping, and the newspaper, by not printing the error, saves its credibility from another beating.

Verify Names

A radio news reporter who was terrible at remembering people's names would greet a familiar face but forgotten name with, "Hi, how are you?" and then slyly add: "By the way, just how do you spell your last name?" The ploy fell apart one day when a person haughtily responded: "S-m-i-t-h." The news reporter, though, should not have been embarrassed because some "Smiths" spell their names "Smyth" and others spell it "Smythe"—and all pronounce it the same way.

The failure to correctly spell a person's name when compounded with the failure to correctly identify the person through age and street address could result in a court suit. The reporter who heard a court official say "Robin Shoemaker of Pilsdon was arrested on sodomy charges" has created a problem when it was not the 22-year-old Robin *Shoemaker* at 136 Bath Ave. but the 53-year-old Robin *Shoonmaker* at 211 S. 10th St.

"Francis" sounds the same no matter if it's a man or a woman's name, but the person's sex does determine the spelling (*is* for men; *es* for women). Is that person's name John R. Nichols or John S. Nichols? The telephone book, the newspaper's files or the city directory can provide the detail. The ultimate source, of course, is the person in the story, who can be queried by telephone. As a matter of policy, a copy editor should check every name in a story even if a reporter swears the check was already made.

Stamp Out Stereotypes

The time has long passed for the news media to cease reinforcing stereotyped views of females, veterans, the United States, people over 60, blacks, Jews and orientals and any other ethnic group whose image is misleadingly preserved in a narrow wedge of description. This is a pitch against *isms*: sexism, ethnocentrism, ageism, racism, xenophobism.

Do not refer to a person's physical attributes as though they were the person. "Stunning women" and "muscular men" are so frequent in pulp novels they've become a cliche. In the news media they are condescending.

Avoid the Vietnam war and World War II syndrome of providing a criminal suspect's military background to the point of creating the impression that a high number of verterans are involved in crimes. That happened after World War II and did not cease until veterans' groups complained. Post-Vietnam reporting created the stereotype of the half-crazed veteran who held people at bay with an arsenal of weapons. Television writers helped fan the image until virtually every Vietnam veteran was considered a dope addict about to shoot up a town.

Keep in mind, too, that America is two continents and several islands large and is not confined to the United States. The wire service reporter who wrote that *Cuban president Fidel Castro came to America today . . .* probably flunked geography. After all, Cuba is part of America and, as the sentence concludes, Castro knew where he was—"I'm glad to be in the United States."

With life spans lengthening and the vitality of people lasting into their eighth and ninth decade, do not use terms that suggest people over 60 are elderly or slow moving or senile. What the body loses in strength over the years the mind gains in wisdom.

Blacks are not chicken-loving lazy dumbbells who couldn't get to work on time without a white man's alarm clock, and Indians are not herded together in tribes eager for the white man's largess. Orientals are not launderers by birth.

Be sensitive, unlike the writer of a caption on a photograph of an anti-Israel speaker. The editor gave the caption this legend—**Shalom,** which is Hebrew for "peace." No anti-Israel speaker would use the word and pro-Israel people would be offended by its use in this situation.

Don't make fun of the way people speak by using headlines like this—**Tickee but no seatee**—for it exhibits an editor's contempt for the ethnic variety that makes up the United States.

Spurn the mentality of the reporter who always identified black criminal suspects as black but never whites as whites and who passed off his ignorance with the line, "If they're not black, they must be white." An editor should remove all references to race unless the race is given as part of a specific description—blue eyes, curly dark hair, 5-6, 160 pounds and white—or is pertinent to the story, such as a minority person being elected to an office previously the exclusive domain of whites. Clearly people such as S.I. Hayakawa, Martin Luther King, Albert Einstein and Eleanor Roosevelt—to name just a few of many—have by their accomplishments debunked the myth that race or religion or sex makes the person. The news media, which have had a hand in perpetuating the stereotypes, are now slowly working to abolish them.

Be a Self-Checker

Except on larger newspapers, a copy editor lacks a backstop—another copy editor to ensure that mistakes were not edited into a story or that a headline fits a story or that a caption is accurate. Good copy editors check their work carefully and with prejudice. They do not say, "I did it, therefore it must be right." At all times they keep their limitations in mind. A self-checker makes the time to do the job well and takes the time to check the job once it's completed.

CHAPTER FOUR

The Written Word

The Need for Graceful Prose

If you have ever walked through a stream with a mucky bottom and your feet stuck with every step so that you had to jerk them to get them out of the mud and move on, then you know how readers feel when they encounter sentences bogged down by wordiness or ambiguity or trips on points unrelated to the main thought. Smooth writing, in other words, equals smooth reading, an essential ingredient in any printed medium competing with television and radio, the easy media to consume. The television viewer merely sits before a moving picture enhanced with sound; that requires no effort. But reading a newspaper or magazine requires some energy on the reader's part, which means the writer must use good writing to reduce the expenditure of energy.

The bridge between the writer and reader is the copy editor, who must carve—but not butcher—each story so that it runs smoothly through the reader's mind. The copy editor works overtime for the reader, ensuring easy reading by deleting cliches, extraneous words, jargon, ambiguities, nondescript adjectives and adverbs. How well the whole stands up, of course, is as important as its parts.

Does the story get right to the point? Is it accurate? Is the lead smooth or does it meander and puzzle? Does the second paragraph deliver on the promise made in the lead? Does the third paragraph continue the development implicit in the lead and second paragraph? Are the direct quotations worthwhile to the story? Are opinions attributed? Is the tone of the story appropriate for the subject matter? Do sentences flow one unto the other? Has the writer drawn the most out of the language?

Those and other questions should confront copy editors every time they edit a story. The errors copy editors fix vary as much as the personalities of the writers, but the principles of good writing and good editing remain unchanged, and it behooves each copy editor to answer to those principles time and time again with concern for the quality of the prose and the exactitude of the message.

The good copy editor does not suffer from itchy cursor, does not edit for the sake of editing, but instead carefully—yet quickly—studies the story to ensure that it performs, that it is the concert of words the writer intended for the reader to enjoy. A good copy editor does not automatically remove verbiage without reason. A mindless copy editor, intent on saving space, would have told President Lincoln to tighten the opening of the Gettysburg Address from "Four score and seven years ago . . ." to "Eighty-seven years ago . . .," assuring brevity but destroying rhythm.

A good copy editor knows that subjects and verbs function best when close together. Search through this example for the impact neutralized by too great a distance between the actor and the action:

> The Barbell Club, which also won't be able to use the facilities during the day even though it donated approximately $1,200 in equipment to the weight room last year, also had no say in the change.

Pity the reader who must stumble over word after word after word—words that don't link directly to the subject. Recognizing the muck at the bottom of such a sentence, the copy editor inverts the order, putting the verb and subject up front and close together, the better to make the point:

> Also given no say was the Barbell Club, which won't be able to use the facilities during the day even though it donated approximately $1,200 in equipment to the weight room last year.

Comprehension advances a big step in the rewrite and transition is aided, almost by accident, because *also* leads off the sentence, thereby linking the previous thought to the new thought.

Points unrelated to the main thought of a sentence fall to the copy editor's cursor. A sentence contains one thought, the copy editor knows, and when a sentence wallows in several, the unrelated points become non-sequiturs. "Born in Los Angeles," such a false sentence might begin, "the deceased was a member of the Barbell Club." The copy editor separates the nativity from the activity and reunites them with their appropriate relatives.

Words get special treatment—almost a fondling—among copy editors eager to oust gracelessness and inelegance from a story. Times have changed since copy editors lost a week's pay for letting into print one misused word, but the punishment might be worth restoring for those who perform slovenly at the terminal.

No copy editor sensitive to the difference between transitive and intransitive verbs would allow either of these headlines: **Girl in red bikini defects Russia** and **Scared Americans evacuate Iran.** *Russia* and *Iran* can be objects of verbs, but the verbs must be transitive. In fact, *evacuate* has one transitive meaning that describes bodily functions, not bodily fears.

One wonders who the bigger fool is when sentences such as this see print—*Lubold was almost near perfect*—the anonymous copy editor who was far from perfect or Lubold, who might as well be "almost near-sighted" or "a little bit pregnant" or "virtually unique." For the reader, the error besmirches the newspaper's credibility, while inside the newspaper, the desk—not the writer—bears the shame. The laughter born in *Former President Gerald Ford breakfasted on Capitol Hill today* does not hide the shortcoming of the copy editor who failed to see the double meaning. As the copy editor's editor later asked: "Isn't Capitol Hill nutritionally deficient?" The copy editor wisely did not respond.

The News Story Leads

Although the inverted-pyramid formula for writing news has fewer and fewer adherents as newswriting styles change, its underlying concepts are still valid. No matter if the story begins with a who-what-why-when-where-how lead or with the subtlety of a novel, the principle remains the same: Does the lead work? The person who can best answer that is the copy editor, the first tester any story comes up against. The copy editor, although required to read the entire story, must decide if the reader, lacking the compulsion of a job, will do the same. If the lead fails, the copy editor must determine why and then return the story to its writer or apply the polish at the desk.

Leads come up short or fail outright for any number of reasons. One guarantee of failure is the imprecise lead that waffles about for 40 words and never settles down to tell the story. Such leads attempt to say too much and are best repaired through excision—cut the facts not required to tell the story's main point and blend them as needed in subsequent paragraphs. In some cases, the excised facts might provide the information for a new paragraph.

Leads without news put readers to sleep. The story that begins *City Council convened last night to discuss next year's budget and last year's unresolved contract with union employees* only to later let out—and there's no more accurate description for such sleepers—that the City Council raised taxes and fired the unionized employees is certain to ensure an unread story. Operating with the news-eager reader in mind, the copy editor reorders the story, often by eliminating the discussion angle for one of precision. *City Council last night raised taxes an average of $20 to pay for hiring employees to replace those fired for not signing a contract.* Such a lead deserves its name—pocketbook—because that's where the reader is going to feel it. Now, the story will probably be read.

Cliché leads dampen reader interest because they display the writer's lack of concern for original prose and their lack of news. "I've read that before," the reader might think when the same old words appear. Consider the family-outing-ending-in-tragedy lead: *A family fishing outing ended in tragedy when a man and his 14-year-old son were swept off a breakwater by the highest surf in eight years yesterday.* A copy editor could remove the cliche with: *The highest surf in eight years swept a man and his 14-year-old son to their deaths from a breakwater where they had been fishing yesterday.* Removing the cliche makes the lead direct, appealing and more original.

Leads lacking comparative data leave readers suspended in a "So what?" state where they refuse to hang on long enough to see what the second paragraph says. A lead that reports the number of deaths from heart disease without comparing that number to the total number of deaths in the population leaves the reader without a yardstick to measure the information. For example: *Heart disease claimed 378 lives in Pilsdon last year, according to a recent report from a Heart Association official.* Is 378 high? Low? How does it compare with total deaths? That information probably hides in the story's body from where the copy editor should dislodge it and place up front. *Heart disease claimed 378 lives in Pilsdon last year—more than any other cause of death, a Heart Association official says.*

A lead piled high with statistics is likely to stupefy readers rather than enlighten them. A story beginning *Four Clive County residents ranging in ages from 17 to 75 died in three traffic accidents within a 12-hour period* suggests the clumsy hand of a sportswriter raised on stolen bases, runs batted in, walks, and, yes, strikeouts than the deft sense of a writer working for the reader.

Leads containing lists—a superficial check-off of major actions taken at some meeting—make the reader yearn for the lead that puts the most important action up front. A lead of lists delays the news and keeps the reader from finding out what happened.

Dependent clauses at the start of leads usually put such leads into the read-me-again category because the clauses appear ahead of the main part of the sentence, the part the clause depends on to make sense. Common to sportswriting, they begin: *Armed with a bat that was heavier than any he's ever handled before, Tiger star "Slugger" Strongarm tapped in the winning run . . .* Another: *Because of the high divorce rate, State Rep. Jonas A. Winston proposed yesterday that the state require engaged couples to wait six months before getting married.* In both, the beginning clauses bewilder the reader because the clauses lack context. "Why am I reading this?" the puzzled reader asks. Rewritten, the second lead might say: *State Rep. Jonas A. Winston has proposed making engaged couples wait six months before marrying as a way of curbing the state's high divorce rate.* (Dependent clauses at the start of any sentence but a lead usually cause none of the same problems.)

Leads that come up short can usually be repaired with information from the second paragraph of the story because that's where the news frequently lies. The writer failed to report first the most current *important* detail. For example: A person has been arrested and taken before a judge for processing and the judge has set bail which the arrested person cannot pay and has been jailed in lieu of. The lead that misses the mark reports the arrest but it should report the person being in jail in lieu of bail. The jailing of a person in lieu of bail usually subsumes the arrest, the appearance in court and the setting of bail, so provide that information in subsequent paragraphs in decreasing order of importance.

Direct quotation leads, especially in hard news (24 hours young or younger) should be paraphrased on the asumption that any writer can improve on the spoken word. To be allowed into print, a quotation lead must be compelling, must still meet the number one purpose of a lead— engage the reader. Quotation leads are also flawed because they lack context. The reader first meets quotation marks, not an attribution tag, and thus does not know who is speaking. Such leads make a reader go by twice (if the writer's lucky enough to get a second chance) in order to make sense out of the direct quotation.

The good lead does more than recite a story; it advertises the story's best points. When a presidential candidate spoke in coal-laden Pennsylvania, one journalist wrote: *Republican presidential candidate John Connally last night said coal could be the key to the solution of the country's energy problems.* But Connally lives in Texas where oil—not coal—is an important fuel. A sprightly lead would can the ho-hum and make something of the contrast. *A presidential candidate from oil-rich Texas said last night coal could be the key to solving the country's energy problems.* That lead points out the contrast between the candidate and the candidate's platform.

A time element can dull an otherwise good lead when placed out front. Newspapers usually do not report hard news older than 24 hours so it's unlikely that the reader—aware of the timeliness of news—needs a time element at the beginning of a story. In fact, given newspapers' trend toward soft or feature leads on news, copy editors have to decide if the time element is necessary in the lead at all. Thus, an otherwise interesting lead should not be tampered with to fit in a time element not crucial to the major point of the story.

This Thursday afternoon lead on a Wednesday morning story by Paula Maynard of United Press International ignores the time element and stresses the human element of a tragedy.

> Six-year-old Travis Crook, stabbed and bleeding, walked with his dog the one block to school with a message for his principal: The boy's mother and younger brother had been slain.

Editors call the preceding a second-day lead because it appears not necessarily in the second day after the news but it is the second lead on the story, the first having been written for an earlier edition or by the competition. Faced with a competitive situation, Athelia Knight of the *Washington Post*, started a stabbing story this way:

> It was about 3 a.m. yesterday when D.C. City Councilman David A. Clarke left a sandwich shop at 18th Street and Columbia Road and began walking home. As he reached 16th and Harvard streets NW, he said he sensed someone behind and continued walking at a steady pace.
> Clarke said that when he reached the walkway to his home at 320 17th St. NW, three men jumped him from behind, punched him in the face and stabbed him twice in the back. Clarke suffered superficial wounds to his back and was in good condition late yesterday at the Washington Hospital Center.

Perhaps the example shows a case of having your hard news and featurizing it too because the headline on Knight's story makes clear what the story is about: **City councilman is stabbed outside his Northwest home.** That shouldn't detract from what Knight did; she told the story from the victim's point of view and her approach makes for a more compelling beginning than this:

> A D.C. city councilman was in good condition late yesterday at the Washington Hospital Center where he was taken after he was stabbed twice by three men near his home early yesterday morning.

That's what used to pass for a second-day lead at third-rate newspapers.

To repair any lead on a VDT, the copy editor should put the terminal in the insert mode and, if necessary, rewrite the new lead *below* the old one. In that way, the old lead remains on the screen for instant comparison. When satisfied with the rewrite, the copy editor sends the old lead to oblivion by depressing the **PARA KILL** key.

The Body of the Story

Once the lead has taken shape, the development of the story concerns the copy editor next. One of the single biggest story organization problems stems from reporters who fail to follow their leads, fail to keep their initial promise to the reader. They instead lapse into background in the second and third (and maybe fourth) paragraphs while the reader hangs around (and a writer should not assume that will happen) waiting for current information. A news story should play up the news, what happened within the past 24 hours, not what happened two days or three weeks ago. Save that for later in the story—or for history books. Another organizational problem develops with the multi-topic story, which begins on one issue then abandons the issue in the second paragraph for another issue. For example:

> Mayor William F. Shanahan says disciplinary action will be taken against police sergeants and lieutenants who, angry over unprecedented layoffs, called in sick or generally ignored prostitutes, gamblers and traffic violators.
> Meanwhile, members of Firefighters Local 69, whose ranks also are to be trimmed by job cuts, planned to set up informational picket lines today outside the fire administration building.
> Local President John Henry said Wednesday members of the Fraternal Order of Police, which represents much of the city's 8,000-member force, would join the firefighters and march to city hall for a joint informational picket.
> "We will do whatever is necessary to save the jobs of our members," Henry said.
> He noted the membership had voted to authorize a strike but said no walkout was planned. Reilly said he would meet today with Shanahan.
> Shanahan's promise of disciplinary action followed a day in which officers in some districts refused to write tickets.

Four paragraphs intervene between the lead and the first paragraph that fills out the lead. The lead and the reader deserve better and the copy editor should make the appropriate changes by shifting paragraphs or creating a sidebar, both of which can be simply accomplished electronically.

News Style

Presenting news to readers who might want information quickly requires the news writer to avoid an episodic bent (and then . . . and then . . . and then . . .) and to condense information as tightly as possible. Don't allow two sentences in backward order when one in news style order will do.

> Hockton proposed that the trustees add a surcharge to the Spring Quarter bill instead of raising tuition. [No news so far; the trustees' vote will be the news.] The motion failed, 14–7. [The news!]

Regrettably, the reporter has forced the reader to hang on to learn the news, which is then poorly presented in a limp sentence that seems stuck on to the end of the paragraph as an afterthought. This rewrite rejects the episodic structure and condenses the information for a quick read.

> A motion by Hockton to place a $35 surcharge on Spring Quarter bills instead of raising tuition failed, 14–7.

. . . or . . .

> The trustees rejected, 14–7, a motion by Hockton to place a $35 surcharge on Spring Quarter bills instead of raising tuition.

The issue here is not sentence length but priority, of letting the reader know quickly what happened. The copy editor who turns episodic writing into news style serves the reader well.

Context

Another trap snaps when a reporter fails to provide the context for any direct quotation. Reading through a story, the reader encounters: "We've asked for Timothy O'Hara's resignation." The next paragraph reveals that O'Hara is the county planning director but doesn't explain why his job is on the line. Three paragraphs later the reader learns it was O'Hara who hired the consulting firm that approved building a county park on chemical-infested land, a problem that should have been detected before the county purchased the land. But the reader doesn't learn that at the right moment. The copy editor, thus, must rearrange or rewrite the story to give the direct quotation context.

Viewpoint

Point of view problems should not be taken casually. When such errors appear, they should be firmly removed from copy. The reporter who writes about "our weather" might confuse the reader who thinks "our" refers to the newspaper. Change "our" to the appropriate name for the area. Similarly, a reporter could unintentionally become part of a story by using the personal pronoun "I" outside direct quotations. Usually, the reporter failed to provide quotation marks, but the copy editor should ensure that the "I" doesn't refer to the reporter.

Fairness must be maintained, leaving it up to the copy editor to check that the reporter is neither under- nor overplaying a story. Likewise, the copy editor must function as a goad when a reluctant reporter holds back because of the fear of offending some sacred cow, whether it be a religious sect, a lobbying group or the publisher's spouse. Similarly, the copy editor should ensure that the reporter did not fashion the story to elicit undeserved display from a prejudiced editor. That often puts the copy editor in the middle, but if copy editors remember that they work for the reader, they'll maintain their balance.

Copy editors must be on guard for unintended opinion, sometimes a product of a bleeding heart or an overwriter (one who makes more out of a story than the facts call for). The story of a 3-year-old harmlessly spun in a washing machine for five minutes does not rate this beginning—*A playful afternoon turned into a nightmare . . .*—when all the child suffered was very slight cuts and bruises and spent no more than 15 minutes in a hospital.

Attribution

Direct quotations provide another spot where a copy editor must maintain vigilance against error. The Iranian student who refers to the United States' acceptance of Iran's former shah as "an *insultation* to the Iranian revolution" doesn't know he has misused a word, but the copy editor does and should repair the damage. The issue, in that case, was political, not grammatical. Similar errors should be fixed rather than published to the embarrassment of the speaker and to what also appears to be the ignorance of the newspaper. Intentional language errors should stand, especially when they are used by the speaker for effect or are typical of the speaker and are used by the writer for flavor.

Attribution tag placement rates special attention from the copy editor, who should make sure that all tags appear as unobtrusively as possible. Bury attribution tags so they're not hanging off the ends of paragraphs or not starting paragraphs in such as way as to disrupt the flow of the story. Within paragraphs, the best place is between two sentences, such as:

> "We've come to the end of the road," *Herlocher said.* "Nothing can go beyond March 1. That's the absolute final date."

Within a sentence the attribution tag fits best at a natural break, as in this example:

> Officials earlier reported only six deaths. Eight of the deaths, *they explained*, went unreported for a time and three people reported dead were found safe.

The tag could begin the sentence but *they* might confuse the reader who momentarily links the plural pronoun to *deaths* rather than *officials*. Tucked inside the sentence, the tag remains out of the way yet still functions as intended. Attribution tags need to begin paragraphs or appear early in the first sentence of a paragraph when the story contains more than one speaker and the writer is shifting from one speaker to another.

Finally, copy editors should ensure that tags not only appear in the right place but that they appear at all. Unattributed sentences in news stories read like opinion—the opinion of the newspaper. But the newspaper wants only to cover the news as fairly as possible and to keep opinion out of the news columns. When anyone on the desk doubts the veracity of anything, senior editors should be consulted.

Tone

A copy editor should also oversee the tone and mood of a story. Keep irreverence from serious stories and confine flippancy to night club acts. Remove unintended slang and colloquialism. The following sentence from a caption on a photograph of people piling sandbags next to a threatening river strikes the wrong tone.

> Building sandcastles is fun but these Tijuana volunteers are not having a good time.

Combining a fun idea with life-saving efforts does not come off well. This headline, about the fatal crash of a jet owned by the Kellog company, should not have seen print: **Kellog jet takes dive.** The copy editor may laugh when seeing such absurdities and that should flash the warning light that something's wrong.

Other Story Types

Not every story in a newspaper is hard news. A good newspaper also contains feature stories, editorials, columns, entertainment and recreation news, reviews of books, theaters and restaurants, and profiles of people in the news. Excepting the editorials and columns, much of the preceding comes under the category of soft news. The name, however, should not detract from soft news' value to the reader. The work is still journalism and should be produced under the highest standards possible. Soft news must be as accurate as hard news and deserves as much attention from the copy desk.

When dealing with soft news and editorial page matter, copy editors must recognize that they are dealing with writing of a different form and probably of a different intent. Granted, all material in a newspaper (even advertisements) aims to communicate, but where hard news may provide timely, limited-use information, soft news can cover a range from entertainment to persuasion. The special sections in which soft news appears add depth to a newspaper.

Whatever writing style a reporter uses, a copy editor bears the ultimate responsibility for the success or failure of that style. The copy editor works carefully to avoid tramping on a writer's style while ensuring that the story is clear to the reader. Soft news, because it is frequently not produced against the tight deadline hard news is, comes in different forms and temperaments, which can cause problems in the hands of the unskilled. An inept writer, far from creating what some would loosely call a work of art, can instead produce a parody of literature. The copy editor must watch for such mistakes, beginning with the lead. Here is the beginning of an in-depth article:

> Helen is a lady with a pleasant personality who always has the time, it seems, to take time out from her canasta games to speak with friends and visitors at the Polk Senior Citizens Center.
>
> Although 84 years of life have taken away some of her hearing, they have not robbed her of the firmness in her voice as she fondly recalls earlier days growing up in Polk and watching the town grow with her.
>
> As a senior citizen and a retiree, she lives on a fixed income but still manages a comfortable life as a tenant in a downtown high-rise apartment building.

By now the reader must imagine this story's focus is senior citizens. The writer has certainly given that impression. Here is the next paragraph.

> In the midst of this picture of tranquility, however, a gray cloud hangs overhead, a harbinger of potential problems. Helen's apartment building is "going condo."

A couple of paragraphs later this sentence appears:

> This is not a scene from a soap opera.

But the writing is. For the writer has gotten off track, has been told to write a soft lead and thinks that such a lead is merely an introduction of one of the characters in the story. The writer has attempted to make drama where pathos exists, but has created a parody instead. The desk should send such a story back to the writer with advice on how to rewrite it.

What has happened in the soft news area has been the adaptation of literary techniques. Journalists strive for drama, for dialogue (rather than just direct quotes), for concrete images, for detail that puts the reader on the scene. Such pure intentions, however, are not without their flaws, for the writer bent on using literary techniques often uses them for their own sake rather than for the sake of telling the story. The result is a lot of irrelevancy. With apologies to the late novelist John O'Hara, this example:

> His pin-striped tan vest nicely setting off his neatly cuffed light blue shirt and brown polka-dotted tie, Francis S. Novinski was not alone as he sat in his chair behind his desk in the expansive, windowless executive office of the Schuylkill-Carbon Agency for Manpower (SCAM) in Gibbsville the other morning.

But neither was he visibly apprehensive as he coolly eyed three Gibbs-ville Standard reporters who were quizzing him on the intent of his newest brainchild, the Schuylkill Comprehensive Management Corporation (SCMC).

The impression he wanted to convey was one of self-confidence. If there was the slightest sign of nervousness, it was in the crossing and re-crossing of his legs.

His angry demeanor of the afternoon before, when he was first questioned on the less than easily comprehended SCMC fiscal management plan which he had submitted to the county as a possible remedy for its money woes, had disappeared.

Novinski leaned forward to answer some questions, swiveled or relaxed backward while responding to others. His "this is my turf" air was evident as he defended the SCMC concept, even though some of his comments appeared to be nebulous and contradictory.

All the story lacks is blue cigarette smoke wafting its way ceiling ward and tough guys Jimmy Cagney and George Raft in the roles of hard-hitting, inquisitive *Standard* reporters. Most of what the writer of the preceding has offered is not relevant to the main point of the story, which is an explanation of Novinski's proposal to solve the county's money problems. Any taxpayer would want to know more about solving money problems and less about Novinski's wardrobe and nervous habits. Again the copy editor sends the story back to the writer with suggestions for rewriting.

Detail in a story is fine, but it must have some bearing on the story. Why mention that the subject of a story chain smokes unless that person is a coal miner with black lung disease, which, like cigarette smoking, impairs breathing, or that person heads a fund-raising campaign to eradicate lung cancer? The details must say something germane about the people in the story. If they do not, the copy editor should remove them.

The same copy editor must recognize when to let a story alone and when to help a story along. Here are the first three paragraphs of a front page story from *The New York Times:*

WHY, Ariz.—It was the sweetest and gentlest of desert evenings, pitch-black except for a sliver of new moon and the light from a hundred thousand stars. Nearby, a coyote scampered among the stately organ pipe cactuses, its occasional mournful howl slicing the silence like a jagged knife.

Presently the stillness was broken by a softer sound, a brief, two-toned whistle. For half a minute there was nothing, then an identical whistle was heard from beyond the rise, followed by a flash of light and an answering flash, the signal that the way was clear. Within seconds, shadowy figures emerged from the desert. Smiling and talking softly, they gathered in a circle near the little-used highway.

After a moment, Bernabé Garay stepped forward. A dignified, cheerful man with a fondness for battered hats, "Don Berna" had led the others here: by bus, third class, from their cloud-high, stone-poor village in the

Sierra Madre; by pickup truck, at danger rates, from the border town of Sonoita to the gap in the barbed wire where, a few hours earlier, at nightfall, they had become illegal aliens; on foot, pressing hard, wary of rattlesnakes and border patrols, to a prearranged pickup point here in the Arizona desert. As it would prove, they had yet to face the greatest obstacles in their journey in search of work in the citrus groves around Phoenix.

The writer, John M. Crewdson, has definitely chosen a literary—but factual—start for his story, which a copy editor helped by simply headlining it: **The Illegal Odyssey of Don Bernabé Garay.** The package comes off as a short story.

Here is another lead, this one on a sidebar about the funeral of an undercover narcotics investigator. The story, written by Doris Wolf, appeared in the *Finger Lakes Times* of Geneva, New York.

> BUFFALO—It was a day the brave men cried.
>
> They came, almost 3,000 of them, to salute a fallen comrade, a man some had worked or trained with, but most never knew.
>
> It was enough that he wore the uniform.
>
> They came to bear witness to undercover narcotics investigator Robert Van Hall, a former Waterloo and Geneva area resident who was killed in a shotgun blast while on a drug investigation in Corning Friday night.
>
> The men wore the somber gray uniforms of the New York State Police, the blue of the Massachusetts State Police, the high brown leather laced up boots of the Rhode Island troopers, the crimson red jackets of the Royal Canadian Mounted Police, the earthy brown of the N.Y. State Department of Environmental Conservation. They wore shoulder patches that read California, Illinois, Toronto, and Border Patrol.
>
> Their badges, silver or gold shields or stars, were bisected with strips of black tape in official mourning.
>
> The uniformed police stood in sharp contrast to Van Hall's fellow plainclothesmen, who wore beards, mustaches and trench coats.

The copy editor who wrote the headline (see Figure 4.1) used Wolf's first paragraph, which took the edge off her story. Since it is a good headline, a better handling of the story calls for deleting Wolf's first paragraph and beginning the story with her second.

A copy editor must also know when to ignore a rule, such as the one that requires identification right after a person is named. In the following story from the *Philadelphia Bulletin*, identifying the person when his name first appears would not only make Warren Froelich's lead clumsy but would get in the way of the story.

> John A. Carr was virtually speechless.
>
> A web of scar tissue, created by massive doses of radiation used to treat his cancerous larynx, tied his two vocal cords together so he could barely speak above a whisper.
>
> What's worse, the web covered almost half his voice box, making it difficult for him to breathe.

Figure 4.1 A well-written sidebar to an undercover narcotics investigator's funeral received special display on the section page of the *Finger Lakes Times* of Geneva, New York. When editors display good writing, they send a message to reporters: Good writing is important.

Doctors told him his only option was complicated surgery, in which his throat would have to be slit, the web cut away, and a plastic triangle bolted in place between his two vocal cords until they healed.

The procedure would have involved a two-week hospital stay and cost more than $14,000.

But then Carr was told about laser surgery.

Soon, his web was literally vaporized through his mouth during a half-hour procedure at Montgomery Hospital in Norristown, Montgomery County.

That night he felt no discomfort, no swelling and saw no blood. His throat—which remained uncut—felt so good, he ordered doughnuts, crackers and a cola which he ate with no ill effects. He checked out of the hospital the following day.

Three weeks later, Carr, president of the Suburban Bank North in nearby East Norriston Township, was anything but speechless. His voice had returned.

As it turns out, the subject of the story is a banker, but his job has nothing to do with the main point of the story—laser surgery. The copy editor who read the story followed a higher rule—common sense.

One effective writing technique tells the story from the subject's point of view. That requires extensive research on the reporter's part, but the result can be very compelling. Sometimes reporters obtain the information, but fail to exploit it. An anecdote deep in a story may be just the thing to begin the story; the copy editor should look for an appropriate anecdote and move it forward.

The subject matter frequently lends itself to an above-average telling of a story. Testimony in a trial reads better when presented in the way it was given in court rather than in the inverted-pyramid form that upsets the suspense. Knowing where to begin the story is also important; the writer must pick up on the story just as it is ready to explode. Anita DiBartolomeo of the *Bucks County* (Pennsylvania) *Courier Times* wrote this story against a very tight deadline one morning:

> In bone-chilling detail, a sobbing Loretta Todt yesterday described to a Bucks County Court jury how she had dozed off watching television last March 19 and awoke as a man crept onto her bed, grabbed her by her nightgown and shot her in the eye.
>
> Mrs. Todt, speaking softly in a cracking voice as tears streamed down her face, said she saw another person standing in the darkened bedroom as her assailant grabbed her.
>
> Mrs. Todt said she was lying in bed, enjoying the television program "Vegas" the night she was shot.
>
> "The next thing I know is that I'm on the bed and there's somebody that's on the bed with me," she said. "The person was sitting on my right side there with me. The man was holding me like this (grabbing at her blouse).
>
> "I heard a thumping sound in which my head went like this," she said, throwing her head to the side. "The last thing I remember is getting up. My head was really hurting . . . I saw the blood all over my pillow, all over the sheets of my bed and just kept thinking 'My head, it hurts.'
>
> "I was looking in the (bathroom) mirror and I just kept seeing my head and the blood and it was all down the front of me. It was on my nightgown," she said as she sobbed. "I came downstairs . . . I looked, my car was gone. I remember coming into the kitchen area to see what time, what night, where Bob was . . . The clock said 11:15 (p.m.) . . . Then it dawned on me. I knew it was Wednesday night, I knew Bob wasn't there."
>
> Mrs. Todt said her 5-year-old son Anthony came downstairs after she had called her neighbors for help. "He was totally wide awake," she said as her 83-pound frame wracked with sobs.
>
> The frail, petite woman testified in defense of her husband, Bensalem special education teacher Robert Todt, 27, who is charged with plotting the

murder attempt by hiring John Chairmonte, an admitted drug addict and former learning disabled student, to kill her. Mrs. Todt, 26, lost her left eye in the shooting.

When asked if she thought her husband was involved in the crime, Mrs. Todt replied, "What I believe is what I believe and I know my husband did not do this."

She said she stared into the eyes of her confessed assailant—Chairmonte—two nights before the shooting when he suddenly appeared in her bedroom doorway.

She was lying in bed watching television and Chairmonte suddenly peered in at her from the doorway.

"All of a sudden, I saw this person coming up the steps and I looked at him and it wasn't Bob," she said. "He came right into my bedroom . . . I saw him looking at me and I looked at him . . . I got scared."

In editorials, copy editors should ensure that the writer's main point is clear, that the point is made without stridency, and that erudition in the writer's style does not come off as condescension in the reader's mind.

In columns, copy editors should remove the personal pronoun I whenever it intrudes on the main point. For example a columnist can say "War is immoral." Since the columnist's name appears on the column, readers know they are reading the columnist's opinion. Columns, especially those written by local people for small dailies or weeklies, are sometimes folksy to the point of parody and the desk should warn the columnist when that is happening. Some columnists need to be steered away from some subject matter (their personal lives) and toward more interesting subjects (other members of the community).

Profiles should not be just biography. If a reporter turns in such a profile, the desk should send it back with advice on how to improve it. Most likely, a copy editor can tell the writer to talk to some of the subject's friends (and enemies) in order to learn more about the subject. Direct the reporter to people who know the subject well.

The sports page represents the greatest potential for good writing and the greatest reality of bad writing. Sportswriters have long had more freedom than most writers in other sections of the newspaper, yet some sportswriters spurned their journalistic mission to produce cliché-filled cheerleading articles. If boosterism and clichés don't do in some sportswriters, synonyms will, for the sports hack does not like to use the same word twice and will go to any ambiguous length to avoid repeating a word. Some people believe that calling a left-handed pitcher a southpaw is good style; infrequent readers, though, must scratch their heads when facing sports page synonyms. The desk must clean up the copy.

In all of this, the copy editor and reporter should remember that stories are written for readers not writers. In a race between the reader's enjoyment and the writer's ego, the writer's ego shouldn't even enter.

Sentences and Paragraphs

Rules about sentences and paragraphs in the news media are based on utilitarian notions, not literary concepts. Journalists lean toward short sentences (an average of 17 to 20 words) because readability experts say that such sentences convey information easily. Still, don't count words in a sentence, but ask first how the sentence reads. That's the test. It's a matter of quality, not quantity.

The most accursed sentences of the lot are the fragment, which usually lacks a subject or verb, and the run-on, a continuous, as the name implies, gaggle of words that seem to never stop. Because so many thoughts make up a run-on sentence, clarity suffers; a run-on offers too much for the easy reader to digest.

The good copy editor, however, does not join a fragment to a whole or halt the run-on sentence without first ascertaining that the "error" impedes reading ease. Fragments can effectively make a point, especially in an editorial or a column. They are not as useful in straight news stories. Some run-on sentences have an ambience of harriedness and can be used to show that. For example:

> Complaining customers seeking refunds pursued him at his office, more than 15 civil suits were filed in small claims court in five days and the state Dental Council and Licensing Board changed its June hearing on the lab from an informal fact-finding to formal investigation which may end up taking away Burchill's license to be a dentist.

Quite a week for one person. Also quite a way to show it.

As for paragraphs, the major rule used to be: Keep them short, say, two sentences, sometimes three, and then only if the sentences are short. Behind that rule was a desire to make cutting stories easier (offset printing methods have negated that reason) and to put white space among the gray columns of type. But that reason too may lose its support as newspapers use other methods to put white space onto pages, including the very simple method of ragged right columns (explained in Chapter 7).

Newspaper utility aside, one old paragraph rule retains its virtue, and that is the one that says a paragraph is (at the least) a series of related sentences, and it is that rule that some newspaper paragraphs violate or ignore. If a paragraph takes three sentences, then the first cannot be about oil in Iran if the second is about a rebellion in Afghanistan and the third is about Muslims in Pakistan—unless the writer makes the relationship clear. If no relationship exists, the copy editor should depress the paragraph key at the end of each sentence to create three paragraphs. If a relationship exists, then the writer or the copy editor must show the relationship through transition.

Transition

Transition is the lubricant of good writing. The lack of it makes the reader stumble and turn away from a story because it seems to have suddenly changed topics without warning. Such an abrupt shift might appear as though two stories joined in the computer and came out as one. (Such an electronic coupling is possible but infrequent.)

Abrupt shifts are avoidable, although a writer might slip when writing against deadline. Then the desk must provide transition, which can improve a story faster than rewriting because one word can perform well by making a lot of words make sense. In fact, journalistic writing avoids long or formal transitions because they delay the reader who is quickly seeking information. By the same token, a story should not come off as a disjointed gathering of paragraphs. The longer the story, the more formal the transition.

In the typical news story (10 to 15 inches), the most effective transitional devices are short. A copy editor can readily change a topic on the strength of one word—*but, however, and, meanwhile*. A change in time or location can also be signalled easily—*later, elsewhere*. Geographical references make effective transition. In a winter storm roundup written for a national audience, the change of location can be heralded with the name of a town. For example:

> A major winter storm pounded the Middle West today, then headed toward the Atlantic Ocean . . .
> [*two paragraphs later*]
> In Des Moines, Iowa, schools closed as 10 inches of snow piled on top of 24 inches left by a storm last week.
> [*four paragraphs later*]
> Commuters in Chicago were kept home . . .
> [*three paragraphs later*]
> By the time the storm reached Cleveland . . .

Each stop along the way comes early enough to alert the reader to a change. The failure to provide transition can make for ambiguity beyond repair, as shown in this example:

> In Laramie, a 53-year-old man allegedly opened fire with a shotgun and killed a youth after the youth threw snowballs at his house, according to police.
> Wyoming Gas Co. spokesperson William C. Freed . . .

At first the reader may believe Freed pulled the trigger but what happened was the writer failed to use transition to advise the reader that the story was shifting from a slaying to a statement on thermostats. The copy desk failed for not catching the shortcoming and fixing it, perhaps by starting the new paragraph with *elsewhere*.

Tightening Copy

Nobody enjoys listening to someone at a party tell a story in 10,000 words when the story-teller could have made the point in 250 words. Newspaper readers are like everyone else—they don't like their time taken up with word-inflated stories. A journalist must get the most information into the least space or time and do it clearly. Every story—regardless of the news medium—should be written as tightly as possible. The goal should be: Leave not one extra word for the desk to remove.

Good intentions aside, the copy editor prunes any word or detail or bulky phrase that would slow the reader or listener. Extra words mean fewer stories; fewer stories make the news package less interesting. The copy editor aims to produce the tightest, fullest package possible—whether it's a weekly newspaper or network news. Consider the extraneous words *(italicized)* in the following nonsensical paragraph:

> Students who do not study *in* two major fields in college miss *out on* opportunities *that* they could benefit from later *on in life*. In a survey, *college* graduates *who responded to a questionnaire* said they regretted not having studied *in* more than one field. *There is* sufficient *enough* time existing *for students*, especially because tuition, when *completely* paid *in full*, pays for any number of credits.

Except for the last sentence (which needs slight rewriting), a good copy editor would rub out the extra words. The remainder of this chapter provides tips on how to do that. (For the curious, the rewritten sentence: *Sufficient time exists, especially because tuition pays for credits.*)

Remove Verbosity

Unnecessary wordage plagues all members of the news team, from the political columnist to the sportswriter. It is even more evident in the broadcast media when anchorpersons and commentators work without scripts and lack an opportunity to edit their speech. The best, though, are skillful enough to speak tightly without a script.

Examples of verbosity include *on the gounds that* for *because* and *in the intervening time* for *since*. Related errors include verbs with unnecessary particles appended to them. They are better reduced to one word, such as *continue on, follow after, miss out, ponder over, slow down, slow up, cancel out, revert back, raise up, slim down, head up, check out.* Similarly, *take into consideration* equals *consider*. The problem also arises with modifiers. *Game-winning run* equals *winning run* and *three separate buildings* equals *three buildings*.

Make Sentences Direct

Indirect writing manifests itself in sentences beginning or containing *it is*/*there is*/*there are*. Those weak phrases can't always go, but not cutting them is the exception. In addition to reducing sentence length, the copy editor who cuts such phrases also strengthens the sentences, a virtue among readers who like their language in good shape.

There are 42 gallons per barrel becomes *A barrel contains 42 gallons. As of this morning there had been only one artist cancel the trip* converts to *As of this morning, only one artist had canceled the trip. There is no tangible evidence to back up the account* is stronger as *No tangible evidence backs up the account. There is a possibility that the U.S. Customs Service may charge Harrison with smuggling* translates to *The U.S. Customs Service may charge Harrison with smuggling* because *may* means *possibility. It was the second such shooting incident in a little over a month* works best as *The shooting was the second in little over a month. There is no death penalty in Panama* gains force as *Panama has no death penalty.*

Copy editors will find plenty of indirectness in local and wire copy because such sentences come easily under the pressure of writing against deadline. On the desk, though, such sentences are easy to repair despite the pressure of deadline. The detached perspective copy editors have allows them to see most damage easier and to repair it faster.

Eliminate Conventional Information

Information readers know simply because it's part of their culture can be deleted. Typically in accident and fire stories, reporters will write or say : "City police, *who investigated the accident,* said the driver fell asleep at the wheel" and "Ladder Company No. 6, *which responded to the alarm,* helped contain the blaze within a half-hour." If the police made the statement and if the firefighters fought the blaze, they had to have investigated or responded. It goes without saying.

Similarly, "The dentist cleaned out the cavity *with a drill*" and "Firefighters fought the blaze *with water.*" When the dentist doesn't use a drill or firefighters don't use water (which can happen), then it might be newsworthy. Otherwise, the tools of most trades are fodder for the editor's cursor.

Strengthen Weak Verbs

Anytime actionless verbs appear, a copy editor should see if they can be replaced with strong verbs. The lead that begins "Four people *are* dead as the result of automobile accidents . . ." gains strength when changed to "Four people *died* in . . ." To say "The city *has* no good water supplies" means "The city *lacks* good water supplies." "He said he *had a poor start* this year" means "He said he *started poorly* this year." With a strong verb, the preceding sentences shed their mealy-mouth image.

Oust the Passive Voice

The passive voice (any form of *to be* and a verb's past participle) represents one of the most anti-news constructions possible in the English language because passive voice hides the actor of a verb, that is, the newsmaker. Consider this lead:

> The awarding of contracts to two firms for supplying furnishings for county-contracted services *was delayed* by the country administration Thursday until it *is determined* who will own the equipment.

In the first case, the passive voice buries the identification of the delayer, and in the second the passive voice enables the lazy journalist to avoid telling who will make the determination. Journalists should report the news, not hide it. The active voice rewrite—which adds a fact and is still tighter than the original:

> The county administration Thursday delayed awarding contracts to two firms for supplying furnishings for county-contracted services until the county controller determines who will own the equipment.

The controller's role surfaced in the fourth paragraph of the story.

Cut Weak Phrases

The flexibility of the English language allows its users to say the same thing in different forms. The copy editor must decide if the form chosen best suits the pace. Often weak phrases can be converted into nouns, as in this: "Seven people *who were at the party* were treated at the hospital" becomes direct when recast as "Seven party-goers were treated at the hospital."

Watch for Redundancies

Reading a story written as follows would be tiring: "The *fiery* flames burned the center *core* of the building where vandals earlier this month had *intentionally* destroyed some offices." The italicized words are redundant because their meanings are inherent in other words—all flames are fiery, the center is the core, vandals act intentionally.

If a person has *sufficient enough time* that person can just as easily have *sufficient time* or *enough time.* Watch for politicians who vow to subsidize something with *public funds such as tax money* because taxes are the only kind of public funds we have. If that promiser is a *Texas state government official* and the newspaper publishes in Texas, *state official* suffices. Watch for the reporter who writes that a judge will *hear oral arguments* when the reporter could have written: *The judge scheduled oral arguments.* Obviously oral arguments are heard. Pay attention for sportswriters who say a football player *quickly sprints.* Until coaches develop slow sprinters, quick sprinters are all they have—and all they really want. And be careful of the bank that offers *free gifts* for a large deposit; after all, if it isn't free, it isn't much of a gift.

Finally, stay awake for those times when a seeming redundancy is needed. Referring to something as a thousand square feet *in size* is redundant but the same phrase can't be cut from this: "She's small *in size* but big *in stature.*" In that sentence *in size* balances with *in stature.*

Compress Wordy Phrases

Provided with a bountiful supply of nouns and verbs, some reporters will use a verb-noun construction in place of a verb. Those who believe in strong verbs tightly writ change such constructions to verbs. For example:

gave approval	approved
make a visit	visit
hold a meeting	meet
get in contact with	contact
get under way	begin, start
express different views	differ

Evaluate Detail with a Cutting Eye

Detail serves an invaluable purpose in newswriting, especially when people can choose between the words of their newspaper and radio station and the pictures and words of their television station. Details enable print and radio journalists to compete against a television journalist who offers detail merely by focusing a camera on something. Despite the competition, however, print and radio journalists should recognize some detail for what it really is—filler—and delete it accordingly. For example: "The defendant stood before the judge and read the seven-page typewritten statement." That sentence can be pared several ways, depending on the circumstances. At the least, *typewritten* adds nothing. It doesn't matter if the statement is typed; in fact, given the increasing number of people who use typewriters, what makes typewritten statements so unusual? *Stood before the judge.* In a court that's usually the way judges are addressed, so four more words of unnecessary detail can go. The kind of detail worth keeping would describe the defendant's mannerisms, delivery style, the judge, and so on.

Omit the Obvious

A 3-year-old boy climbs into a washing machine and his sister closes the door, thereby activating the machine. The reporter, though, wants to make sure the reader understands the sister's presence and bogs down the story this way: "According to Todd's 7-year-old sister, Amy, *who was with the boy,* the washing machine started when she shut the door." Since she could not have done it by remote control, the italicized phrase adds nothing. Cut it.

Similarly: "The biology of sex, Biology 341, has been offered every winter for the past nine years and is continually filled *with students.*" What else could fill a class?

Unpile Prepositional Phrases

Under "Oust the Passive Voice," you saw a lead containing four prepositional phrases. Here is the active voice rewrite with the prepositions in italics:

> The county administration Thursday delayed the awarding *of* contracts *to* two firms *for* supplying furnishings *for* country-contracted services until the country controller determines who will own the equipment.

Notice how the phrases pile one atop the other until it becomes difficult to figure which phrase modifies what. Carefully edit such writing to remove the ungainly mess.

> The country adminstration Thursday delayed awarding contracts to two firms that would supply furnishings for county-contracted services until the county controller determines who will own the equipment.

Converting prepositional phrases into possessive or modifier forms usually removes the problem, although be careful not to pile too many possessives or modifiers in a row lest you replace one problem with another. Here are two good conversions: *The battle appeared to be the most significant issue of the decade* becomes *The battle appeared to be the decade's most significant issue; Requirements for the certification of paramedics will be upgraded* converts to *Paramedic certification requirements will be upgraded.*

Knock Down Stone Walls

A stone wall in any form of news reporting is a sentence or paragraph that does not advance the story by offering news. In this example, the second paragraph is the stone wall.

> Pilsdon City Council last night raised real estate taxes 1 mill in order to pay for a new street sweeper.
> The council met in its chambers at 8 p.m. and was called to order by Mayor Joseph Picciano.
> The city needs the sweeper, City Manager James T. Owens said, because an unusually high number of storms have left streets dirtier than in past years.

When stone walls are as clear-cut as that one, the paragraph-delete command on the editing terminal removes the blockade. In some cases, re-writing may be necessary to blend some of the information in the second paragraph with news in the third.

Edit Elliptically

Sometimes the repetition of a word between sentences is unnecessary: its unwritten or unspoken repetition is understood by the reader and listener.

> The grant program *receives* the most federal funding; institutional programs *receive* the least.

Even though the second *receive is* plural, an editor can still safely delete it because the reader provides the correct form.

> The grant program receives the most federal funding; institutional programs the least.

The elliptical approach works well in lists:

> Guiser said strokes caused 67 deaths; hardening of the arteries, 17; rheumatic heart, 10; high blood pressure, 6.

Imagine how boring the sentence would be if *caused* and *deaths* were repeated in each grouping.

Faulty elliptical usage causes problems. For example, this extract from a caption:

> Two youngsters passing a gasoline station are *unconcerned* with the near-$2 price of premium. You can bet motorists are.

The caption writer meant: "You can bet the motorists are *concerned.*" But since the reader supplies the missing word from the previous sentence, the caption really says: "You can bet motorists are unconcerned."

Related complications arise with names in possessive form in which the writer believes that the name will carry over to the second thought. For example, this headline: **Simeon's conviction upheld; will reappeal**. That says the conviction will reappeal, although the headline writer thought it said Simeon will. It's a case of trying to make a modifier change to a noun elliptically. In that case, this rewrite: **Simeon's conviction upheld; he'll reappeal.**

Drop Unnecessary Pronouns

Part of elliptical editing is omitting some pronouns at the beginning of clauses. *The editor who is highest in my esteem edits all copy carefully* can be tightened to *The editor highest in my esteem edits all copy carefully* with the deletion of *who is*. Likewise, *that, which* and *where* sometimes can be deleted provided their omission does not create a cacophony as in *The fire chief said when the fire company arrived flames were spilling from all sides of the building.* The fire chief did not say that *when* the company arrived but after the fire. Insert *that* for clarity: *The fire chief said that when the fire company arrived flames were spilling from all sides of the building.*

No Story Is a Formula

Unfortunately, some people have developed the attitude that a story for a newspaper or a broadcast can be written or edited only one way. Editors addicted to formulas count not only the number of words in sentences but the number of syllables in words. Four syllables and more and a word is out. No lead can be longer than 15 words. A 16-word lead? Rewrite it.

Those same editors insist that the inverted-pyramid style of newswriting be followed to the point of absurdity, absurdity being the turning of an interesting story into a dull one. The inverted pyramid is functional and utilitarian, but editors should recognize it as the basis for newswriting, not for the form all newswriting must take. The narrative approach to newswriting—especially with stories not of a breaking nature—may be the salvation of a print medium facing the appeal of television, Home Box Office, Teletext, specialty magazines and home computer terminals. Not only will some rules be broken, survival will dictate they be discarded.

Similarly, the advice given in this chaper, in fact, throughout this book, should be measured against common sense. Form should dictate function. If the inverted pyramid works best on a story, use it. By the same token, the narrative approach to story-telling may not work if the result is too long to engage the reader on the run. All rules require the copy editor to blend the practical, the theoretical and his or her experience to learn what works best.

Suggested Reading

The following list of books is useful when applied to this and the following chapter:

Best Newspaper Writing, Roy Peter Clark, ed., Modern Media Institute, 1979, 1980, 1981.

The Careful Writer, Theodore M. Bernstein, Atheneum Publishers, 1973.

Language Skills for Journalists, R. Thomas Berner, Houghton Mifflin, 1979.

Writing in Style, Laura Longley Babb, ed., Houghton Mifflin, 1975.

The Treasure of Our Tongue, Lincoln Barnett, Alfred A. Knopf, Inc., 1967.

CHAPTER FIVE

Language Skills for the Desk

The Function of Our Tongue

A nationally syndicated columnist once told a group of journalists that one of their holy duties is preserving the English language against decay through misuse. The columnist did not suggest that the journalists lock in to a set of rules and never bend them; instead, he said that journalists could preserve the language by using it correctly. Meeting that challenge lies with the copy desk more than with any other position in journalism, for while the reporter may experiment with words, it is the copy editor who judges if the experiment succeeds or fails.

The people who work on the copy desk may not know how to parse or diagram sentences, but they do know that the English language is alive and changing and that they must consider that tension when editing. They appreciate the language's flexibility: How it allows—even encourages—nouns to become verbs and verbs to become adjectives even if for only one unheralded use. That doesn't mean copy editors tolerate linguistic experimentation that baffles or that they allow free-form writing, which means no form at all. Free-form writing, in fact, is a modern Tower of Babel in which each person's personal style (if "style" is the right word) confounds the language a thousand times more than the biblical act credited with creating the multitude of languages.

Today's copy editors know that the first function of the language is communication, a process in which the writer/speaker and the reader/listener understand messages and needs. Carefully written prose the reader cannot understand serves no one, especially the person who labors to put the words down. Puzzled, the reader can stop reading after one labored sentence with little time invested. The writer, of course, stuck it out till the end.

The area in which language has changed more than any other is semantics—what words mean, which is not as easy as consulting a dictionary. Words mean different things to different people at different times. Thus, copy editors are not so much reaching for a dictionary to define a word as they are ensuring that the context the word appears in makes the intended meaning clear.

Words mean what a society wants them to mean, and even within that society, subgroups can apply words to mean the opposite of what society at large considers them to mean. Just one example: In legal circles a "sanction" is a penalty; society in general uses "sanction" to mean approval.

Quibbling? Of course! That's what good copy editors do. They challenge. They doubt. They split hairs and then split them again. They don't let go of a precise meaning—a needed meaning—just because some dictionary lists as one of the word's 17 meanings some faddish dilution only one generation uses—and uses seldom at that. Good copy editors are always fighting a rearguard action against changing semantics, not because they are fuss-duddies but because they sense the need to preserve distinctions society might let slide through ignorant misuse.

A necessary difference exists between *convince* and *persuade*, between *disinterested* and *uninterested*, between *oral* and *verbal, hopefully* and *it is hoped, affect* and *effect, among* and *between, currently* and *presently, new* and *recent, compose* and *comprise, refute* and *rebut, damage* and *damages, farther* and *further, allude* and *elude.* Some purists have reluctantly given up on *presently* and *hopefully,* conceding that they are overwhelmed by the wave of imprecision that seems to be sweeping the country. (Every generation has faced the same wave. One wonders if the wave is regenerative every 30 years or so or part of a continuum.)

But the issue goes beyond the preceding list because, as far as journalists are concerned, correct language usage is not a matter of being right or wrong—of lexical rectitude—but of being precise. The journalist who searches for the exact word is probably the same one who seeks out the minute details of a behind-doors session held by a city council. It is a matter of doing a job well.

Here are five examples of writing not done well. The first shows an idiom common to the country at large.

Testifying before the committe on drug abuse, Joe Bernard, who has had four of his 11 children addicted to drugs, told the committee to push for more money to fight drug abuse.

That father sounds as though he made his children take drugs, which, as the reader can infer from the remainder of the sentence, obviously is not the case.

Less common is this example, which shows that some writers believe all words about death are synonymous with the word *death*.

> The spokesperson said cardiovascular diseases caused 378 fatalities last year.

But *fatalities* are unexpected, more common to highways, while people with cardiovascular diseases represent a group of people expected to die sooner than the population at large.

With polls so popular, reporters must be attuned to writing stories that do not overstate what polls do.

> A poll issued today by Republican Harrison T. Heartbreaker proves he can beat Democrat Robin Earache in the U.S. Senate race in November.

Polls don't *prove* anything; they *indicate*, a suggestive, not an absolute, word. Language aside, copy editors should demand to see proof of validity of any poll before publishing a story about it.

Within political systems not everyone agrees and sometimes they form a disagreeing group but do not leave the larger group. The dissenters represent a *faction*. Knowing that, ponder this abuse:

> Various factions in the community met to discuss vandalism problems in the North Side.

Some of the people represented the schools, others the local Chamber of Commerce. Still others were residents. They didn't disagree with a larger group on anything; they did agree to do more to fight vandalism. No factions there.

Finally, a greatly overused word:

> The senator formulated his re-election plans.

Formulated sounds so much like artificial mother's milk that that is reason enough not to use it. Besides, it's of more use to chemists than journalists. Try *made* or *developed* or *devised*.

Unlike the earlier examples of misused pairs, the preceding five examples won't show up in a usage book. That's fine. The point is not that copy editors should have at their fingertips a dozen usage books, but that they should have in their brains a sense of the language, of how the meaning of words change. Such a sense comes from reading a lot—including those usage books, but also books from different periods, by different authors, from different cultures and generations. Copy editors must be as hip to the language of Elizabethan England as they are cognizant of the jargon of the current generation of teenagers.

Modern Conventions

Because copy editors are in the language business, they have to know the rules of grammar. Copy editors, in fact, are expected to know more about those rules than reporters, who often write and punctuate by instinct. Copy editors need more than instinct to do even an average job.

Many who read newspapers or listen to radio and television cannot recite the rules of grammar nor could they fix an incorrect sentence. But publish or broadcast a mistake and news consumers will react, not necessarily with the correct answer but with discomfort. They sense something's wrong although they're not sure what or why. Readers and listeners expect good language from their news media. They do not want sloppy usage; they look up to the usage in the news media and are critical when the usage is shoddy.

What follows is an abbreviated set of guidelines on the conventions of modern English. Many books have been written to explain grammar, so what follows should be taken as nothing more than a capsule coverage of the volumes of insights, guidelines and rules. For the most part, what follows covers the more unusual errors copy editors see. It assumes a basic knowledge of the rules.

Subject-Verb Agreement

Anyone who cares about language knows that subjects and verbs agree in person and number, that a singular subject takes a singular verb and so on. The same people also know that the only time a present-tense regular verb changes form is in the third person singular where most verbs add *s* to the first-person form. Thus, in conjugating the verb *know*, a user needs only two forms—*know* and *knows*. The conjugation: I know, you know, he/she/it knows, we know, you know, they know.

Copy editors have to be alert to the sentence structure that shadows the subject from the verb and misleads the writer in selecting the verb number. Here are some examples.

> "The American journalists' *interference* in the internal affairs of Bolivia and their biased *reporting*" was the cause of the expulsion, the foreign minister said.

The preceding shows a compound subject (italicized) in a direct quotation followed by a linking verb (*was*) and a singular predicate nominative *(cause)*, which logic says agrees with the subject. Since *cause* is singular, the subject must be singular, thus the verb is singular. But verbs agree with subjects, not predicate nominatives, so the verb for this example must be *were*. (As you know from "Strengthen Weak Verbs" in the previous chapter, however, you can make a better sentence by discarding *were the cause of* and substituting *caused*. Much more direct.)

The same problem in a different form:

A spokesperson said 3,200 gallons less propane were used this January.

This time the subject (*gallons*) appears plural, is usually plural, but is being considered here as a single unit and, thus, gets a singular verb. Monetary figures also are frequently treated as single units.

The kidnapping victim's father told the caller that $500,000 is a lot of ransom to pay for a journalist.

The next example:

A total of 47 persons were placed in local employment through the efforts of the State Job Security Bureau last month, the bureau's director announced.

The sentence shows the intruding plural prepositional phrase (*of 47 persons*), which has led the writer to use a plural verb. Writers' fingers move faster than their subject-verb agreement recall, so it behooves the copy desk to watch for such problems. The writer got in trouble because of the misapplied newspaper style rule that forbids figures at the start of a sentence. The rule, however, does not say *number*, but many misread it that way. Thus, rather than start a sentence with a spelled-out number, misled writers insert flabby phrases such as *a total of*. Flab becomes the lesser of two evils, however, when the spelled-out number would twist the best of tongues. This is OK:

Forty-seven persons were placed . . .

. . . this isn't . . .

One thousand two hundred sixty-five local turkeys will not see the light of day tomorrow . . .

Similiar errors:

A *variety* of changes are taking place . . .

A *quantity* of moon rocks are missing . . .

In both, the subjects (italicized) are singular so they must get singular verbs.

A variety of changes is taking place . . .

A quantity of moon rocks is missing . . .

Problems with Pronouns

To avoid linking a pronoun to an unintended antecedent or creating a comical sentence because the wrong pronoun gets used, copy editors should triple their guard every time they see a pronoun. The question ought to be: What does that pronoun refer to? For example:

> Reports on what triggered Sunday's violence differed. *It* appeared, however, that *it* began when snipers opened fire with automatic rifles . . .

Those two italicized pronouns do not refer to the same noun. The first *it* represents an indefinite use, which is OK in weather reports ("It will be warm tomorrow.") but not very useful in clear writing. The second *it* refers to *violence* in the preceding sentence, but because *it* appears twice, the reader may be confused. The solution: Repeat the antecedent rather than use a pronoun.

> It appeared, however, that the violence began . . .

Although some editors frown on repetition, it proffers a wide path of clarity when the only other choice is a swamp of ambiguity.

Watch for pronouns doing double duty, that is, referring to different antecedents in another sentence or paragraph.

> Randy Sampson, who served as Thompson's managing editor, said the late editor showed his ability to lead shortly after assuming the editor's post.
>
> "Newsrooms are often the battlegrounds of immense egos and *he* managed to pull us all together when the egos clashed," *he* said.

One pronoun used twice, two antecedents, an unknown number of confused readers. Since changing the *he* in the direct quotation would have been tampering with a direct quote, the copy editor should have changed the second *he* to the name of the speaker. Pronouns have enough problems finding antecedents within the same paragraph; relying on them to refer to another paragraph could be the downfall of a sloppy copy editor.

Doubling up can occur within a single sentence. For example:

> The press has to make the public understand that First Amendment issues affect *them* as much as *they* affect the press.

Pronouns tend to affix themselves to the closest noun that agrees, so in the preceding example the first pronoun must refer to the *issues*. That means the second also refers to *issues*, there being nothing else agreeable nearby.

> The press has to make the public understand that First Amendment issues affect *issues* as much as the *issues* affect the press.

Imagine the reader who just did that! Clarity can be achieved through the repetition of the correct nouns.

The press has to make the public understand that the First Amendment issues affect the *public* as much as the *issues* affect the press.

In this example the problem may be with an idiom, not a pronoun, although fixing the pronoun removes the idiom.

The pilot told investigators *he* was not at first aware *he* was dangerously low on fuel.

The sense of the sentence survives the idiom, but a copy editor wanting to avoid listening to someone's dumb joke about the pilot's fuel tank would change the sentence:

The pilot told investigators he was not at first aware *the plane* was dangerously low on fuel.

Pronouns and antecedents, like subjects and verbs, agree in person and number. Thus, a reference to *senators* takes the pronoun *they* while a reference to a doctor takes the pronoun *she* or *he*. But in some sentences the correct pronoun is not clear-cut.

The first indication of trouble came when Arizona State University officials questioned $500 worth of telephone calls on ——July bill.

In the original, the writer chose *their*, feeling that the antecendent was *officials*. The copy editor, feeling that the real antecedent was *Arizona State University*, changed *their* to *its*. The copy editor's editor, wanting to leave no doubt, change the *its* to *Arizona State University*. That's the lesson of pronouns: Use them cautiously so there is no doubt.

Verbs, Deadlines and Tense

The verb tense that appears most frequently in hard-news stories is the past tense, which says the action in the story happened once and is now over. The city council meeting, the congressional hearing, the collision of two automobiles, the bankruptcy of a store, the death of someone in the community—all are written in the past tense.

The person who is credited with reviving Pilsdon after the Great Depression *died* last night in his sleep at the age of 92.

But when journalists are looking to put immediacy or timelessness into their stories, they turn to the present and present perfect tenses. Those tenses offer the reader the sense that the story is now, not yesterday. The writer of a feature story about a man who raises prize-winning gladioli realizes that the story does not take place in one discrete period but encompasses many hours or days—even years—in the subject's life. That calls for present tense treatment, which engages readers at the moment they begin the story and makes them feel a part of it, as though they are watching it take place.

> Ralph Baker *does* not putter around his garden in the popular image of someone who *fusses* over every bloom and bug around. Instead, Baker, who *raises* prize-winning gladioli, *commands* his garden.
>
> "Turn more toward the sun," he *says* sternly to one budding plant, "and you'll find the warmth to grow."
>
> "Get out!" he *shouts* sharply to a bug sneaking up on a bud just peering above the mounds of earth that *separate* the rows of gladioli.
>
> The bug, enemy that it *is*, *is* given a gentle heave-ho from the garden on Baker's finger rather than a puff of bug spray from the can of insecticide he *carries* with him but never *seems* to use.
>
> "God made the bugs, too, you know," Baker *says*, explaining why he *evicts* bugs rather than *kills* them.

Even though the reporter may have written the feature story based on one morning's interview, the reporter still treated it as timeless by using present tense. The reporter is suggesting to the reader that Baker acts like that all the time, not just during an interview.

The present perfect tense provides journalists with the proper vehicle to write a timeless lead on a timely event. The reporter who wants to stress the action or even the implications of the action spurns past tense (and its attendant and sometimes intrusive time element) for the present perfect.

> A group of citizens unhappy with unchecked growth near their homes *has formed* an organization to lobby the City Council for strict zoning laws.
>
> Called Happy Acres Homeowners, the group organized last night at the Jefferson Elementary School, which serves Happy Acres.

In the lead, the perfect tense removes from the reporter the obligation of using past tense, and allows the reporter to key on the issue—the formation of the group. When the reporter uses the past tense in the second paragraph, he or she affixes the time element. That type of organization makes a great deal of sense in a newspaper, a medium in which the reader expects to find information of a timely nature. The logic is: Why give the reader the time element in the lead when the reader already has some idea of it? The time element is not the news; hide it. If the writer does not do the hiding, the copy desk should. The copy editor, after all, is the fine tuner of all writing.

Present tense overuse (if not abuse) shows up in future tense situations, such as a Wednesday story containing this phrase: *The president speaks Thursday to* . . . Its origin is unknown, but the use now occurs so frequently it is a fault in all three news media. The future tense provides well in such situations.

For some future events, future tense not only fails but would be incorrect. For example, it's 8 a.m. and the afternoon newspaper plans to publish a story about an event scheduled to occur at 2 p.m. that day. The reporter writes: *Striking teachers will vote on the proposal today . . .* The problem is, by the time the newspaper reaches subscribers *and is read,* the evening will be over. In fact, the readers who watch the 6 o'clock news on television while they read the newspaper will be confused when the newscaster gives the results of a vote the newspaper said was going to happen. In such cases, the write should hedge: "Striking teachers *were ready to* vote on the proposal today . . .'' The hedge gets the newspaper off the hook; if the event does not transpire, the newspaper did not promise it would but merely said the event was scheduled. The reader understands that the newspaper does not control events.

Given the immediate nature of broadcasting, radio and television journalists don't usually face this problem unless they sense something planned may never take place. A good example is a threatened strike that could be cooled by a last-minute agreement. The 6 o'clock news treats such a prospect this way:

Members of the Paper Clip Assemblers Union *are* set to strike at midnight tonight, but last-minute negotiations might resolve the differences and head off the strike.

Note the present tense (italicized). A newspaper reporter would have to use the past tense for the reason cited earlier.

Parallel Construction

Items joined by a conjunction (*and, but, or*) should be parallel; that is each item should appear in the same form as the others. Consistency of form makes not only for easier reading but also for clarity. Here is an unparallel sentence:

A doctor makes a diagnosis after *examining* a patient and after she *studies* the results of tests.

The verb connected by *and* should be in the same form, either gerund or third person. The gerund:

A doctor makes a diagnosis after *examining* a patient and *studying* the results.

Third person:

A doctor makes a diagnosis after she *examines* a patient and *studies* the results of tests.

A less clear violation appears in the following:

The old bonds will remain available until June 30 at financial institutions and through payroll savings plans until Dec. 31.

The affront here is not to the rules of grammar but to the logic of the reader who when reading the first two prepositional phrases (*until . . . institutions*) expects the next two to follow in the same date-place order. At first glance the sentence suggests that the bonds will be available *until June 30 at financial institutions and through payroll savings plans . . .* To ensure clarity, a copy editor would make the halves of the sentence parallel.

> The old bonds will remain available until June 30 at financial institutions and until Dec. 31 through payroll savings plans.

The sentence mends another way.

> The old bonds will remain available at financial institutions until June 30 and through payroll savings plans until Dec. 31.

False Series

The absence of a necessary conjunction or the inclusion of a surplus verb creates a false series. In the following the series appears to contain four items.

> The premier today pledged (1) to disband the secret police, (2) cut off oil to Christian nations, (3) release all prisoners not accused of murder or theft and (4) introduced a new minister of state.

The absence of *and* between items (2) and (3) created a false series in which the reader would rightfully expect all four items to begin with infinitives (written and elliptical). But the fourth item is not really part of the series and should be severed.

> The premier today pledged to disband the secret police, cut off oil to Christian nations and release all prisoners not accused of murder or theft. The premier also introduced a new minister of state.

Principles Behind Modification

Words and phrases intended to modify other words and phrases function best when they are next to or as close as possible to what they modify. Given that principle, a copy editor should always check that modifiers pass the test. The misplaced modifying phrase in the following is italicized.

> Fourteen people were injured in the five-alarm fire, *including four firefighters.*

The italicized phrase modified *Fourteen people* and should appear immediately after it.

Fourteen people, including four firefighters, were injured in the five-alarm fire.

Another example, this one a headline: **Talks are slow with striking teachers.** The failure here is to make clear what the talks are about; the modifying phrase is misplaced. Put correctly: **Talks with striking teachers are slow.** But adhering unconsciously to the close-as-possible rule can create problems, as in this headline: **Women included in resumption of draft possible.** The writer followed one rule at the expense of another—always be clear. A rewrite: **Women may be included in draft resumption.**

Another typical modifier out of place is the infamous dangling participle, commonly used by careless writers to begin a sentence when they haven't thought through what they're going to put in the middle or the end of the sentence. For example:

> *Seeing a butterfly alight on one of his gladioli,* the garden was examined for more by Baker.

The dangling phrase (italicized) modified *garden* but should modify *Baker.* To salvage the sentence, a copy editor would not move the modifier but the word modified.

> Seeing a butterfly alight on one of his gladioli, Baker examined the garden for more.

(Note also the removal of the passive voice.)

Adverbs are modifiers seldom used in newswriting, although some of them, such as *only,* serve to clarify information for uninformed or unknowledgeable readers. A non-sports fan, for example, would need a signal that a basketball team that scores 35 points is not very productive. The sentence might say: *The Maple Syrups scored only 35 points.* But in those circumstances, where the facts speak for themselves, a copy editor should remove *only.* For example: *The president of the union said the vote was 20,212 in favor of a strike to only 1,210 against.* The reader needs no adverbial assistance to figure out the one-sidedness of that vote.

Another frequent *only* problem is placement. In speech, people say: "I only have three dollars to my name." On paper, though, *only* should appear as near as possible to what it modifies. *Only* correctly in place in the previous example results in: *I have only three dollars to my name.*

Specific references to facts not yet introduced in a story represent still another modification problem. A lead that says a city council raised taxes "at last night's meeting" is not only wordy (*last night* will do) but also assumes the reader knew before reading the story that the council met. The reader has to be told, has to be introduced to the meeting before the writer can call it "last night's meeting."

Likewise, the story could not later turn to another topic and begin like this: *In other business, the proposal to require the curbing of dogs was presented to the council for the first time*. The fault lies with *the* referring to something the reader hasn't yet been told about. Change *the* to *a* and the introduction is accomplished. Then the next reference can be to *the proposal* because the reader knows about it.

Punctuation

Myths about punctuation marks are as numerous as stories about gruff copy editors. In trying to explain some punctuation marks, teachers have linked them to breathing—a period is a full stop (inhale and exhale), while a comma means a short pause (inhale and exhale faster). The gruff copy editors should be so miscast. Actually, punctuation marks represent tools for writers to show the end of a sentence, a compound sentence not joined by a conjunction, a question, a phrase in apposition, a compound modifier, the beginning of a list or summary, the insertion of explanatory matter, possession and who's speaking. But no huffing and puffing.

The Period.   The end of a sentence is marked with a period, a function most writers accomplish successfully without thinking. Period abuse, in fact, arises not at the end of sentences but within them, and with abbreviations, especially those created locally. The wire services' stylebooks list the abbreviations and punctuation of several national groups and leave clear advice for local creations: If the abbreviation creates an unrelated word, insert periods between each letter. Thus, to sway the reader away from pronouncing its abbreviation, the group Youth Entertaining Common Hopes would use periods—Y.E.C.H.—or (more wisely) change its name.

Do not place spaces within such abbreviations or initials because a typesetting machine keys on space codes to justify lines and a space would make it split the abbreviation or someone's initials between lines.

> One writer I admire is C.D.
> B. Bryan, author of "Friendly Fire."

The author's name is C.D.B. Bryan. Note that the period went inside the quotation marks. It always does.

The Semicolon.   Its name aside, the semicolon is not half a colon, but rather functions like three-fourths of a period. It most commonly separates a compound sentence not joined by a conjunction. Thus: *The president chose to take the weekend off; Congress, on the other hand, uncharacteristically convened both days*. The biggest mistake writers make in such a sentence is using a comma for a semicolon. The semicolon does have a comma-related function in separating complex items in a list. For example: *Police identified the dead as Kenneth R. Sweeney, who was driving the car; Jonathan A. Swanson, owner of the car; Julian Anglais, a Gibbsville automobile dealer, and Ellen T. Macungie, owner of a shoe store in Clive.* The semicolon becomes a comma before a conjunction in such circumstances. Generally, place semicolons outside quotation marks.

The Question Mark.   Few copy editors have to ask when to employ the question mark; with one exception, it always appears at the end of a question. The exception is the paraphrased question. *The mayor asked if she could yield the gavel so she could speak to the assembly.* No question mark.

Depending on circumstances, question marks can go inside or outside direct quotes. Inside:

"What does this tax measure mean to the oil companies?" the senator asked.

Outside:

Which word don't you understand: "philanthropist"?

The Comma.   Writers usually don't have to be told when to use a comma; sometimes they have to be told when not to. Inappropriately (as already noted) some writers use the comma for a semicolon. If the abusive writers would remember that commas define relationships within a sentence and that semicolons appear *between* sentences, the writers would stop making the error.

Apparently afraid a collision may occur when two modifiers appear side-by-side, some writers cushion the modifiers with a comma. That can be done only when the modifiers are of equal rank. *The bright, red fire truck gleamed in the sunlight.* To test the comma, replace it with *and. The bright and red fire truck gleamed in the sunlight.* Obviously the modifiers *bright* and *red* are not equal; *bright* modifies *red.* No comma. Equality exists in the following so the comma prevails: *The glassy-eyed, limping man said nothing when a police officer approached.*

The comma creates a series where none exists when a writer puts in commas where dashes belong. *Other sources for heating homes, natural gas and electricity, have also experienced at least small declines.* The writer, aware of the use of the comma to set off a phrase in apposition, thought no further in punctuating that example and created sources that heat homes, that heat natural gas and that heat electricity. What the writer meant was that natural gas and electricity are sources for heating homes. Dash it. *Other sources for heating homes—natural gas and electricity—have also experienced at least small declines.*

Another comma error appears when a phrase calls for two commas yet the writer uses only one. Such a situation can arise with apposition or clauses; the problem is that the writer forgets the second (usually) comma, resulting in: *J. Edgar Hoover, the long-time director of the FBI is no longer the revered man he was at his death.* The missing comma would appear after FBI. Some comma-droppers omit the mark at the beginning of a clause: *Oakwood Manor which until last year had no paved roads, now has paved roads and a community swimming pool.* Place a comma between *Manor* and *which.* Commas, by the way, always go inside quotation marks.

The Hyphen.   The copy editor who remembers that a hyphen connects words and that a· dash separates will correct many of the errors associated with those two punctuation marks. The hyphen's major use is linking compound modifiers. It is especially important when the unlinked modifiers might engender another meaning. Compare these headlines:

> **Race fixing trial begins**
> **Race-fixing trail begins**

The first suggests a trial that has something to do with race; the second says clearly that the story concerns a trial about someone who tried to fix a race. The hyphen makes the difference.

Hyphens occasionally appear where commas function better. *Heart attacks were the leading cause of death at 257 followed by strokes-67, hardening of the arteries-17, rheumatic heart-10, and high blood pressure-6.* Convert the hyphens to commas and remember the function of semicolons in some series: *Heart attacks were the leading cause of death at 257; followed by strokes, 67; hardening of the arteries, 17; rheumatic heart, 10, and high blood pressure, 6.*

The Dash.   The trick that copy editors have to pull with the dash is getting reporters to write it correctly. On a typewriter, the dash does not exist but can be created by typing two hyphens. On a VDT, that won't work because VDT keyboards contain a dash, usually found by shifting the keyboard and striking the hyphen key. The copy desk must be extra careful that hyphens are hyphens and dashes are dashes.

Primarily a dash sets off a phrase a writer wants stressed or signals a summing up in much the same manner a colon does. An example first used under "The Comma" shows the setting-off use: *Other sources for heating homes—natural gas and electricity—have also experienced at least small declines.* A summing up: *The batter struck out to end the game with two men on base—that's what her entire season was like.* A similar use appears in the introductory paragraph to "Verbs, Deadlines and Tense."

The dash and colon are sometimes interchangeable when used to signal the beginning of a list. The dash offers more stress because it is a bolder mark; the colon, on the other hand, does its work quietly. *The*

president told members of Congress they must accomplish three things—
help balance the budget within two years, reduce congressional spending,
provide for a tax cut.

The Colon.   The interchangeability of the dash and colon does not extend to all functions of the colon. For example, the colon can be used—
seems almost required—between long introductory phrases and direct
quotations.

> The editor, who stood before the members of her staff to tell them about
> the closing of the paper, said: "I regret to tell you I have been able to con-
> firm a rumor we have all been hearing—we are closing."

Colons cause non-punctuation problems when a writer or editor is
unsure how to treat the first letter of the first word following the colon—
capitalize or lower case. The rule is this: If what follows is a complete
sentence, capitalize. The other half of the rule: letters in lower case for
words or phrases.

Parentheses.   The punctuation marks that set off secondary information
in a sentence are seldom used in newspapers because of their disruptive
nature. Sometimes a reporter uses a direct quotation that is not complete enough to be clear and the reporter parenthetically provides the
clarifiers.

> "Now you know that (Harry) Hinder (last year's champion) played the most
> stupendous game (of raquetball) he's ever played (in single's competition),
> but wait till you see him next (in double's play)," the director of the ra-
> quetball tournament said.

Because such insertions make a sentence jerk along instead of smoothly
flow, they should be avoided. The desk should flag such sentences and
require the reporter to rewrite them. In general parenthetical inserts
should be discarded through paraphrasing.

Because parentheses say that what's contained within is secondary
to the main point of a sentence, they should not be used in this circum-
stance:

> Strokes caused 67 deaths. Other noted killers were hardening of the arteries
> (17), rheumatic heart (10) and high blood pressure (6).

The figures in parentheses are part of the news and should not be hidden.

The Apostrophe.   A writer shows possession usually by adding *'s* to a
singular word and just the apostrophe to a plural word ending in *s*. The
desk must be alert for those writers who add *s'* to non-standard plurals,
such as *people*. It is *the people's right to know* not *the peoples' right to*
know.

Quotation Marks. The exact words spoken by a person are encased within quotation marks. Words quoted within a direct quotation are placed in single quotation marks.

"I called you 'lazy,' among other things," the mayor screamed at the police chief.

When a VDT does not contain double quotation marks, the user must strike the single quotation mark twice to create a double mark. Furthermore, some VDTs contain opening and closing quotation marks (called "left" and "right") for the (respective) beginning and ending of direct quotation. The desk must watch for closing quotation marks erroneously used at the beginning of a direct quotation—and vice versa.

Some Facts on Spelling

One of the marvels of the electronic age is the computer that can spell. It matters not how many misspelled words a writer inputs, a properly programmed computer will correct all except homonyms before they see print.

At last, the story goes, people who cannot spell can still work for newspapers; the computer will take care of them. Any salesperson peddling such nonsense deserves not to get the contract because the pitch is deceptive. The computer is not the cure-all for bad spelling. A good analogy is the pocket calculator that provides the wrong answer because a piece of dust is making a microprocessor malfunction. Only someone aware of the mathematical principles involved would spot the error because such a person would have an idea what the answer should be. The spelling computer needs the same backstop.

The spelling computer suffers from a more serious flaw—it recognizes misspelled words only if the misspelling has not become another word, such as *effect* for *affect*. The journalist who writes about a *board of trusties* could have been assigned to a university or a prison beat—the computer wouldn't know and thus wouldn't be able to fix the misspelling. That leaves the correction to the copy editor, the human computer programmed to know the difference between *trusties* and *trustees* and countless other possibilities. In addition, the good copy editor knows the so-called rules of spelling and the exceptions (the noun is *fire* but the adjective is *fiery*) and the exceptions to the exceptions.

Running through a list of rules here would consume time and produce a marginal yield. Entire books have been devoted to spelling rules and copy editors still find the best book of them all to be a good dictionary. In short, however, here are some good spelling rules:

When seeing a word for the first time ever, a copy editor should look it up.

When absolutely certain of the spelling of a word, a copy editor should certainly look it up.

When in doubt about the spelling of a word, a copy editor should look it up.

A copy editor should compile a list of words he or she has particular difficulty recognizing as misspelled. Such a list spares that editor the time of searching through a dictionary.

Making sure words are spelled correctly is only one of a copy editor's many duties and the harried editor might consider it last among equals and therefore not worth as much attention as checking facts. But the fact is, a spelling error is a major fact error. It reflects harshly on the credibility of the newspaper. It makes the reader wonder: If a newspaper cannot spell correctly, how can it report any better? The few moments spent checking the spelling of a word are worth it to keep that reader's mind at ease.

CHAPTER SIX
Headlines

Aid to Readers

Children do not want to grow up to be headline writers, but many head-line writers approach their work with a child-like delight and glee because they know that if they do their job well, they will attract attention. That is one of the functions of a headline—to attract the reader's attention and draw the reader into reading a story. Most importantly, the headline must tell what the story is about. When you consider how little time anyone devotes to a newspaper and then how little of what appears in a newspaper gets read, the challenge to headline writers is immense.

The headline serves the reader in a number of ways beyond just attracting attention and telling what the story is about. The size of a headline enables the reader to evaluate the importance of a story. When combined with story position on a page, a headline says to the reader: "In the opinion of the editors, this story is more important than that story but not as important as this story." In this bigger-is-better world, the larger the headline the more important the story. That is why the lead story of the newspaper contains the largest headline not only on Page One but the largest headline on any page. Some newspapers have rules that reserve a certain size headline for the lead story of the day only—and no other page editor may duplicate the size.

A good headline gets right to the point. It tells and sells the story to the reader. As editors have often said, a Pulitzer prize story is not a prize unless it is read. Getting the reader to start reading is the job of the headline writer. Stories with poor headlines don't get read. In major cities, stories with good headlines can ensure extra street and newsstand sales for newspapers. Figure 6.1 shows how the *Naples* (Florida) *Daily News* competes with two other newspapers vying for the tourist eye. "Naples has three newspaper sales boxes on every corner," says Jeff Lytle, who lays out the front page. "We have to get attention."

The good headline is direct, and while the rest of this chapter contains many examples of good and bad headlines, this one example should be remembered throughout. First, the indirect headline:

**60 dead, 300 injured
as earthquake strikes**

That headline does not directly connect the dead and injured with the earthquake; it leaves the reader in doubt about what happened. But a direct headline makes the connection, leaves nothing to chance for that reader on the run.

**Earthquake kills 60,
hurts 300 in Colombia**

That headline leaves no doubt about what the earthquake did and where it occurred. In a present tense, active verb, the headline puts the story out front. If the reader does nothing more than read those seven words, the reader will still know something about the story. That's the mark of a good headline.

Another mark of a good headline is how well it relates to the lead. Occasionally, a headline writer will base the headline on information deep in the story, which confuses the reader because the headline and

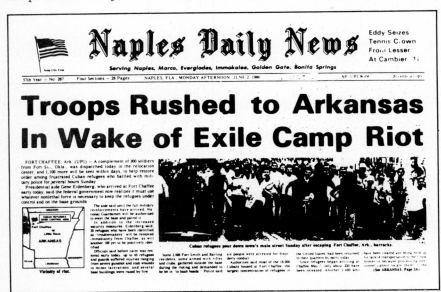

Figure 6.1 Faced with a competitive newsstand situation, the *Naples* (Florida) *Daily News* uses large headlines every day to catch the eyes of passers-by. (Copyright 1980 Collier County Publishing Company)

the lead don't match. If a headline writer believes the lead of the story is incorrect, the writer should inform the chief copy editor. Also, a headline on a feature story—which often builds to a climax—should not steal the punch line. The writer who spends three pages weaving a story will not appreciate the headline writer who gives the story away in three or four words.

In Error, They Glare

A newspaper's most vulnerable spot is the headline. The qualified privilege that extends to a reporter's story on a court case does not protect the headline writer. Good attorneys caution editors that a libel-safe story means nothing if the headline fails. Over the years letters to the editor of different newspapers have revealed reader unhappiness with misleading headlines. Usually, the writer begins by saying: "The story was accurate, but . . ." and then goes on to complain how the headline distorted the story and gave a lasting misimpression. So true. If the reader takes in nothing but the headline and the lead, the headline is sure to be remembered.

The reader's retention aside, courts have found in favor of plaintiffs in libel suits even when the story was accurate and the headline writer's intention was not to slur anyone. This headline—**Bid specs reported 'rigged'**—cost a newspaper $10,000 even though the writer was trying to say the specifications favored (were rigged in favor of) some manufacturers over others, not that anyone was fraudulent (which is what *rigged* suggests). Intentions don't count.

A thoughtless headline can deflate any claim of fairness and objectivity when it seems to take sides. For example, **Student protests mar decade's start** was the headline on a story recapping the 1970s. Perhaps it's matter of perspective, but some would argue that had it not been for the student protests, a senseless war would have gone on longer than it had. The merits of that point aside, the headline should have been neutral. Changing *mar* to *mark* would have done that. In another case, when protesters were arrested for trespassing at the Statue of Liberty, a headline writer convicted them before they faced a judge: **Protesters trespass on Statue of Liberty.**

Headlines thoughtlessly placed on a page can combine to give an unintended meaning; for example, stories about prostitutes and a political candidate that appear side by side so that the one headline reads into the other in this fashion:

Prostitutes identified   **Watson runs for office**

Even if the reader realizes that Watson is not one of the prostitutes, the damage has still been done.

Then there's the two-faced headline, such as these from a school board's proposal to restructure the system for students in grades 7 through 12. **School board considers regrouping secondary students into 2s,** one headline said, suggesting that all students would be paired off. Said another: **Secondary students may undergo change.** One editor quipped: "To what? Primary students." And, if you don't like the results of a trial, express your feelings in a headline such as this: **Jury hung in Mesmer murder case.** What kind of deal is involved in **Mubarak offers U.S. bases?** Has the president of Egypt been given the right to give away U.S. bases? No; he's offered bases in Egypt to the United States. The headline says it both ways.

The more seriously flawed two-faced headline is the one with a ribald meaning. What is one to think of **Dick should veto studs, Carson says** and **Dick will fill vacancy, court rules**? The reader is expected to know that "Dick" is a governor's first name, but that isn't clear. The headline writer would have served all readers better with **Gov. should veto studs, Carson says** and **Gov. will fill vacancy, court rules** The same headline writer also wrote: **Delinquent water, sewage customers are fingered.** The writer meant they were named. The sexual connotations aside, the writer misused "sewage," which is what the system gets rid of. The writer meant "sewerage," which means the system and for which there are customers. After all, who would want to buy sewage?

One two-faced headline that never saw the light of print: **Leaking is a Washington habit.** The same, though, can't be said for **Doctor discusses disease with lucky victims** in which the "lucky" means the victims who didn't die. A copy editor for the late New York *World-Telegram* wrote this headline and readout:

> **Ford lays off 50,000 men**
> **as strikers cut off parts**
> **Action halts**
> **nearly all**
> **production**

The way to keep such headlines from getting into print is to ensure that every headline is read by someone other than its creator. A dirty mind helps too.

Writing Seductive Headlines

A good headline is alluring; it doesn't smack the reader over the head but instead seduces the reader into reading the story. A good headline stimulates readership. A good headline is a pleasure to read even though the reader may not say: "That was a good headline." In fact, the reader never notices good headlines. Good headlines do not call attention to themselves but to the stories they accompany. Copy editors can learn to write good headlines but only if they do not view headline writing as a distasteful chore that precedes sending a story to production. Instead, the writer must see headline writing as putting the finishing polish on a jewel. The attitude of the headline writer helps determine the quality of the headline.

On a story about a shortage of beef, a writer grabbed the readers with **Don't beef—there isn't much.** Who could complain? When a home economist announced that despite rumors the price of hamburger was not going to $2 a pound, a writer caught in the spirit offered: **$2 per pound 'burger report pure baloney.** When NBC and the Nebraska Educational Television Network settled a dispute over logos, one headline announced **All's well that N's well,** the dispute having been over the similarity in the N-styled logos of both stations. When the FTC took the egg industry to task for alleged false advertising, one newspaper's readers learned: **FTC cracks egg ads.** When a U.S. president who had just been shown in photographs slipping on a piece of ice outside the White House later said something he shouldn't have, a headline writer touted the story with **President slips on his tongue.** The headline worked because the image of the president slipping on the ice was still fresh.

The next two headlines sprang from the mind of the same person, suggesting that the good headline is not a one-shot occurrence but a matter of the writer's attitude. The positive attitude produced **Buying a watch needn't tick you off** and **Zipper case closed with happy ending.** The writer graduated from college into a desk job then moved on to a larger paper and another desk job. In college he was a Newspaper Fund copy desk intern at *The Wall Street Journal.*

The copy editor bent on writing good headlines does not quit after the first attempt. Second-rate headline writers would accept the following on a story about the R-factor, which tells how well insulation insulates: **Energy department gives insulating tips.** For the reader, the headline guarantees instant sleep. Knowing such a headline would have a high yawn factor, the writer produced: **Insulating means learning the fourth R.** Intriguing. Given a story saying that the U.S. Supreme Court had ruled that police with warrants to search public places, such as a bar, may not also search the patrons, another writer wrote: **Supreme Court rules against unreasonable search, seizure.** Sounds like it's right out of the Constitution. A jauntier headline: **Cops with search warrants may not frisk elbow-benders.** The problem with the second headline is that it lacks overt attribution; the *may* implies something legal but the reader doesn't know who said it.

The headline writer goes beyond the obvious to produce a good headline. When a judge ruled that police could not cross municipal boundaries in hot pursuit of speeders and the newspaper produced a story saying the police were not happy with the ruling, a headline writer wrote: **Police cool to ban on hot pursuit.** The writer of the story praised the headline writer, who replied: "But it was the obvious head." Likewise, a profile on Jim McKay, among other things the host of a television program called "Wide World of Sports," cried out for more than this headline: **Jim McKay: his wide world.**

To be understood a headline should not require the reader's familiarity with another medium. The headline writer who relies on the reader knowing some television jingle or watching some television program could write a poor headline if the reader never watches television. This rule, however, carries with it an important exception—the headline a reader can understand on two levels. Such a headline is fine if the reader understands the intended meaning. For the reader who also sees the secondary meaning, it's a bonus. This *Washington Star* headline, about the Milwaukee Brewers, a baseball team, serves as an example: **The Brewers That Make Milwaukee Famous.** Seen on a sports page, that headline makes sense. But to those who are familiar with the pitch for Schlitz beer, the headline reveals more because Schlitz advertises itself as "The beer that made Milwaukee famous." The reader who doesn't know about Schlitz beer still receives a good headline. Those who know the Schlitz motto appreciate the headline more.

Mixed metaphors and strained puns detract from headlines. This one, **Curtain rises on Bears' question marks,** drew this comment: "Keep curtain risers on the Arts Page and question marks in the grammar books and that way you won't mix them." Sports headline writers are especially vulnerable to mixing metaphors because so many sportswriters have destroyed the language already and one more piece of sloppy work doesn't seem to matter. The way to measure the headline with a pun is to submit it to the groan test—if another reader groans, scrap the headline; three groans, scrap the writer.

Headline Rules

Headline writing follows a lot of practical rules intended to help the neophyte. Some rules, of course, bend better than others and some newspapers ignore them altogether, relying instead on intuition. The newspapers read that way too. Intuition is best applied in unfamiliar situations, which is not what headline writing is.

The best headlines are written in the present tense because the present tense provides the reader with a sense of immediacy. **President signs tax bill** involves the reader; **President signed tax bill** turns the reader away because it sounds like old news.

Frequently, present tense, active voice headlines count better, that is, allow extra room for the writer to say more. This passive voice headline counts 33$\frac{1}{2}$—**Vienna's largest store destroyed in fire**—while its present tense, active voice counterpart counts 31$\frac{1}{2}$. In some situations a difference of 2 could mean a headline that does not fit, which makes it unusable.

Do not blindly follow the present-tense rule. Headlines containing time elements usually sound better in past tense. For example, **Personal income rises in October** would not make a lot of sense in November. Better to use past tense: **Personal income rose in October.**

Use only commonly understood abbreviations and then be careful. Is **Reps request inquiry** about Republicans or representatives? More common abbreviations include FBI, CIA, U.S. U.N. Avoid regionalisms, such as CLUM, which stands for Civil Liberties Union of Massachusetts but which when used in a headline is clumsy. And what is the reader to make of **CLEP tests set for 2 dates**? It sounds like a venereal disease.

The need for attribution in a headline parallels the need for attribution in a story. If without attribution, the source of information is unclear or the headline sounds like the newspaper's opinion, then attribution is mandatory. That's one of those rules that doesn't bend. When needed, attribution works best at the end so it does not impede the message. Compare:

Authentic letter from	**'Free us from this**
American hostages to	**terrible situation,'**
home asks, 'Free us'	**hostage letter asks**

The headline with the attribution at the end reads better. The first headline buries the news at the end. With attribution, the challenge to the writer is to avoid writing similar-sounding headlines such as these:

**Bottled water contains
arsenic, N.Y. officials say**

**Missing valve caused
leak, NRC official says**

Since the same person wrote those, she could have avoided the repetition by using a different form of attribution.

**N.Y. officials find
arsenic in water**

**NRC aide cites missing
valve as cause of leak**

In headlines with kickers or drops, repetition can dull the message because the readers get a feeling of old news when they see words repeated. For example, a page editor ties two storm stories together with a main headline and a drop headline for each story. The main says:

Storms kill 10 on Pacific Coast, 6 in Hawaii

The stories contain these respective headlines

Thousands lose power in icy Pacific storm

Freak winter storm hits Hawaiian Islands

With so many words repeated, it's apparent the writer was not working hard to produce a good set of headlines. This rewrite not only removes the repetition but shows how to link stories with ellipses:

16 die as storms belt Pacific Coast, Hawaii
Thousands lose power in icy onslaught . . .
. . . flooding, high winds, surf plague Islands

Figure 6.2 shows the use of ellipses in headlines.

Putting an abundance of modifiers in front of a noun can muddle any headline. For example, **Windfall profits tax phaseout pushed back** hides the verb and leaves the reader wondering if "phaseout" might not be it. (The verb is two words, phase out, but readers don't always spell when they read.) The writer would not have had a problem if the writer had used present tense: **President delays windfall phaseout.** Given that a tax on windfall profits was a major news item at the time, the reader would understand the rewrite without *tax* and *profits*.

When writing multi-line heads, some headline writers attempt to

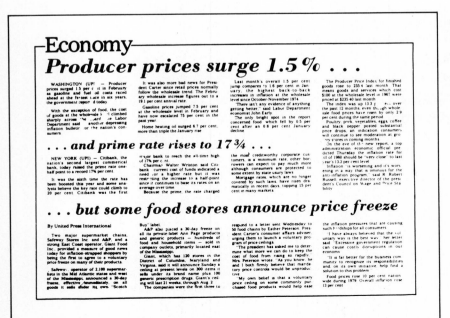

Figure 6.2 Related stories are sometimes linked through the use of ellipses in their headlines. This example comes from the *Telegraph Herald* of Dubuque, Iowa.

make each line stand on its own. That way the reader is not jerked along, unsure how the headline fits together. To write such headlines, the writers avoid "bad breaks," the splitting of a phrase whose parts cannot stand alone. One example:

**Pat leaves White
House very sad**

If the reader reads the headline line by line, the reader is in for a jar.

Pat leaves White

The possibilities at this point are endless and the reader may stop to figure them out or the reader may go to another story or the reader may read the second line as a unit unto itself.

House very sad

The emphasis has now switched from Pat to the House. The House of Representatives? Will the reader re-read? No.

A more typical example involves the splitting of an infinitive between lines.

**Senate rejects plan to
end free prescriptions**

Some editors frown on such breaks and urge their writers to avoid them. Some editors and professors consider the preceding rule nothing but superstition. Certainly common sense should remain the primary rule in determining headline clarity. Whatever, an absolute taboo in the category of bad breaks is this:

**Psychologist Erich
Fromm dead at 79**

Names should never be split between lines of a head.

Headline writers have created their own slang (called "headlinese") when they have needed a short word to take the place of a big word that won't fit. Unfortunately, headlinese isn't always clear, as one 9-year-old showed one day after looking at **A's down Yankees.** "Does that mean the Yankees lost?" she asked. When the reader has to ask, the headline is no good. Given the use of horizontal layout in which headlines are easier to write because they go across the page instead of down in narrow vertical columns, writers can more easily avoid headlinese. In horizontal layout no writer can have an excuse for this: **House axes tax slash; vows $ probe.** That has an Attilla-the-Hun quality to it, which makes it hard to read.

The following headline is almost hard to believe: **Wrestler nipped in state finals.** Does it mean the wrestler was bitten? Some headline writers opt for words such as *cut* for *reduction* and *Mideast* for *Middle*

East. But **Troop cut seen in Mideast fray** defies explanation because of the headlinese.

Not all slang, of course, should be avoided. In this headline the use of *up,* as slangy as it is, provides a snappy cadence the headline would otherwise lack:

**Federal aid to cities up,
but not up with inflation**

Headlines that begin with verbs sound like commands to the reader and are best avoided. What is the reader to make of **Charge man with murder?** And this headline, although it has a national tabloid essence to it, actually comes from a staid small-town daily: **Has her house burned but her cheer's back.** Because the headline begins with a verb, it sounds as though the woman intentionally burned down her house, which was not the case.

Just because a headline should not begin with a verb does not mean it should lack a verb altogether. Verbs are the locomotives of thought, and without verbs, thoughts go nowhere. The following doesn't move: **Growing awareness in U.N. of Third World dependence.**

A headline must be clear. Fathom this: **Egyptian fat cat class expansion charged.** If you figured from that the rich are getting richer, you have more patience than most readers. Consider this: **False sex scandal rumored.** Why would anyone bother to spread a rumor about a "false sex scandal"? How far would such a rumor get? "Psst. Wanna hear about a false sex scandal?" False sex scandals aren't any fun.

Colon headlines create problems because of the multiple use of a colon. Consider these three colon headlines:

**Heinz, Green: Similar views on national issues
Vorster: No urban black rule in South Africa
Hearst: 'Rebel in search of a cause'**

In the first, the colon functions as an equals sign or replaces a verb. The headline says Heinz and Green have similar views. But in the second, the colon functions as a signal for an attribution tag. In other words, Vorster is making the statement about black rule. Thus, the third headline must be a direct quotation from Patty Hearst. Wrong. The direct quote is about Hearst, not by her. The confusion results from the multiple functions of the colon. Here are some more:

**Public: Strong work force needed to keep U.S. great
Suspect: 'I messed things up' in other kidnapping attempts
Studies: Saccharin users face low risks
Social Security: Everyone's involved but few understand system
Austerity threatens Newgate: historian**

Some editors wisely ban colon headlines while others insist that their use be clear and consistent throughout the paper. To achieve consistency means not mixing some of the preceding usages. That seems to be the only way to avoid confusion.

Like leads, headlines should be specific. The tip-off to a say-nothing lead is the word *discuss* as in *City Council last night discussed raising taxes.* The same word tips off the reader to a say-nothing headline as in **Candidates discuss Social Security proposals.** A better headline would tell what the candidates said. Similarly, this headline, **U.S. Supreme Court upholds FCC stand,** says nothing because the reader does not know what the FCC's stand is.

Question headlines deserve the same gimicry label given question leads. Don't try to con the reader into a story with a question headline, such as **Cigarettes harmful to infants?** After all, the headline should be telling the story, not raising questions. **Smoke harms infants, doctor says** would be an acceptable rewrite.

Uncommon words should be avoided.

**Androgynous
management
suggested**

After that, this headline—with its long word for *dies*—doesn't look so bad.

**Councilman
succumbs
at meeting**

Obviously, *succumbs* was picked to fill out the line. That's padding, which should be avoided.

Labels usually fail as headlines because they merely sit atop a story and do nothing. Their staticism turns off the reader. Something like **Bike rodeo at Catoctin** says nothing and **Today's weather** says even less. What about the bike rodeo and the weather? That's what the headline should answer. Some labels, on the other hand, can be effective, such as **Skateboard industry: a high roller.**

Single quotation marks take the place of double quotation marks in headlines because the double marks are space consuming and unattractive in headline type.

Forget the style rules when using numbers in headlines. In some newspapers, no number is spelled out; always use the figure. In other newspapers, the loneliness of the figure 1 has earned it special status— spell out when used alone. Regardless of the rule, when using the pronoun *one*, spell it out.

And does not appear too often in headlines. Instead, the comma substitutes.

Woman shoots husband, drunken friend

Headlines, of course, follow the rules of grammar. Logic doesn't take a backseat just because a writer can't make a headline fit. This is a poor head: **Resident injured in fire, destroys home.** It sounds as though the resident destroyed the home.

Likewise, commas do not disappear, as one did in this headline:

**Bullet pierces house
barely misses woman**

To avoid a *house barely misses woman*, insert a comma after house.

**Bullet pierces house,
barely misses woman**

This does not conclude the many rules for writing headlines. More rules appear later in this chapter.

Headline Styles

Headline type comes in many designs (called "faces") but for many reasons few are used for headlines. Aesthetically, a mix of headline faces on a page detracts from the design by calling attention to the mixture. The mix also detracts from the content of the headlines. An editor striving for a simple, functional look would not mix a lot of headline faces. The editor might—to set it off—use a different face on a headline on a column or news roundup on the front page. Too, the editor might use a different face on the editorial or lifestyle page. Practically, though, storing a large variety of headlines is a task. Also, the news department does not use a great many faces because most are set aside for the advertising department where variety of display type among advertisements helps set the ads off from one another—a preferable result in advertising.

Figures 6.3 and 6.4 show two type faces and their relative sizes (the figures have been reduced). Compare the Helios with the English. The English type contains serifs while Helios does not and is said to be sans serif. (Compare the letter *d* in both and note the additional lines at the top and bottom of the English *d*. Those lines are serifs.) The serifs make it easier for the eye to pace along a line of type. But since headline type is much larger than story (body) type, the eye aids are unnecessary. Modern headlines are sans serif.

Modern style headlines also appear in what is called downstyle; that is, the first letter of the first word of the headline and of proper nouns are capitalized. Newspapers went to downstyle headlines because type experts say downstyle duplicates the way body type is set, which is easier to read. After All, How Easy Is Reading This Sentence, With Every

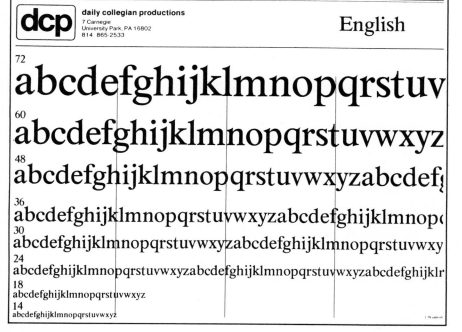

First Letter Of Every Word Capitalized? Downstyle headlines avoid the problems these two upstyle headlines have:

Dr. Robert Going
To Speak

Phils To Name Green Manager

Perhaps the reader will figure out who Dr. Going is, but will even the most understanding of fans forgive the Phillies' management for hiring a green manager? Experience should count for something. (Green, by the way, was the manager's last name.)

A standard headline over the years has been the *banner* or *streamer;* it spans the top of the page from left to right. Figure 6.1 shows a banner, although its two lines are an exception and are used only on significant news stories. The typical banner contains one line. Note how uncluttered the banner in Figure 6.1 is; the writer tells the story in a few words. Good headlines, no matter the size, use as few words as possible. In fact, if a headline sounds wordy, the editor who assigned it might consider increasing its size, provided enough body type exists to balance with the headline.

Figure 6.5 shows a variety of headline styles, including some in up-style. Underneath each headline appears a typical way of slugging the headline copy so the copy editor knows which size headline to write. In the system used here (and newspapers have different systems), the first figure in the slug indicates the number of columns; the second figure, the size of type; the third, the number of lines. The banner in Figure 6.1 would be marked 6-60r-2. The *r* stands for roman. If the headline had been *italic*, the assigning editor would have placed an *i* next to the number indicating the size of type.

Another conventional headline is the kicker, usually a one-line headline with a second line (the kicker) appearing above it in half the type size and in a different style. That is, if the main line is roman, the kicker is italic, and vice versa. A typical kicker on a 36-point headline would be 18 point.

The kicker adds zest to the headline. Good headline writers, however, do not rely on the kicker to complete the main thought of the headline because a make-up editor may have to drop a kicker if a space problem appears. Thus, the headline writer avoids a kicker that reads into the main line as though it were the first line of a head. A headline writer uses a kicker to explain a main line. This kicker does not do that:

New contract doesn't solve anything
Striking bus drivers face new problems

The kicker should say what the problems are.

Manager wants strikers to rebid jobs
Striking bus drivers face new problems

Baylor news staff quits in protest
6-48r-1

Leftists Ease
Death Threats
2-36i-2

Going, gone
for goodies
at Adolphus
1-30i-3

Silcox cranks up House campaign
2-24i-1

**Productivity rises 1.7%
for federal employees**
1-18r-2

Apologetic Reagan says
'no slur was intended'
by joke about ethnics
2-36i-3

Figure 6.5 Although the trend in headline capitalization is toward downstyle, some newspapers still use upstyle. This illustration shows up- and downstyle in various headlines.

Kickers usually extend no more than midway above the main line. A kicker that is half the point size of the main line will count approximately the same as the main line. A 36-point headline that counts 26 over three columns would carry an 18-point kicker that would count virtually the same. But because it's half the size it would extend only half the distance. Figure 6.6 shows a kicker from the New Haven., Connecticutt, *Journal-Courier*. Some newspapers underline kickers for emphasis, but in a modern, airy format, the underline is unnecessary.

Related to the kicker is the tag, which, as the name suggests, tags the story type for the reader. Figure 6.7 shows a tag. It can be distinguished from a kicker by its lack of color and its label function.

Modern offshoots of the kicker headline are the over-under and the reverse kicker. The over-under (Figure 6.8) seems to have merely switched the lines of the typical kicker, but a closer look reveals that the larger line is really almost a title and the line beneath it tells the story

Similar incident, no arrest cited in letter

Ambrogio claims double standard

Figure 6.6 A kicker headline which could be designated as k18i/3-36r.

Spring Training

Cerone, Watson use bats to ignite Yankees, 8-7

Figure 6.7 A tag over a headline labels the content or subject of the story rather than functioning as a kicker would. Despite that, the headline is marked the same way—k18i/3-36r.

Pageant the road to a dream

Bourne woman hopes for career break

Figure 6.8 One reverse application of the kicker headline is the over-under, which could be marked 3-36i/k18r. Some editors also call this style reverse kicker, a style shown in Figure 6.9.

in headline style. Also, the smaller line extends more than halfway across the width of the larger line, which makes it an easier headline to write. The smaller headline does not fill out the line, which results in air at either end that helps set it off.

The reverse kicker (Figure 6.9), on the other hand, uses larger type on the top line but that type does not extend the entire width of the headline. Usually, too, the reverse kicker is a catchy phrase or, looked at another way, a brightly written tag. The underline, which some editors justified in a typical kicker headline as a means of setting off the kicker, is dysfunctional in the reverse kicker. After all, the larger of two type sizes hardly needs anything else to set it off. The underline is distracting.

A closing note on over-unders and reverse kickers: Unlike the normal kicker and its half-size rule (24 kicker on a 48-point head), the modern styles sometimes ignore that and step up one size from half. Thus, a 48-point reverse kicker might appear on top of a 30-point headline instead of 24.

Next comes the hammer, which is a reverse kicker but in all capital letters (Figure 6.10). Such headlines should be used sparingly because all capital letters are hard to read. By virtue of their size, hammers impress the reader with their importance, but that can be diluted with too many hammers on one page.

Carny Knowledge

Central Florida Has a Love Affair with a Fair

The Missing Musketeer

Yankee Spring Training Camp Seems Empty for Mantle, Berra and Ford Without Martin

Figure 6.9 Two reverse kicker styles show that commonly the top line performs more a subject function than a story-telling function.

STRIKE?

Baseball union leaders call for April 1 contract deadline

Figure 6.10 The distinguishing characteristic of a hammer headline is the use of all capital letters.

The over-under, the reverse kicker and the hammer have spawned other varieties. Note the headlines in Figure 6.11. The *Yakima* (Washington) *Herald-Republic* has no name for its style although Mario R. Garcia, an associate professor of graphic arts, calls them tripod heads. Graphics director Kurt E. Smith says the style came about from his managing editor's quest for a headline that was not restrictive to the writer or uncommunicative to the reader. Smith says that sometimes the editors call the bold-faced (*i.e.,* darker) headline a "banger." At one time *Herald-Republic* layout editors put a 60-point banger on the lead head but they decided that it was too strident and have since cut back to 48 point. The type is Future.

Still another style shows up in Figure 6.12. Technically, the *Herald-Republic* head belongs with the others in Figure 6.11 but receives billing

Bye-bye, birdies Fleeing city growth, San Juan Capistrano's famed swallows head for a peaceful haven — and bring a sticky problem in their wake

Rules/*Bumper crop this year*

'Lifetime of love': That's what adoption agency line waited for

Figure 6.11 With a "banger" at the side, a different style of headline has evolved. Although its name varies from newspaper to newspaper, it remains a variation of the "wicket."

Settlement
City agrees to pay
$30,000 to widow

Hidden cameras
Video tapes of alleged theft to be allowed as evidence

Figure 6.12 A variation of the over-under, reverse kicker and hammer headlines is this style from the *Yakima* (Washington) *Herald-Republic*. The darker type is called a "banger." (Copyright 1980, *Yakima Herald-Republic*)

here because of its similarity to another style, which lacks a universal name. *The Evansville* (Indiana) *Courier,* according to its news editor, David Rutter, calls its style "Khadafy." Rutter says he casually named the style. "After explaining what I wanted done with the headline on a feature story about Libyan politics," Rutter says, "the slotman asked that I codify the style with some catchword. The name 'Khadafy' stuck." (Khadafy was the last name of Libya's president at the time.)

The *Courier* uses the style only on feature stories. The tag words (a banger by any other name is a tag word) are set in Newton type while the remainder (Rutter calls it "the tail") is Univers type. The *Courier* sticks to a 36-point Newton tag and a 30-point Univers medium tail. "It is designed to catch the eye, not give you a headache," Rutter says. "If the size difference varies greatly between the components, it tends to become disjointed."

The Louisville *Courier-Journal*'s version of a Khadafy (not shown) uses ellipses instead of a colon. At Evansville, Rutter says, the desk uses ellipses, dashes and colons for variety.

At the *Pottsville* (Pennsylvania) *Republican,* news editor Chuck Buchanan calls that newspaper's style a "sidesaddle hammer." Buchanan uses a 60-point banger with a 30-point tail (not shown). He has also reversed the style, putting the tail ahead of the banger and calling it a "reverse sidesaddle hammer."

The Bend, Oregon, *Bulletin,* which uses Future Demibold Condensed and Future Medium, has no name for its style. "We are so computerized," editor Robert W. Chandler says, "that nothing has names any more—just a string of numbers which means nothing to anyone excepting our computer."

The preceding has not been an exercise in name-calling but was done to show that although headline styles may not vary, their labels do. As with other facets of journalism, individual newspapers have their own names and you should not depart from this book with the feeling that it has used universal labels throughout. Universality is impossible. What should not be lost on you is the evolution in headline styles and the opportunity that presents imaginative copy editors to create other styles.

The sidesaddle headline frequently appears when the story sits in such a location that the headline will not clash with a headline below. Typically, that is above an advertisement that spans six columns. In circumstances such as an ad that leaves only two or three inches across the top of the page, using the space-saving sidesaddle style is imperative for the editor who wants to publish a lot of story. The alternative is a small (24 point, perhaps) headline, which most editors would not run across six columns because it would be too wordy.

Sidesaddle headlines, when used on an open page, appear with boxed stories so that the headline does not conflict with other headlines on the page (Figure 6.13). The box also keeps the story type from running into other stories.

The drop headline is making a comeback—a "comeback" because it appears to be a variation on the deck style of headline writing. In deck style, a story carries a main headline and several subordinate headlines immediately beneath the main head. They are called "decks." *The New York Times'* front page exhibits this style, which dates back at least a century. The new form carries only one deck, which editors refer to as a "drop."

OSU headed to Tempe?

The pairings and seeds for the NCAA basketball tournament will be announced today.

And most people — including Oregon State coach Ralph Miller — believe the Beavers will probably be assigned to one of the two sites for first round play in the West, Ogden, Utah, or most probably Tempe, Arizona.

In either case, Oregon State, the Pac-10 Conference's top representative, will probably be the top seed at the site and receive a bye to the second round.

Games at Ogden will be played March 6 and 8, and games in Arizona will be played the 7th and 9th.

It's believed that Oregon State will go to Tempe so that Weber State, which is also likely to be a seeded team, will be able to play at home in Ogden.

It's also believed that Oregon State will probably wind up in the same region with either or both Washington State and Arizona State, something that Miller said he thinks is "stinko."

One Pac-10 source said Saturday that the NCAA committee was considering this lineup in the West:

At Tempe — South Alabama (the Sun Belt Conference champion) vs Loyola-Marymount (the top-seeded team from the WCAC) in one first round, and Washington State (the Pac-10's third representative) vs Utah State (winner of the Pacific Coast Athletic Association).

Oregon State would get a bye to the second round and face the winner of the South Alabama-Loyola game. Weber State would get a bye and face the winnner of the WSU-Utah State game.

At Ogden — Arizona State (the Pac-10's second representative) would face University of Nevada-Las Vegas (an independent) in the first round and Purdue (the Big Ten's third representative), would face University of Texas El Paso (the Western Athletic Conference's second representative) in the first round.

Notre Dame (independent) would get a bye and face the winner of the ASU-UNLV game, and Brigham Young University (winner of the WAC) would get a bye and face the winner of the Purdue—UTEP game.

Figure 6.13 A sidesaddle headline appears to the left of a story when placed in such a way that it might clash with other type, a sidesaddle headline and the story it appears with should be boxed.

The style shown in Figure 6.14 is virtually nothing more than an over-under headline, although the layout editor dropped it into four columns of type so that the top of columns one and six are even with the top of the drop headline. The problem with such a style, some experts say, is that readers are trained to return to the far left to begin a new line and may have problems finding the drop because it begins a column in. The reader may go right to the lead, missing the drop. On the other hand, the larger type may help guide readers. A single-column drop head style appears in Figure 6.15.

Another useful function of drop heads arises when an editor is relating two or more stories to a main headline. (Figure 6.16) shows two examples. Note that the drop heads are written below the maximum count

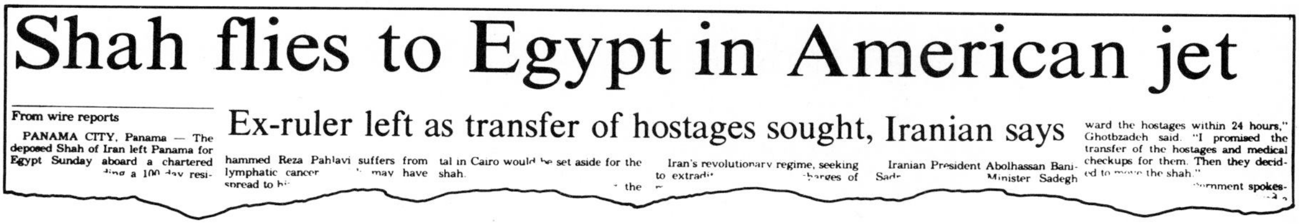
Shah flies to Egypt in American jet

Ex-ruler left as transfer of hostages sought, Iranian says

From wire reports

PANAMA CITY, Panama — The deposed Shah of Iran left Panama for Egypt Sunday aboard a chartered

ward the hostages within 24 hours," Ghotbzadeh said. "I promised the transfer of the hostages and medical checkups for them. Then they decid-

Figure 6.14 This style of drop headline is an over-under headline in which the under headline is "dropped" into the story.

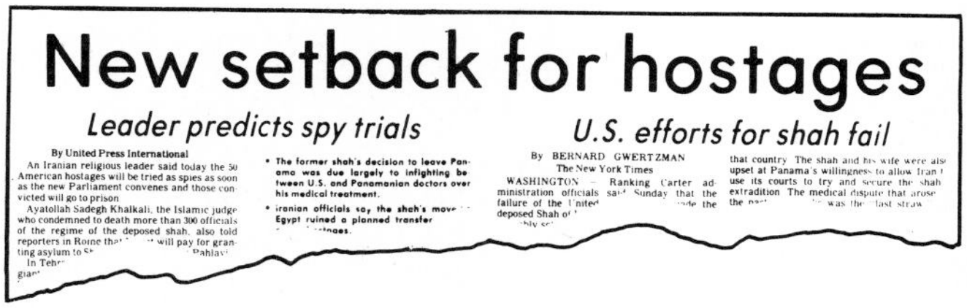
New setback for hostages

Leader predicts spy trials

U.S. efforts for shah fail

By United Press International

An Iranian religious leader said today the 50 American hostages will be tried as spies as soon as the new Parliament convenes and those convicted will go to prison.

By BERNARD GWERTZMAN
The New York Times

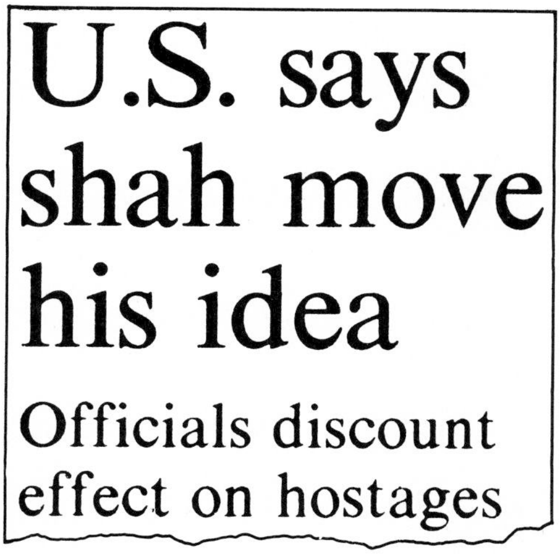
U.S. says shah move his idea

Officials discount effect on hostages

Figure 6.16 Related stories appearing under a common headline receive their own headlines too. By contrasting italic and roman type or by using a generous amount of white space between, editors avoid headlines that run into each other. Still, too much of this clutters a page.

Figure 6.15 Another version of a drop headline shows how modern editors are adopting the old deck style of headline writing. The danger in such headlines is wordiness—too much headline to read for that reader in a hurry.

so that air separates the headlines. That keeps them from reading into each other. Faced with three drop headlines, an editor might make the center one italic, which creates a contrast that helps separate the headlines. Drop heads can be overdone in this function and should be used sparingly to avoid a cluttered look. Also, such treatment forces the reader to choose between elements of apparently equal value and so the reader may not know which one to read first.

Figure 6.17 shows what might be called gimmick heads. While the two shown here may not offend, other gimmick heads could. The problem lies with the fact that the reader may consider the gimmick as cute

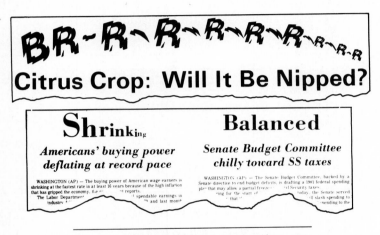

Figure 6.17 A little imagination can create a once-in-a-lifetime headline style. Headline designers, though, should guard against creating a headline no one understands. The headline style should not get in the way of the message.

or may not understand what the editor is trying to say or may misunderstand the intent. In any case, the headline fails. Approach gimmick heads with caution.

Finally, 6.18 shows a variety of standing heads. Such headlines take their name from the fact that they do not change from day to day; that is, they stand as is from day to day. Standing heads, like section flags, look better in a type other than the family used for headlines. Using a different family on standing heads tastefully sets them off from headlines. Standing heads, by the way, do not substitute for headlines. The reader uses standing heads as guides to the news but expects a headline beyond the label to give the news. The headline that says **Tomorrow's weather** doesn't serve the reader quite as well as the one that says **Blizzard coming.**

Stocks, commodities

Sports scoreboard

Business report

Figure 6.18 Standing headlines have that name because they remain the same day after day.

Figuring the Count

Every headline family counts differently so the following system represents just one of several in the industry. Learning a new system is not difficult; most copy desks put together a headline chart that gives the size for every headline the system can produce. All the writer has to learn is what individual lettters and figures count. On top of that, the computer tells the writer when a headline is off.

Generally, most lower case letters and figures count 1, even though an accurate measure might show that some letters count three-quarters or nine-tenths. In most headline counting, editors use as a basis $1/2$, 1, $1^1/2$ and 2, and then don't worry about the counts that might fall in between or under. The law of averages helps headline writers.

The letters and figures that do not count 1 include "fat" letters such as *m* and *w*, which each count $1^1/2$, and "skinny" letters such as *l*, *i*, *f*, *t*, which each count $1/2$ along with the figure 1. In some systems the letter *j* counts 1 whether it is capital or lower case.

Generally, capital letters count $1^1/2$ except *M* and *W*, which each count 2. Even *L*, *I*, *F*, *T*, which one would expect would increase by $1/2$ when capitalized, counts $1^1/2$ per letter with the exception of the *I*. *I* counts 1. Spaces between words can count $1/2$ or 1, depending on how much spacing the typesetter has been programmed to allow. The computer allows the editor at the terminal to fudge a little on the spacing if necessary to fix a tight headline. Most punctuation counts $1/2$ except ?, %, and $, which count 1.

Sophisticated electronic editing systems have eliminated the guesswork in writing headlines. A sophiticated system allows for the writing and sizing of the headline. In one system, when the headline writer is finished, the VDT will flash a figure that tells how many counts remain. If the remainder appears as a positive number, the headline writer is done. If the figure has a minus sign before it, the writer must rework the head. In another system, the terminal shows a number and then subtracts from it as the headline is written. If the headline is long, the letters that go beyond the maximum count blink. In still another system, if a writer produces a 48-point headline that is slightly long, the writer can instruct the typesetting equipment to produce a 47-point headline, which then might fit. If not 47, then 46-point. The ability to change headline sizes a point at a time was not possible in pre-electronic systems. Around the newsroom, this ability is referred to as "rubber type." Whatever method, once the writer has a satisfactory head, the proper commands are pressed and the headline comes out in type with the story. The headline, of course, appears in the headline type of the newspaper and the story appears in the newspaper's body type.

The major counting rule of headlines is: Do not use headlines that exceed 50 counts. Anything longer is wordy and difficult for the reader to grasp. Generally, a reader will skip over a headline that takes more than 20 seconds to read. Some editors might allow the 50 count-rule violated when the headline includes a kicker, but a headline of 50 counts with a kicker will equal about 100 counts and will still take a long time to read.

Some newspapers also have rules about minimum lengths for headlines. Usually, the minimum is found by taking one-half the column count for that headline size and subtracting it from the maximum count. Thus, if a headline has 8 counts per column and the maximum count is 26, the minimum count would be 22 (8 divided by 2 equals 4; subtract 4 from 26).

Multi-line headlines are written so that each line falls within $1\frac{1}{2}$ or 2 counts of each other. Such a rule avoids ragged looking headlines and assures smooth reading.

Finally, those who assign headline sizes know that some counts are virtually impossible to write and that asking a writer to produce a one-line head that counts 18 maximum or three lines of eight counts per line is unfair. Thus, a headline can have too many or too few counts. Each newspaper has its limits and new copy editors learn them easily and immediately.

CHAPTER SEVEN
Design

The Way it Was

Newspapers of yore are distinguishable from their modern successors by their multitude of vertical columns of type which created visually displeasing long gray lines. The same newspapers also stand out (in the wrong way) for their almost unreadable narrow columns of type and the many column and cutoff rules about a page. The vertical layout of olden newspapers stemmed from mechanical limitations that did not allow type to be spread horizontally across a page. But even after the improvement of presses, many newspapers retained their vertical formats so they could stuff Page One with a lot of stories—most of them continued to another page or another section. Such an approach resulted in a front page of 14 to 16 stories and some newspapers went as high as 30. With so much on a page, the layout editor produced a page in which most stories appeared the equal of all others, leaving the reader in doubt as to where to begin reading.

If vertical layout had any value, it was that the approach required little imagination or thought and a page editor could send a sloppy page dummy to the printer, who could be relied upon to place the stories correctly row on row on row. Story placement, of course, was intentional but not creative and was based on many inflexible and archaic rules. On inside pages at uncaring newspapers (and this still happens today) stories were selected because they filled a space not because they were of value to the audience. Those stories that did not fit were cut because, as a cynic once said, "a newspaper story is written in such a way that when it comes to an ad, the rest of the story can be thrown away without harm."

Narrow columns of type contributed to the gray appearance and because the columns were narrow (as narrow as $1\frac{1}{4}$ inches), the stories contained a high number of end-of-line hyphens, which are barriers to reading ease. The column rules—those dark lines that kept one column of type from running into another—upheld the newspaper's image as a rigid, dull product. Fortunately, all that has changed.

The Way It Is

The operative difference between yesterday's newspapers and today's is more than the difference between the meaning of two words, *layout* and *design*. The modern newspaper is better planned than its predecessor; editors pay great attention to the package, from length of story to style of caption. That is design. The concept behind modern newspaper design envisions a visually pleasing product that will attract readers and draw them into reading the newspaper. The modern product must appear pleasing enough to compete with television, radio, magazines, leisure time, children, home chores, social functions and whatever else people can do with their available time. Newspaper design continues the concept of good editing, which is done with the reader uppermost in mind. Today's editors polish words and then create attractive formats for those words to appear in.

Design gives order to a newspaper and sets priorities. A poorly designed newspaper tells the reader that the editors don't care; a well designed newspaper, on the other hand, tells the reader how much attention the editors pay to the product, how careful they are with their work. The design tells the reader what the newspaper is worth. The design also gives the paper its personality. Simplicity, clarity and focus guide the editor in designing the daily news package.

The modern format derives its attractivenesss from a modular design (see Figure 7.1) in which stories square off so that each column of type in the story is the same length as the others. The stories, for the most part, run across the page rather than down. Those stories that go down the page without subheads are short—eight inches or less. White space has replaced column rules. The columns of type are wider and the type is larger, all of which makes the paper easier to read.

Deep vertical modules have not disappeared altogether. When used at a great depth (more than eight inches), they often appear in the form of photographs, which the eye can easily scan, or in the form of news roundups with subheads. In fact, pages without vertical modules appear listless for they lack the tension so necessary to attract the reader. One critic calls pages lacking vertical modules "layer cakes" because that is what they look like.

Figure 7.1 Modular design typifies modern newspaper design. Each story appears as a rectangular unit, which is easy on the eye and easy to read.

The necessary tension comes from the contrast between the horizontal and the vertical. A page of all horizontal modules bores the reader; but set vertical and horizontal modules against each other and the conflict will attract readers. The modern newspaper designer, in other words, must have a sense of geometry.

The Package Concept

In another time newspapers were figuratively thrown together without much thought as to what went where after Page One. Local and foreign news appeared on the same page with a feature story. Smaller newspapers published obituaries on the front page. (The obituaries were considered local news.)

Today, though, the product is well planned. The newspaper not only has a purpose, it projects that purpose. It has become a package of information. The *Statesman Journal* of Salem, Oregon, packages obituaries and similar informaton on one page. Special pages extend beyond obituaries to include pages and whole sections dedicated to certain kinds of news, such as foreign or sports. In essence, the concept behind the typical metropolitan Sunday newspaper now shapes dailies everywhere.

Newspapers have become compartmentalized. The reader can find various calendars of events in one spot; all general news together; features in still another but unified spot. Larger newspapers contain sections or parts of sections on the arts and entertainment, on business and lifestyle.

Within a section, editors practice packaging. Figure 7.2 shows the *Times-Union* of Rochester, New York, presented here to call attention to the package of three stories about the Middle East. The reader did not have to read throughout that day's issue to learn about the Middle East; *Times-Union* editors packaged the Middle East news for the reader. Realizing that not every worthy story can fit on Page One, some editors package a second front page.

Related to the package approach are section flags and indexes, which help the reader sort out the information. They are discussed later.

Editors also provide their readers with a high number of news stories by packaging them in roundups on a special page. In addition, editors break stories apart into sidebars not only to rid themselves of bulk but so readers can focus on all or parts of an event as their interests dictate. Magazines have long used sidebars as an effective way of telling a long story through a variety of short stories.

Present-day newspaper packaging is evolving. Who knows, one day editors might decide to publish only current information on their early pages and put background later in the paper where the reader who needs it can find it and the reader who doesn't can skip it. For that matter, maybe all background information will be stored in a computer, subject to accessing on home computer terminals by only those who want it.

Elements of Design

The designer works with modules that are easily created on a sophisticated VDT system which allows a story to appear—with headline—in the module size determined by the design editor. For the design editor needing a wrap around some visual element, a pagination terminal makes the task easy and accurate.

The standard newspaper design of the early 1980s is the six-column format (see Figure 7.1). Some newspapers, however, use a five-column or a four-column format. The five- and four-column formats, though, allow

Figure 7.2 Keeping related stories together—in this case, on the Middle East—makes reading the paper easier.

for few stories and, as will be noted again, publishers and editors are seeking formats that remain attractive while carrying relatively more stories than the skimpy formats of the 70s.

Editors do not agree on whether to continue stories from Page One to later pages, although the feeling is that the reader should not be made to turn any page to finish a story. Television and radio news programs do not require the reader to work so hard, the argument goes, so newspapers shouldn't either. But other editors say that necessity dictates continuing stories, especially if the editors are to get a reasonable number of stories and useful graphic elements on the front page. To ease the burden on the reader, editors who continue (or "jump") stories put them on the back page of the first section, which makes turning back and forth easier. Research conducted at Indiana University suggests that jumped stories lose a higher number of readers than non-jumped stories, that stories perceived as boring lose readers regardless of whether they're jumped, and that subject matter can override the question of whether a story is continued. If the reader is interested in the subject, the reader will follow the story to the end, jump or no.

To achieve unity, designers concern themselves with three major elements—art (any visual element), type (including headlines) and air (functionally, white space). Some designers might argue for placing color in the cagetory of major design element, but so far few newspapers have distinguished themselves with the good *news* use of color, and its use is suspect among some editors. Other elements include boxes and rules, section flags and indexes. Also important is production quality. No matter how well designed the page, it will not work if the photographs are spotty or the type is crooked. Quality of the finished product, of course, directly relates to the quality of the designing editor's work.

One element not always considered with the others is advertising, yet poorly planned advertising display detracts from the effort of the news designer. Although the concept runs contrary to popular practice, horizontal placement of advertisements presents a sensible hole for a news designer to use without detracting from the sales pitches. After all, the reader buys the newspaper for the advertisements too and will want to read those. No doubt a total page well designed works to the advantage of the advertiser a lot better than a page laid out with old-fashioned principles blindly in mind. If a page looks ugly and the reader skips it, the reader skips the news *and* the advertisements. When advertisers become aware of that, they'll pressure newspaper advertising managers to change.

By necessity, this chapter contains a large number of newspaper pages, and while a particular page may be presented to show just one element of design, you should not focus on that aspect alone. Also look at other elements and at the total page.

Type

The design editor who selects the wrong type for a newspaper story can assure as much non-readership as a dull headline or a dull lead. A story type (more commonly called "body type") needs serifs, distinctive markings at the tops and bottoms of letters. Those markings provide fixation points for the eye to set upon when reading horizontal lines of printed matter. Sans serif type, on the other hand, is optically even weighted (the strokes of the letters are the same thickness), which creates a lack of contrast so necessary for the eye to distinguish between letters.

Likewise, the space between lines should provide the eye with enough room to return from the end of one line to the start of another without encountering and being distracted by the second line. Lines too close together don't allow enough space between them for the eye to move uninterrupted to the next line. The typical leading in a newspaper is one point, meaning a story will be set 9 point on 10 point (or "9 on 10"), which ensures a half point of space top and bottom and a point of space when two lines appear one above the other. The wider the line of type and the larger the type size, the more leading is necessary. The most common body type sizes range from 8 point to 11 point, although the use of 8 point appears on the wane as reader-conscious editors aim to make their product easier to read.

The optimum length of a line of type is from 16 to 18 picas. Newspapers occasionally violate that dictum to create, say, a two-column box that might run 25 picas wide. At that width, the type size should be no smaller than 10 point. Too many stories set beyond the optimum length tire readers.

The smallest body type used is 5 or 6 point, which frequently appears on sports pages for boxscores or other statistical matter. Some sports editors place all of their statistical matter in 5 or 6 point bold face (for legibility) and keep it confined to one page or section of the page called "The scoreboard" or "For the record" or whatever. Some news editors, unfortunately, set lists such as court proceedings and meeting or state house schedules in small type and then wonder why nobody reads them. The small type (so-called "agate") is hard to read and is best avoided. Given the high median age of newspaper readers and the rising median age of the country as a whole (30 in 1980), editors will no doubt have to discontinue using small body type altogether because the older reader will have trouble reading quantities of it. Some editors believe that only the most rabid fan spends any time reading small type on the sports page.

One of the most current typographical changes in newspapers has been the adoption of ragged right columns of type. Most newspapers justify their columns of type so that each line lines up with the preceding line on both the left and right sides. That requires end-of-line hyphenation, too much of which diminishes readability. Ragged right, on the other, requires little or no hyphenation and injects more air (white space) onto a page. Ragged right use in newspapers may be a trend that will fade. Whatever happens, ragged left typesetting of body type should be avoided because it deprives the eye of a common return point line after line of reading. To avoid fatigue, the eye needs the common return point.

In selecting type—be it for a story or the headline on a special page—beginning editors often make the mistake of selecting an inappropriate face. For any story, the type should be easy to read. Figure 7.3 shows two type families—Murray Bold and News No. 2. Murray Bold might be appropriate for a couple of one-line captions on a picture page

Murray (12 point, ½ point leaded)

Whatever your present method of composition may be, Compugraphic can put greater speed, capability and quality at your fingertips for the lowest possible cost. CG offers a wide variety of typesetting equipment, all incorporating the latest electronic techniques for maximum reliability. In addition to a wide choice of typefaces from the extensive basic typeface library, CG has a typeface development program that is the most active in the industry. Typesetting, today

ABCDEFGHIJKLMNOPQRSTUVWXYZ&
abcdefghijklmnopqrstuvwxyz   1234567890

Murray Bold (12 point, ½ point leaded)

Whatever your present method of composition may be, Compug raphic can put greater speed, capability and quality at your fin gertips for the lowest possible cost. CG offers a wide variety of typesetting equipment, all incorporating the latest electro nic techniques for maximum reliability. In addition to a wide choice of typefaces from the extensive basic typeface library, CG has a typeface development program that is the most act

ABCDEFGHIJKLMNOPQRSTUVWX
YZ&   abcdefghijklmnopqrstuvwxyz   1234567890

News No.2 (8½ point, 1 point leaded)

WHATEVER YOUR PRESENT METHODS OF COMPOSITI on may be, Compugraphic can put greater speed, capability and quality at your fingertips for the lowest possible cost. CG offers a wide variety of typesetting equipment, all incorpora ting the latest electronic techniques for maximum reliability. In addition to a wide choice of typefaces from the extensive ba sic typeface library, CG has a typeface development program that is the most active in the industry. Typesetting, today and in the future, requires equipment that will meet the ever incre

ABCDEFGHIJKLMNOPQRSTUVWXYZ&
abcdefghijklmnopqrstuvwxyz   1234567890

News Italic No.2 (8½ point, 1 point leaded)

WHATEVER YOUR PRESENT METHODS OF COMPOSITI on may be, Compugraphic can put greater speed, capability and quality at your fingertips for the lowest possible cost. CG offers a wide variety of typesetting equipment, all incorpora ting the latest electronic techniques for maximum reliability. In addition to a wide choice of typefaces from the extensive ba sic typeface library, CG has a typeface development program that is the most active in the industry. Typesetting, today and in the future, requires equipment that will meet the ever incre

*ABCDEFGHIJKLMNOPQRSTUVWXYZ&
abcdefghijklmnopqrstuvwxyz   1234567890*

News Bold No.2 (8½ point, 1 point leaded)

WHATEVER YOUR PRESENT METHODS OF COMPOSITI on may be, Compugraphic can put greater speed, capability and quality at your fingertips for the lowest possible cost. CG offers a wide variety of typesetting equipment, all incorpora ting the latest electronic techniques for maximum reliability. In addition to a wide choice of typefaces from the extensive ba sic typeface library, CG has a typeface development program that is the most active in the industry. Typesetting, today and in the future, requires equipment that will meet the ever incre

**ABCDEFGHIJKLMNOPQRSTUVWXYZ&
abcdefghijklmnopqrstuvwxyz   1234567890**

News No.3 (9 point, 1 point leaded)

WHATEVER YOUR PRESENT METHODS OF COMPOSITI on may be, Compugraphic can put greater speed, capability and quality at your fingertips for the lowest possible cost. CG offers a wide variety of typesetting equipment, all incorpora ting the latest electronic techniques for maximum reliability. In addition to a wide choice of typefaces from the extensive ba sic typeface library, CG has a typeface development program that is the most active in the industry. Typesetting, today and in the future, requires equipment that will meet the ever incre

ABCDEFGHIJKLMNOPQRSTUVWXYZ&
abcdefghijklmnopqrstuvwxyz   1234567890

News Bold No.3 (9 point, 1 point leaded)

WHATEVER YOUR PRESENT METHODS OF COMPOSITI on may be, Compugraphic can put greater speed, capability and quality at your fingertips for the lowest possible cost. CG offers a wide variety of typesetting equipment, all incorpora ting the latest electronic techniques for maximum reliability. In addition to a wide choice of typefaces from the extensive ba sic typeface library, CG has a typeface development program that is the most active in the industry. Typesetting, today and in the future, requires equipment that will meet the ever incre

**ABCDEFGHIJKLMNOPQRSTUVWXYZ&
abcdefghijklmnopqrstuvwxyz   1234567890**

News No.4 (10 point, 1 point leaded)

WHATEVER YOUR CURRENT METHODS OF composition may be, Compugraphic can put grea ter speed and quality at your fingertips for the low est possible cost. CG offers a wide variety of type setting equipment, all incorporating the latest ele ctronic techniques for maximum reliability. In ad dition to a wide choice of typefaces from the ext ensive basic typeface library, CG has a typeface

ABCDEFGHIJKLMNOPQRSTUVWXYZ&
abcdefghijklmnopqrstuvwxyz   1234567890

Figure 7.3 Ease of reading determines which type the editor uses. For a short line, Murray Bold would not offend the eye. A longer story, however, would at tract more readers when set in News No. 2. (Typefaces courtesy of Compugraphic Corporation)

but it would turn readers away if an entire story were set in it.

In order to set off a story, to make it stand out from other stories, editors use wide measure. Wide measure—also called "bastard" or "odd" measure—is any non-standard width in the newspaper. Preferably it should be wider than standard. Figure 7.4 shows wide measure under the headline **Leftist militants free 5 hostages in Bogota.** The photograph to the left of the story also is not standard width. Wide measure is an attractive and easy way to set off a story, but a page filled with a variety of wide measures appears disharmonious.

Figure 7.4 The designer of the *Minneapolis Tribune* built in air between paragraphs and around bylines. (Copyright 1980 Minneapolis Star and Tribune Company)

Air

Air in a newspaper provides a subtle background for the other design elements on the page. To be legible, type needs the right amount of air between letters and lines. Some editors try to crowd out air because they feel they must squeeze in every last letter as if it didn't matter that the lack of air will make the page illegible.

Examine Figure 7.4, the front page from the *Minneapolis Tribune*. Note how the editors space out stories between paragraphs; how bylines and datelines are set flush left to create white space; how much air appears between the lines of a headline.

When wide enough, air functions as a divider. Skinny column rules, which once separated columns of type, were dropped in favor of wider strips of air between the columns. But the one pica of air that keeps lines of 9-point type from running into each other is not enough to separate two headlines. Headline type needs a larger divider.

Like any other design element, air must be used consistently. A page with a lot of air at the top and crowded graphics and type at the bottom does not show a consistent use of air. Spread it around.

Modular Format

A modular page is not only easier to read but it also imparts unity. Unity is the end that comes from the good use of the elements of design. The page becomes a unified collection of modules (stories and photographs). Figure 7.5 shows one of many modular pages that appear throughout this chapter.

Behind the modular approach is knowledge of the Golden Rectangle, a proportion said by the Greeks to be the most pleasing. The proportion approximates 3 to 5. Any page full of modules beholden to that proportion, though, might lack the tension so necessary to stimulate the reader to dig into the page.

In part, that tension comes from violating the Golden Rectangle principle by creating modules that defy the 3 to 5 proportion. Vertical more than horizontal elements best violate the principle and photographs more than stories appeal to the eye in such cases. A deep photograph or other graphic is easier to read than a deep column of type. When a deep column of type is used, subheads help break up the gray and make the module less formidable. Figure 7.5 shows such a roundup down the left side.

If possible, no module on a page should be the same size as any other. Each deserves its own distinctive size. A page of many-sized modules generates the tension mentioned earlier. Also to be avoided are square modules; with every side the same, square modules are static.

Figure 7.5 A well designed page presents itself as unified. Modular organization of news content provides the reader with easy-to-read story blocks.

Photographs

Photographs are discussed more thoroughly in the next chapter so just a few brief comments appear in this section. Photographs should not be used to prop up a large headline unrelated to the photograph. Sloppy layout editors will stick unrelated headlines and photographs together and confuse the reader, who will try to figure out what the headline and the photograph have to do with each other.

Conventional wisdom says photographs should be anchored to the top or bottom of a page or to a nameplate or headline but should not be allowed to float unconnected to anything. Photographs surrounded by stories but unconnected to anything confuse the reader; thus, the anchor advice is sound, although like any other advice it should not be followed blindly. When violating the "rule," some editors box the photograph and its caption. Whatever approach is taken seems to be more a matter of training the reader than following an absolute.

Photographs deserve the same kind of play a comparable story would get. If it's a major news photograph, play it big. The reverse is not quite as true, though. Tiny photographs in a large format such as newspapers' lack communicative quality. Even a bad photograph looks better played large. (No editor should use a bad photograph, but if a bad photograph is all an editor has to help tell a story, the editor should use the photograph.) Finally, never publish on the same page two photographs of the same size. They will offset and diminish each other's impact. One of them must dominate the other. "Mug shots" (photographs of a person's head and shoulders only) do not come under this rule.

Caption Styles

A photo caption's first function, of course, is to complement the photograph not look pretty. But a caption whose design gets as much earnest attention as its message will add immeasurably to the appearance of a newspaper. Generally, a caption must contrast with the body type. If they are the same—same column width or same type size—the caption will be lost. What is desired is a caption that stands out so the reader can easily find it. It is not difficult to avoid the same column width as the body type's, especially when the caption is set in wide measure. Also, to help contrast the type should be larger than the body type, meaning, for instance, that a 9-point body type mixes best with a 10- or 11-point caption.

Captions sometimes appear in stacks, although every effort is made to minimize the number of stacks so the reader finds the caption easier to read. Several of those minimizations will be discussed presently. Editors attempt to balance the stacks of a caption by having each stack match line for line. With a sophisticated VDT system, that mission is easily accomplished. After writing a caption, a copy editor can press an appropriate command key (**JUSTIFY,** perhaps) and the caption will appear on the screen exactly as it would appear in the newspaper. If the copy editor wrote a caption that requires two stacks, it will appear before the copy editor in two stacks. If the second stack is a line short, the copy editor can rewrite the caption to balance the stacks.

Air plays an important role in displaying captions. To help float the caption in a background of air, the design editor indents all captions a minimum of one pica on each side. Captions so indented stand out better than those that run from one edge of the photograph to the other.

The standard caption style appears in Figure 7.6. The legend (or "lead in") appears in all capital letters. One legend is also bold face. Most

ALL EYES WERE ON THE ACTION Friday night in the Butte Civic Center as the Anaconda Copperheads tangled with the Butte High Bulldogs. The visitors were impressive in racking up a 74-42 in Western Division Class AA basketball, breaking a four-game winning streak by the Bulldogs in the series. Story and another picture on Page 6. (Staff photo)

— Staff photo by John E. Hall

SCHOOL PICKETS — Sam Houston Elementary students and parents picketed school administration offices Monday to protest busing students while renovations were being made at the school. A majority of the school's students also boycotted classes Monday.

Figure 7.6 Some photograph captions begin with words in all-capital letters. Such a beginning is called a "legend."

non-traditional caption styles are merely a variation of the traditional. Two other traditional captions are the nameline (Figure 7.7) and the one-liner (Figure 7.8). The nameline shown appears in italic type; other newspapers use either a larger or a bolder type to make namelines contrast with body type. The one-liner usually appears in a type larger than normal caption type. Editors use one-line captions when they must span a great distance with few words. The editors know that using the regular caption style would result in a caption a half-stack short of covering the distance.

Archbishop Romero

Figure 7.7 A nameline is just what the word says—a photo caption made up of only a name contained on one line.

Trucks in trouble: Fording Los Angeles freeway, left, jackknifing on I-90 near Livingston

AP Laserphoto

Figure 7.8 A one-line caption works best when an editor must span a long distance with a few words. Some newspapers flush left such captions while others center theirs.

Figure 7.9 shows two caption styles that are a variation of the all-caps legend. In these, the legend is set in headline type and appears above the caption. Besides being more eye-appealing, this style also puts more air into a page design. It's a good style when consistently used throughout the paper. Figure 7.10 shows a variation on the variation. In this example, the caption has been indented so that it fits in one stack instead of two. Another way to cut down on a lot of stacks in a caption is to put the legend in headline type alongside the caption. Figure 7.11 shows a sidesaddle caption. If larger type had been used for the caption, the caption writer should have set it in one stack to make it easier to read.

Given a five-column photograph but not many words for a caption (although more than enough for a good-looking one-liner), the editor opts for the caption that appears at the side of the photograph (Figure 7.12). The rules that affix the caption to the photograph are optional unless confusion would result without them.

Capital Journal photo by Gerry Lewin

They've got the right number

SILVERTON — It's been a learning process all the way since students in Lois Estell's first grade class at Eugene Field Elementary School here got used telephones from Continental Telephone. They're learning how to dial their own home phone numbers in case they get lost. The teacher said the students also are learning numbers generally by dialing numbers. When Estell, shown here at the rear of the classroom, says "Ring!" the children pick up their phones and answer properly. In the foreground are Larry Lawton, right, who lives with the Brad and Marilyn Agenbroad family in Silverton; Stephanie Carlson and Julie Harris.

TODAY Photo by Maurice Rivenbark

Reminder of David

A jacketed man braves the cold weather and deteriorating conditions at a Melbourne pier damaged by Hurricane David's powerful gusts last September. The pier is part of a senior citizen housing project.

Figure 7.9 Legends turned into overlines appear in headline type.

St. Petersburg Times — ERIC MENCHER

Shadows on the pier

Rays of bright sunlight peeking through the railings at the municipal pier surround this sightseer with a pattern of light and shadow. Following several days of cooler-than-normal weather, sunshine has returned to the Sunshine State, much to the delight of northern visitors.

Figure 7.10 To help set off the caption, a design editor can indent the caption but flush left the overline.

Wedding
bells

More than 300 people attended the first annual Bridal Affair Sunday at the 4-H exhibition building in Marion. Thirteen local buissness sponsored the four-hour affair, which consisted of a style show and booths displaying all the things a

C-T Photo by Greg Fisher
new bride might need from garters, to a trip to paradise. Many came with bells ringing in their ears, with hopes and plans for the future, and for others it was an afternoon of memories.

Figure 7.11 A legend can also be placed at the side of a caption. Although this example shows two stacks of caption type, a more appealing appearance would have been achieved had the caption been set in one stack.

A Lenten performance

Sandy Muy was among a group of students from Louisville's Youth Performing Arts School who played yesterday during a noon concert at Christ Church Cathedral in Louisville. The performance by two ensembles was the first of a series of Lenten concerts at the cathedral.

STAFF PHOTO
BY GAIL FISHER

Figure 7.12 Instead of placing a caption underneath a photograph, an editor can place it at the side. Note the use of the rule to "tie" the caption to the photograph.

Boxes and Rules

In newspapers, boxes function as containers of information. They're found most frequently around feature rather than spot-news stories, although an editor may box a short late-breaking story to give it more attention. Boxes are also useful to set off features, series roundups and briefs. Figure 7.4 shows one use of a box.

Some boxes come with squared-off corners while others have rounded corners. Rounded corners break up the straight lines of a page but they are harder to paste on and are unpopular with production people.

Boxes are sometimes used with photographs. The *Telegraph Herald* of Dubuque, Iowa, for example, wraps a box around a photograph and part of its caption to link the photograph and caption. Still other newspapers place a box around the edges of a photograph for emphasis or when it is not related to a story. Some design experts disagree with that because they say a photograph already draws attention to itself and needs no help.

Because boxes are visual elements, editors try to keep them from bumping each other and from being next to photographs. The editors feel that boxes side by side or next to photographs compete with each other.

But boxes have taken an interesting turn in page design. As Figure 7.13 shows, boxes now surround entire pages and with cutoff rules form what is considered some of the leading page design of the 1980s. Notice how the *Dallas Times Herald* uses a double rule between unrelated stories but uses only air to separate related stories.

Another variation of the boxed page shows up in the *Times Union* of Rochester, New York, (Figure 7.14) and *The Morning Call* of Allentown, Pennsylvania. Both newspapers box each story on a page rather than make each story share column or cutoff rules with other stories the way the *Dallas Times Herald* does.

The semi- or half-box results when rules are used top and bottom but not at the sides of a story. One popular rule in such cases is the Oxford rule, a line of two point parallel to a line of one point. Note: Printing equipment that can set a story and headline in a boxed module now exists, reducing the production problems that boxes create.

Graphics

In their drive to improve their appearance, newspapers have added a new position to the news desk, that of the graphic editor or graphic journalist or graphic artist. In another era, an editor assigned a story to a reporter, who wrote it. The story was then shown to a photographer, who took photographs, and to an illustrator, who was expected to produce illustrations. Today the editor assigns the project to a reporter, photographer and graphic journalist, who work together to produce a unified result. Also, the graphic journalist is no longer concerned with illustrating the story but with helping tell the story.

Figure 7.13 and Figure 7.14
Newspapers are increasing their use of column rules—the dark lines that appear in the columns between stories. Rules between the bottom and top of stories are called cutoff rules.

The artist who designed the graphic element at the right side of the page in Figure 7.15 was interested not only in a visual presentation but also in simplifying a complicated story—the procedure for firing a tenured high school teacher.

Maps make excellent graphic elements and are available from a surprising number of sources, especially the wire services but also state and local government officials. When publishing a story about an unfamiliar location, for example, a newspaper can use a map to provide a perspective.

Editors of small newspapers may feel that they cannot afford a graphic journalist and thus avoid using any graphics. But simple graphics are available to any newspaper with a photographer. In a hypothetical case, a newspaper is running a series on energy and wants to produce a graphic logo to accompany the story daily. That way, the reader will recognize the story without first having to read it. The assumption is that the reader will want to find the series and the logo will help. Two possible graphic elements appear in Figure 7.16. Simply by treating photographs as black and white drawings, the camera operator who helps make plates for the press can create local graphics. Just ask the camera operator to drop the screen used to make a photograph look like a photograph in print.

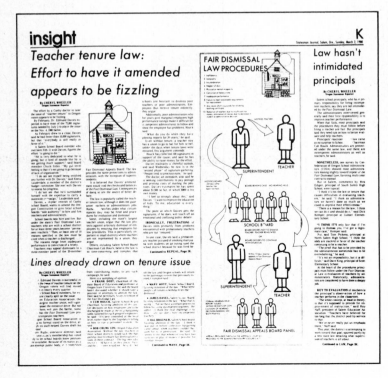

Figure 7.15 A complicated story—in this case, the dismissal of a tenured school teacher—becomes easier to understand when a flow chart graphic appears with it.

Figure 7.16 Unscreened photographs (making them pure black and white) make effective graphic elements to accompany a series. (Department of Energy photographs)

Extracted Quotes

When an editor believes a story contains a compelling direct quotation that helps tell the story, she will extract it from the story and set it in larger type. The quotation also remains in the story, of course. Figure 7.17 provides examples of extracted quotes. Extracted quotes should contrast with the body type. Some editors achieve that with bold face type; others use italic. Still others use a different type or a small version of the newspaper's headline type.

Extracted quotes are miserable failures if they appear *after* the quotation in the story. Such failures occur when extracted quotes are used throughout a story in the same manner as subheads—to break up the gray. There's nothing wrong with breaking up the gray, as long as the breakers appear logically. The reader who reads a quote in the body of the story and then encounters it set off in larger type finds the placement illogical.

Refers

The word is pronounced *ree-fer* and it has nothing to do with cigarettes. Refers point the reader to related stories elsewhere in the paper. They are part of the package concept. One typical refer appears with a story and says, "See related story on Page 7." Such a refer does not direct the reader well because the reader may have to figure out which story on Page 7 the refer means.

Instead, the editor who wants to serve the reader repeats the headline of the story referred to and then gives the page number. When the reader turns to Page 7 and sees five stories, he'll know which one he was directed to. Figure 7.18 shows how *Today* in Cocoa, Florida, processes refers. Typographically, refers are much like extracted quotes and can be handled in a variety of ways limited only by the editor's imagination.

Nameplates and Section Flags

Some newspapers have gone quasi-modern—that is, adopted a six-column, no-column-rules format but retained their nameplate, which was set in Old English type around the turn of the century. The editors who argue against changing their nameplate contend that the readers need the old style to maintain identity with the newspaper. The editors say that with a straight face even though, for example, professional sport teams, which have enjoyed increasing fan loyalty, are not bashful about changing uniforms and team logos every five years.

Just sentenced, man kills himself in jail

By MARCIA A. SLACUM
St. Petersburg Times Staff Writer

CLEARWATER — A 31-year-old man shot himself to death in a holding cell in the Pinellas County courthouse Thursday, moments after he was sentenced to four years in prison for bank robbery.

It was the first time such a suicide has happened in 33 years.

As bailiffs took his fingerprints and led him out of the courtroom, Douglas Leon Bafford mumbled that he wanted to stop to use a restroom before going to jail.

He was placed in a holding cell, where a bathroom was available.

LESS THAN a minute later,

> 'Oh God! They didn't search that man before he went in there?'
> — Judge Harry Fogle

courtroom spectators were startled by a loud bang that sounded as if it came from the hall.

Two bailiffs raced out of the courtroom and found Bafford on the floor of the holding cell. Sheriff's deputies said Bafford shot himself once in the chest with a 38-caliber handgun.

Shortly before he died, Bafford, his arms braced against the cell floor, appeared to be trying to raise his body out of a pool of blood that was forming on the floor under his chest.

Bafford had been free on bond before appearing in court to be sentenced, and he apparently brought the gun with him to court. He was dressed in slacks and a sports jacket.

PERSONS WHO are not in custody before sentencing are not searched, judges said.

After the shooting, attorneys and witnesses jammed the hall outside the holding cell, while bailiffs rushed for help.

Bafford's attorney, Richard Rahter, began pacing the hall and shaking his head. He was speechless.

Pinellas County Chief Circuit Court Judge Harry Fogle, who had sentenced Bafford, left the bench.

"Oh God! They didn't search that man before he went in there?" said Fogle as he rushed into the holding cell.

THOUGH Bafford seemed calm throughout the sentencing, Fogle said he "appeared disappointed" not to get probation.

Rescue workers arrived and tried unsuccessfully to treat Bafford. He died on the holding cell floor.

In 33 years, Bafford is the first person to commit suicide immediately after being sentenced, Fogle said. Bafford's record gave no indication that bailiffs needed to take extra precautions, he added.

Bafford moved to Clearwater from Baltimore, Md. several years ago. His parents were being notified late Thursday of their son's death, a sheriff's spokesman said.

Rahter, the last person to talk

with Bafford, said Bafford had been nervous about going to court.

"HE WAS obviously nervous," Rahter said. "He was sweating and he told me he was nervous. I had told him he was probably going to get some prison time."

Although court records show that Bafford was charged with armed robbery of a bank, Rahter told Fogle there was no evidence that his client had had a weapon. Bafford only drove the getaway car, Rahter said.

Bafford and Myron Mall of Largo were charged with robbing the Countryside Community Bank in North

See JAIL, 15-B

Calls Key to Vanished Brevardian

By JOAN REUS
TODAY Staff Writer

Dana Maria Lindenberg's nightmare began Feb. 7 when she picked up the ringing phone at her Miami mobile home.

"Dana, I know you're alone," the man said.

The words that followed were so obscene, she later would refuse to tell her co-workers at Norwegian Caribbean Cruise Lines Inc what the man said.

There were at least nine more calls that night from the same man — an "older man" who knew her name and apparently knew her boyfriend was out of town on business.

When she phoned to wish her mother, Donna Hyland of Merritt Island, a happy Valentine's Day a week later, she mentioned the calls only casually and said that since the calls had stopped, there was nothing

> 'I go to the mailbox over and over and hope there's a ransom note'
> — Missing Woman's Mother

to worry about.

Her mother wouldn't know until later that the calls had so terrified Lindenberg that she cried while telling co-workers about them.

The 20-year old Cocoa

Beach High School graduate also didn't tell her mother that the tires on her small yellow Toyota had been punctured the day after she received the calls.

On Feb. 18, Dana Maria Lindenberg vanished.

Worried friends went to her mobile home two days later to find the doors open, the lights still on.

A grilled cheese sandwich sat in a frying pan and a glass of lemonade was on the table next to personal letters she had composed and checks written to pay utility bills.

Lindenberg's car sat in

See VANISHED,
Back Page This Section

DANA LINDENBERG
. . . disappeared Feb. 18

Schools may balance budget

By JERI KORNEGAY
Citizen Patriot Staff Writer

The Jackson School Board may be able to balance its budget without damaging "most of the programs Jackson Schools are so proud of," Supt. Richard H. Escott told the board Monday night.

He said no additional operational millage would be necessary.

At Escott's urging, the board plans to make its final decision on his proposal, which was discussed at a Wednesday study session, before the month is out.

Board members seemed pleased with most of the proposal, but balked at plans to trim the maintenance budget by one-third and to substitute some classes at the Career Center for classes now taught by the school district.

An estimated $818,650 can be cut from the budget, Escott said, "without affecting the educational program we have." He guaranteed the board would not have to disrupt the K-5 program for five years if it accepts his proposal.

The budget, if not cut, would run

> 'No additional operational millage will be necessary.'
> Richard H. Escott

> 'We're doing a very outstanding job in this area. I guess I've got to retract my position a little bit.'
> Richard Surbrook

about $1 million in the red, according to Richard C. Powell, district finance director. State law mandates a balanced budget. Teacher retirements and leaves, and state aid may make up the remaining $200,000 gap in the budget, Escott said.

He suggested closing Ridgeway, Blackman and Griswold elementary schools for a $200,000 savings. He offered the board alternatives of closing Dibble and Wilson schools, but argued against them.

ESCOTT SAID Ridgeway students could be moved to Dibble without disturbing classes and

friendships. Schools contiguous to Griswold would absorb that school's population. Blackman students would probably go to Longfellow and Bennett.

"There is no teacher elimination in this proposal whatsoever," he said, but added that the Wilson Basic School principal would be dropped.

That principal has charge of only five classrooms, so Escott recommends adding Wilson School to the McCulloch School principal's jurisdiction. The Basic School would remain intact at Wilson.

The police Youth Services program in the middle and high

schools should be eliminated, Escott said."Police protection is a function of the police department," he said. That program is costing the district $45,000 this year, but federal funding runs out and the bill will be $108,000 next year.

An "alternative" presented last month to reduce by one-third the skilled trade services of painters, electricians, plumbers and carpenters was retained in Escott's Monday suggestion. This $186,827 cut sparked concern from trustee Richard Surbrook, who heads a committee in charge of the rebuilding of Withington Stadium.

In trimming $139,000 from the general contract bid for Withington Stadium, the committee had planned on using district personnel to do much of the sub-contract labor.

"WE'D HAVE TO find some other source" since a reduced skilled trade labor force would not be able to handle the Withington work, Kenneth Lautzenheiser, di-

Please turn to Page A-2

City's state projects in danger

By the Citizen Patriot Staff and Lansing Bureau

State officials say financing of state-supported building projects — including three in Jackson — is threatened by a near collapse of the national bond market.

Projects endangered here are the new downtown state office building, the new Foote Hospital and a proposal to convert the Otsego Hotel into apartments for the elderly.

All the Jackson projects are dependent upon raising money through the sale of tax-exempt bonds by state agencies.

Instability in the bond market could paralyze state construction projects throughout Michigan, officials say, including the construction of office buildings, college facilities, low income housing and hospitals.

"The situation is very grim," said state Budget Director Gerald H. Miller, adding: "The market right now is in a state of near collapse and that clearly will impact state

> 'The market is in a state of near collapse and that clearly will impact state building plans.'
> Gerald H. Miller
> State budget director

building plans."

Foote is seeking to finance its new hospital through the state hospital finance authority; the Otsego development relies on backing of the Michigan State Housing Development Authority, and the state office building will be financed by the state building authority.

Hospital authority spokesman Thomas J. Letavis wasn't quite as pessimistic as Miller this morning, saying that while bond interest rates have climbed by a percentage or more over the last couple of weeks, the bonds should still be marketable.

"Within the next couple of weeks, as things stabilize, we should be able to sell bonds," he said.

He said inflation has gone up sharply over the last several weeks, and investors are waiting for a plateau to be reached.

The sale of Foote Hospital bonds isn't scheduled until fall. Hospital officials acknowledge that rising interest rates would mean that hospital rates would increase so that the debt could be retired. But the officials don't see those additional expenses threatening the project at this point.

Sale of bonds for the Otsego project also

is months away, even if the state housing authority approves it. The proposal — made by American Development Corp. of Los Angeles — is being reviewed by the authority.

However, state Budget Director Miller said that, because of the bond market situation, the state may be unable to sell bonds to finance the Otsego project, as well as proposed projects in Bay City, Dowagiac, Alma and other cities. The same may also be true, he said, of the following state projects:

— Office buildings in Jackson, Flint and Saginaw.

— The planned $210 million University of Michigan replacement hospital. The building authority also was to be used for this project.

— An $11.4 million fine arts building at

Please turn to Page A-2

Figure 7.17 Compelling quotations can be extracted from a story and set off in a variety of ways.

Brevard Braces For Cold Snap

- Rare snow blankets Middle East, 3A
- Twisters rip Broward County; 1 dead, 4B

By TODAY Staff Writers
and Wire Services

People in North Florida were frolicking in rare snow Sunday. But citrus growers further south braced for freezing nighttime temperatures that could ruin half this year's crop and kill the tender blooms of next year's.

And from Mississippi to Virginia, a record-breaking storm spread a deadly mantle of snow and ice on roads and sent temperatures plummeting. At least 25 deaths were blamed on the storm.

"The wolf is at the door right now, the way it looks tonight," said Earl Wells, spokesman for Florida Citrus Mutual, the state's largest cooperative of citrus growers.

He said growers throughout the vast Citrus Belt of Central and South-Central Florida were being warned about the expected freeze, but added that if wind kept up overnight there was little that could be done to protect the groves.

The cold was left in the wake of a violent, wet, tornado-spawning front that moved southeastward through the erstwhile Sunshine State.

Arctic air brought snow flurries all across the northern sections, from Pensacola to Jacksonville and as far south as Gainesville. Damp flakes piled up about half-an-inch deep on grass and trees in some locations, but quickly melted from roofs, pavement and sidewalks.

Though snow was not reported in Brevard and Indian River counties late Sunday, winds gusted to an average of 35 mph while mid-60s morning temperatures dropped to 44 and 45 degrees by late afternoon.

Gusts of 60 mph were recorded in North Brevard but no damage was reported.

National Weather Service forecasters at Daytona Beach predicted continued cold today and Tuesday with warmer temperatures arriving later in the week.

Low temperatures of 24 to 28 degrees were forecast Sunday night for farming areas of the Space Coast. A freeze warn

See SNOW, Back Page This Section

Ford Comes Out of Political Closet

- Bush expands Iowa lead over Reagan, 6A
- Voters don't agree with polls on Kennedy, 7A

LOS ANGELES (AP) — Former President Gerald R. Ford says that Ronald Reagan cannot win the presidency because he is too conservative and that he would himself become a candidate if offered a "broad-based" invitation from the Republi-

TODAY's Chuckle

The most delightful benefit of being bald is that one can hear snowflakes.

can Party.

Ford said he would have to make up his mind about entering the presidential race by about April 1.

Reagan and George Bush, on the Republican campaign trail in Massachusetts, both invited Ford to join the fray.

The former president said he had received a growing number of requests that he become a candidate, but he was not yet convinced they represented a "truly broad-based" feeling in the GOP.

"If there was an honest-to-goodness, bona-fide urg-

ing by a broad-based group in my party, I would respond," Ford said. "As of today, the party hasn't asked me."

Ford, who succeeded Richard M. Nixon as president in 1974 and lost a bid for election to the presidency in his own right in 1976 against Jimmy Carter, made his comments about the 1980 campaign in an interview published Sunday by The New York Times.

Asked if he believed Reagan could not win, Ford replied that "it would be an impossible situation" because Reagan is "perceived

as a most conservative Republican."

"A very conservative Republican," he said, "can't win in a national election."

Newsweek reported Sunday that Ford has been saying he would reappoint Henry Kissinger as Secretary of State if he became president. Newsweek said Ford considers Kissinger perhaps the best secretary of state in U.S. history.

Reagan said in Boston that Ford should "pack his long johns and come out here on the primary trail with us."

Figure 7.18 To help the reader find related stories inside the paper, an editor uses refers. The best kind repeat the headline from the story referred to in order that the reader can find the story easier.

Modern editors not only have redesigned their nameplates to fit the times, they have also installed section flags or logos to help the reader through the paper. Using section flags represents a segment of the package concept, of thinking through the entire product and telling the reader where each section is.

The newspaper's section flags create an image consistent with the front-page nameplate. The section flags don't have to be the same as the nameplate but they should project a relationship to the nameplate.

Modern section flags also appear in the same place as the nameplate—at the top of the page. In the late 1960s and for most of the 1970s, the floating nameplate and section flag were popular. They could be moved around the top half of the paper. Then some newspapers stopped doing that. Redesigned nameplates were kept at the top of Page One, and the section flags were made in the image of the nameplate and kept at the top of the section. Occasionally a newspaper will lower its nameplate and run a single story above it. That doesn't happen on inside pages, although there's no reason why it couldn't.

Indexes

The package concept that lies behind the better newspapers manifests itself early in the paper in the form of an index or what is really a detailed table of contents. The index tells the reader what's in the package and provides a brief summary of the entire paper. The index has to be complete enough to tell the reader what's inside and that what's inside is worth turning to. The index promotes the content of the newspaper. It sells the inside.

Indexes are put together in various ways. The most common is by the location of the news, such as local, state, and so on. Other indexes merely tell what's inside without any categorization. Still other indexes are broken up by subject matter—politics, religion, entertainment, lifestyles. Other indexes combine elements of location and subject (see Figure 7.19).

A good index is well written. Treated as an after-thought, an index reveals an uncaring newspaper and suggests that the content is no better. The index should be intriguingly written; it should give more than the one-sentence lead of every story in the paper. In fact, one difficult index to write would take the form of a story; items would be related and transition provided between items. But making the index an attraction such as just described also means giving someone the time to write it and it means putting the paper together soon enough so that the writer has a sense of the total package. The idea is good but executing it might be sloppy and time consuming.

The indexes shown in Figure 7.19 all run down the side of the page and are anchored—that is, they appear in the same place daily. Other newspapers, such as the *Providence* (Rhode Island) *Journal-Bulletin*, anchor their indexes across the top of Page One. The index of the *Yakima Herald-Republic* moves around the page.

Color

Two types of color appear in newspapers. The full color photograph is called ''process'' color while the color border on a box, for example, is

Figure 7.19 Better organized newspapers provide indexes so readers can readily find what interests them.

called "spot." Process color is much more expensive than spot color and needs more planning. Often the fault with color photographs is that they are used just because of their color. The color photograph that engenders the reaction "good color" instead of "good photo" suggests where the editor's priorities are. They certainly aren't with the news. A good color photograph should appear in a newspaper because it has something to do with the news, not because it's colorful. Now that more and more newspapers are able to process color photographs in-plant, newspapers should be trying for more spot news color photographs.

Spot color has also been abused or misused. In some cases, it appears in headlines, giving the newspaper page the appearance of a circus poster. In other cases, the same color shows up every four or five pages, as though the editor required that color be used even if no one had a reason. Overused color shows up in every other graphic element on a page. All of that color spoils the impact. Finally, the spot color on the front page matches the spot color in a later advertisement, meaning the advertiser paid the paper's color costs that day or that the only reason the paper uses color is because an advertiser also uses color. Not very original.

The best spot color is functional; it is not used for its own sake but because it can help make a story clear. Color can be invaluable on a map in setting off certain areas in different colors to distinguish the areas. A zoning map in color would certainly aid its user. Whether color is circusy or useful depends on how an editor uses it. The difference in application shows a difference between bad and good editors.

The Future

In redesigning a newspaper editors have been faced with a problem—how to do it so the new design causes the least shock to the reader. Editors assume that readers are conservative and don't like surprises. That has led to three attitudes on redesigning a newspaper. Two of them are consistent with the conservative interpretation of reader tastes and the other is more radical. The conservative approach calls for redesigning from the inside out or a section at a time, leaving the hard news section for last. Both approaches—best described as mitotic—result in a gradual change that will not affront the reader. Also, mistakes don't glare as brightly in the gradual approach. The radical approach is to redesign in one major step—overnight. Editors who inform readers about design changes and their reasons ahead of time usually win reader acceptance quickly.

It is hard to say which way newspaper design will go. Today's styles—while innovative—have their roots in old newspaper or magazine design. The box approach shown earlier is a modern application of column and cutoff rules. As noted later, content is changing in the face of static circulation and rising competition from other media and different modes of news delivery. A lot of what happens to newspaper design will be determined by which medium newspapers feel the most pressed by. Newspapers will adapt their design to compete. Figure 7.20—an experimental redesign of the Rochester *Times-Union* by J. Ford Huffman—suggests magazine competition.

The problem with a fixation on design arises when all that editors concern themselves with is appearance. Newspapers that look good but

Figure 7.20 This experimental design of the *Times-Union* of Rochester, New York, presents a magazine appearance.

read bad are not newspapers. Design should never come at the expense of content. After all, the message is in the medium. Furthermore, design should not dictate news play. No editor should feel badly about ripping apart a good design in order to provide worthwhile fast-breaking news.

Another concern future design editors must face is the rising cost of newsprint—the paper on which newspapers are printed. Gone are the days of cheap paper and lots of air and few stories on Page One. Publishers are demanding good looks tightly packaged. Figure 7.21—an experimental redesign of the *Chicago Tribune* by Tony Majeri—speaks to the problem. Majeri has produced a good-looking (albeit conservative) format that allows for a relatively high story count and a respectable table of contents. Majeri's format calls for eight stories while the more typical horizontal, modular format of the 1970s allows no more than six modules—and that includes photographs. Seven modules seems a fair compromise if jumps are allowed. Disallowing jumps reduces the number of modules and decreases the variety of news.

It has long been suggested that the newspaper of the future will carry a front page that is nothing more than a table of contents of the major stories of the day, which appear throughout the paper. Figure 7.22—an actual Page One from *The Morning Call*—turns an idea into reality. Whether the reader would accept such a newspaper day after day remains to be seen.

Figure 7.21 Given the need for a "high" story count on Page One, Tony Majeri produced this experimental redesign of the *Chicago Tribune*.

The Mechanics of Design

Laying out a dummy and keeping a copy schedule are necessary bookkeeping chores that keep the daily production schedule moving and provide a view of what the day's issue is shaping up as. Figure 7.23 shows the dummy—a miniature version of what the design editor wants Page One to look like. Figure 7.24 shows the copy schedule that accompanies the page. The copy schedule is a list of the stories, photographs and other graphic elements scheduled for a particular page or section.

Design editors may rough out a page before actually fitting it together, but they send a precise, polished dummy to production.

Standard design practice calls for the top of the page to be dummied first. The top includes the lead story and photograph of the day.

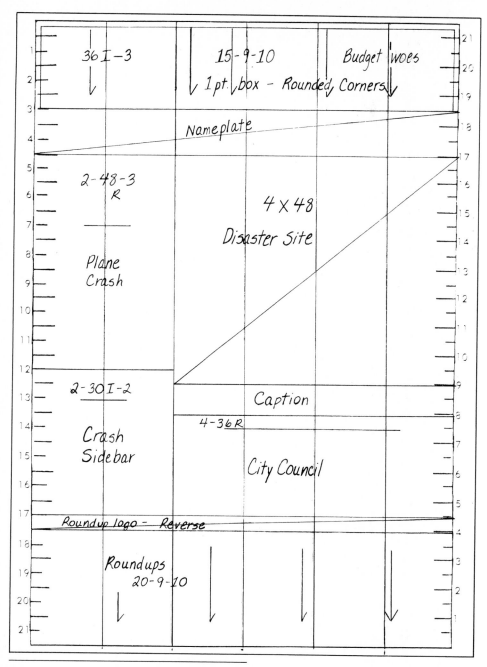

Figure 7.23 The dummy is a schematic of what the design editor wants the page to look like.

COPY SCHEDULE

Page # __1__   Date __5-19__   Editor __Williams__

Slug	Head size	Story Size	Copy Editor	Special Instrs.
Plane Crash	2-48-3 R	10	O'Ryan	w/art 4×48
Budget Woes	Sidesaddle 36 I-3	15	Bonner	15-9-10 1pt. Box 5 on 6 w/head
Crash Sidebar	2-30 I-2	8	Di Bui	
City Council	4-36 R	12	Bonner	
Roundups	24 -	20	Di Bui	20-9-10 Reverse logo

PHOTO SCHEDULE

Slug	Publication Size	%	Caption Writer	Special Instrs.
Disaster Site	4 × 48	132	O'Ryan	w/ lead story

Figure 7.24 A copy schedule enables an editor to keep track of all stories on a particular page. Copy schedules, of course, can also be kept for sections, such as supplements, special tabloids or Sunday magazines.

Second to get dummied is the bottom, where some editors place their second lead story. This particular dummy has across the bottom a news roundup set in wide measure, which must be noted on the dummy and the copy schedule. The bottom is dummied after the top so the page has a strong foundation. The middle of the page—while last—should still receive the same attention and skill the editor gives the top and bottom. The news content on a page with advertising across the bottom is designed from top to middle since the ads provide the foundation.

The largest headline on the page belongs to the lead story. The lead story, as in the case in Figure 7.23, is not always at the top of the page. The editor who designed 7.23 placed a boxed story with a sidesaddle head above the paper's nameplate then put the lead story and its related photograph below the nameplate. It will stand out because it has such a large headline.

The copy schedule maintains continuity on the desk, especially if several editors are involved and if several editions or sections are planned. The editors who put out the state edition may not be the ones who edit the late-night final and they'll need a copy schedule to keep track of the earlier work. Even on a small newspaper, a single editor should keep at least a rough schedule, just to have an idea where the stories for that day's issue are.

The desk editor fills in the copy schedule as each story goes to a copy editor. A story not logged in at the time an editor decides to use it could get lost. Special instructions remind everyone if a story has an accompanying photograph or if it is set wide measure or if it has a sidesaddle head or subheads. Although not shown on the dummy, the page editor has assigned subheads for the news roundup and the copy editor who does the roundup will produce a 20-inch piece with subheads intact. They won't have to be inserted later.

Doing copy schedule work on a VDT system has its advantages. An editor can tell the computer how many inches are available and the computer can tell the editor how many inches have been used every time a story or photograph is logged into the copy schedule. It's the same principle as keeping a running checkbook—you always know what kind of shape you're in.

Be it the mechanical or artistical side of design, newspapers are changing, perhaps faster than they've ever changed before. The good newspapers, however, will make changes that not only improve their bodies but also their souls. Redesign will not be done without regard for content and ultimately for the reader's needs. Newspapers that never lose sight of the reader have won half the battle.

Suggested Reading

Contemporary Newspaper Design: A Structural Approach, Mario R. Garcia, Prentice Hall 1981.

Newspapers on this page are *The Philadelphia Bulletin* (above), *The Bulletin* of Bend, Oregon, and *The Sun* of San Bernardino, California.

The newspaper pages displayed on pages 162–164 show many of the elements of modern design. Notice the use of modular design, indexes and other reference devices, the use of type to match a picture page's theme, wide measure, boxes and rules, and white space. On this page are the *Providence* (Rhode Island) *Journal-Bulletin* and the *Yakima* (Washington) *Herald-Republic.*

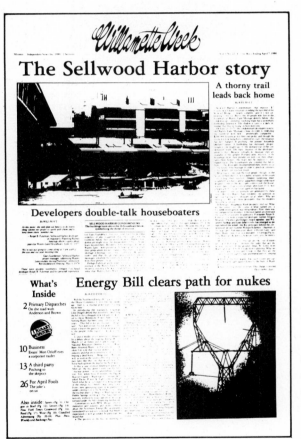

Newspapers on this page are *The Minneapolis* (Minnesota) *Tribune* (top left), the *Willamette Week* of Portland, Oregon, and the *Banner Graphic* of Putnam County, Indiana.

CHAPTER EIGHT
Photographs

Photographs Have a Purpose

Photographs are not just something to fill in space or to make pages attractive. Photographs function the same way stories do—they present the news. An editor who considers photographs as filler—something to avoid bumping headlines or to disguise an unimaginative design—will publish a poor newspaper. If the overall news package is to succeed, editors must give the same attention to photographs that they give to words.

Photographs are not just illustrations on a page. A photograph with a story ensures a higher readership for the story than had the story run alone. The reader sees the photograph first and is attracted to the story through the photograph. Often a good photograph can lift a story from the routine or save a writer weak in description. The story accompanying Figure 8.1 might say members of a Nazi party rally in Chicago's Marquette Park beat a black counter-demonstrator and that a white man attempting to intervene was roughed up. But those words don't begin to say what the photograph, taken by Larry Ruehl of *Daily Southtown-Chicago*, says. The photograph freezes the action and allows the reader to study the event. The reader can take a few seconds or many minutes, and the longer the reader spends with the photograph the more the reader will get out of it.

A photograph transports the reader to a different time or place. The photograph of Dresden, Germany, (Figure 8.2) was taken in 1946, one year after British and U.S. planes bombed the city and killed 135,000 persons, more than the number killed in the atomic bomb attack on Hi-

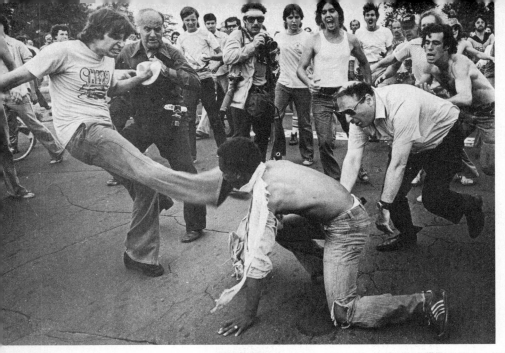

Figure 8.1 A photograph immediately tells readers what the story is and frequently does it with more impact than words can have. (Photograph by Larry Ruehl of *Daily Southtown-Chicago*)

Figure 8.2 Few people saw the destruction that overwhelmed Dresden, Germany, during World War II. But photographs, including this one, tell the story of that destruction to the many who never saw it. (United Press International photograph)

roshima. Few people saw the destruction, and to most of the readers of this book, the event is part of a war that took place before they were born. But the photograph remains to help tell the story.

One photograph can evoke any of many human emotions. It is hard to imagine anyone who would not be touched by a starving victim of civil war in East Timor (Figure 8.3). Emaciation is not pretty.

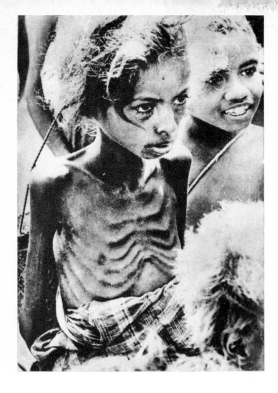

Figure 8.3 A photograph can evoke many emotions in its viewers. This one shows a starving victim of a civil war in East Timor. (United Press International photograph)

Too often photographers are unfairly accused of trying to be artistic rather than journalistic. That happens. But the good photographers are photojournalists; they know they are helping to tell the news and they photograph accordingly. That their work rises above the mundane should not detract from it. When their photographs fail as a news conveyor, editors should reject the work the way they would reject a story that fails. It is, of course, easy to require a reporter to rewrite a poor story, but it is impossible for a photographer to reshoot a news event already a part of history. For that reason, a photographer who produces quality work is worth more than a reporter who has to rewrite. Getting it right the first time is an essential ingredient of good photojournalism.

Good editors respect good photographers the way they respect good reporters. Good editors would no more butcher a photograph than a story. Mutual respect inspires editor, reporter and photographer to strive for all-round understanding and quality. To engender better use of photographs, various top editors have added a new person to the news staff—the picture editor. At larger papers, the person is a photographer; at smaller papers, a copy editor may double as picture editor. No matter, the mission is the same—enhance the visual personality of the paper and then protect it against those who would, for the sake of a windy story, reduce a photograph one or two columns just to get in all of the words.

A photograph worth using is worth using at a size that will engage the reader. The *Everett* (Washington) *Herald* practices that philosophy, using large photographs the way word editors use large type: good display for everything. Figure 8.4 shows a *Herald* sports page in which the photograph takes up more than a third of the page. Note, too, that the page contains only three stories; the editor did not cram it. And if a story needs five or six photographs to be told well, an editor should use them. It's similar to using sidebars to help tell a major news story.

In selecting photographs, editors should not be swayed by a type of photograph that won an award. According to Lil Junas, one-time Arkansas News Photographer of the Year and author of *Cardon Creek, A Photographic Narrative*, photographs showing tragedy and violence win awards more readily than any other type of photograph. Junas studied the Pulitzer Prizes and the Pictures of the Year (awarded by the National Press Photographers Association and the University of Missouri School of Journalism) and found that 54 percent of the winners showed tragedy or violence. With the Pulitzers only, the tragedy/violence among winners rises to 63 percent. A look through back issues of *Editor & Publisher*, a trade magazine for the newspaper industry, supports Junas' research. Prize-winning or major news photographs depict assassination, violence, death, mass suicide, protests. *E&P* headlined one presentation of photographs this way: "Mostly grim."

But the attitude of judges and editors may be changing, for another issue, while still showing photographs of grim scenes, also heralds a photographer who produced an unobtrusive yet touching essay on a child dying of brain cancer. For that, George Wedding, then of the *Palm Beach Post*, received the World Understanding Award from the National Press Photographers Association, the University of Missouri and Nikon Inc., a camera manufacturer. Another photograph, this one from the portfolio of Chris Johns of the *Topeka Capital-Journal*, shows a father kissing his child through the plastic wall of a bubble that protects the child from infection. A tender moment hard to put in words.

Words cannot substitute for the good photograph. For example, in 1976 *The New York Times* used these words in a story about Vice President Nelson Rockefeller: "After protesters showed they were able to drown out his speech, Mr. Rockefeller then gestured three times with his finger." Did he point? Beckon? Raise his pinky? Flash the *V* for victory? The words don't tell. A photograph of Rockefeller gesturing was taken by Don Black, then of the Binghamton, N.Y., *Sun*, and the photograph moved on the Associated Press and United Press International wirephoto nets. One of the papers receiving it was the *Times*. Rockefeller was also a former governor of New York and since he had gestured in New York, a student of journalism might assume that the *Times*—prideful of itself as a paper of record—would publish the photograph. Not so. The *Times* turned down the photograph because it was not tasteful and because the gesture could be explained in words. But the words (". . . Rockefeller then gestured three times with his finger") don't make clear which finger Rockefeller gestured with or that Rockefeller gave political credibility to

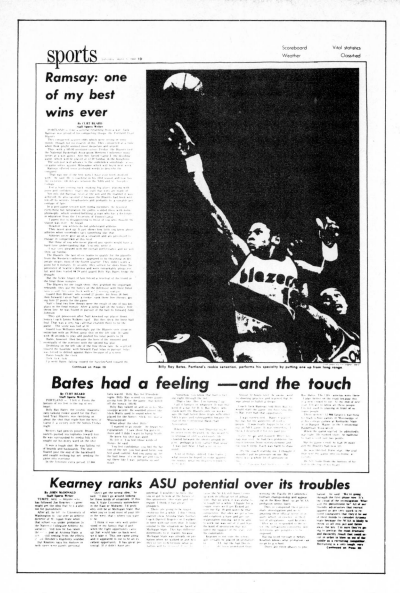

Figure 8.4 A good photograph poorly used loses much of its impact. This photograph deserves the play it has received. (© The Daily Herald Co.)

an obscene gesture. Even a later allusion in the story doesn't make the point the way the photograph does. The photograph (Figure 8.5) makes the action credible. The reader sees it happening.

Interestingly, Black doesn't hold up the Rockefeller photograph as his finest. In fact, he says he was in the right place at the right time and was not even sure Rockefeller had made the gesture or if it was on film. When Black, director of photography at the Salem, Oregon, *Statesman-Journal*, discusses his work, he cites Figure 8.6 as an example of a good photograph, one he is pleased with. Black likes that photograph because "it is more universal—it's a look at a facet of life that needs no words to augment it, and the communication and impact don't depend on who these people are, but on what is happening. If the mayor of Binghamton

Figure 8.5 Some editors chose not to use this photograph of Vice President Nelson Rockefeller but attempted in writing to tell what he did to a crowd of hecklers in Binghamton, N.Y., in 1976. Words were no substitute. (Don Black photograph)

had given 'the finger' to the crowd that day rather than the vice president, there would have been no interest outside of our circulation area. The birth picture, on the other hand, has been published all over the world in numerous magazines and is a better example of the type of involvement and communication I would like to see in all my pictures.''

Photographs that do not communicate include those of a line of people receiving a check or being sworn into office or being congratulated for something. They are derisively referred to as "stand 'em up and shoot 'em" or "execution at dawn" or "grip 'n' grin" photographs. Given a choice between a photograph of the president of the United States addressing a group as part of an event to show off newly installed solar

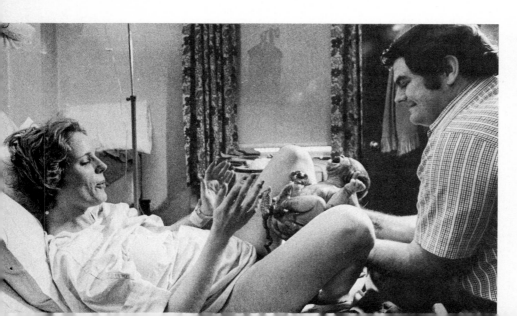

Figure 8.6 A good photographer wants a photograph that has meaning in itself. Don Black, who also took the photograph in Figure 8.5, cites this one—of a father delivering his wife of their child—as a photograph with meaning. The Rockefeller photograph resulted from Black being in the right place at the right time. (Don Black photograph)

panels at the White House or a photograph of the president showing off solar panels, a good editor should choose the second picture. The second picture shows more than a head, a microphone and the presidential seal; it shows the president doing something.

An editor must also decide what effect the shape of the photograph will have. Horizontal photographs generally produce a calming effect on the layout while vertical photographs, because of the contrast they offer, stand out. Such an effect will not happen every time, but the new editor should remain aware that horizontal and vertical photographs often give off different sensations.

Photographs in series or semi-series help the reader understand an event by giving a sense of a continuum. A series of photographs helps the reader better understand what happened. Series photographs are especially popular in sports where the sequence details a particularly spectacular play. When the action is moving from left to right, run the series horizontally on a page. When the action is moving right to left, run the series vertically, which is easier on the reader.

Taste and Ethics

A distasteful or unethical story must be read before anyone will react to it. A newspaper can publish such a story but few may notice because the story hides among the advertisements and carries a bland headline that attracts no attention. A photograph, though, requires none of the effort of reading; it can be taken in with a glance and its impact imparted immediately. A photograph needs no headline, and a reader does not have to read five or six or seven paragraphs into a photograph to learn the details. The photographic story appears in an instant; one sweep of the eye usually makes the story clear.

What does the reader make of a series of photographs that show firefighters searching a creek for the body of a boy who fell through thin ice, that show one of them carrying the boy's body to the shoreline, that show the dead boy's mother tearfully watching the unsuccessful rescue attempt, her grief understandably heavy on her face? The first question that might arise is how intrusive was the photographer? If the photographer was heavy handed and pushy in getting the photographs, the family's privacy has been shattered and later apologies will not change that fact. But what if the photographer shot the scene from a distance, did not poke a camera in anyone's face and did not behave obnoxiously while trying to get the photographs? The next issue, then, is whether by publishing the photographs the newspaper invades the family's privacy. Is the photograph worth it?

What of the newspaper that publishes a photograph of the body of a woman who has been hit by a train? Her body lies across the tracks and the camera angle makes it appear she was decapitated. In that case, friends of the family and the family felt badly about the photograph and expressed their dismay to the newspaper.

The *Poughkeepsie* (New York) *Journal* also received criticism for publishing the photograph of a man who had been shot and was near death as paramedics attempted to save him (Figure 8.7). The photograph, taken by chief photographer Robert V. Niles, shows a man who was shot-gunned in the stomach and who died approximately four hours later. But what if the man had not died? Would that soften the impact of the photograph? Would it mean something else to readers to know that the victim was under indictment on a drug charge? In other words, does the victim's possible criminal background make a picture of his dying fair game for publication? What, instead, if he had been the mayor of Poughkeepsie—a well known public figure? What if he had been a nobody? Also, what of the man's family? Must they be subjected to such a photograph? Editors must consider many things before deciding to publish such a photograph.

Figure 8.8, from the Fort Myers, Florida, *News-Press*, shows an injured child and her distraught family watching paramedics work on her while a helicopter prepares to land and take the child to a hospital. The child, who had gone into a street to retrieve some books she had dropped and been struck by a car, was alive when the *News-Press* published the photograph. She died a few days later. Only one complaint reached the managing editor, Harper says, and that was to say that the photograph was in poor taste. On the other hand, Harper says a police sergeant and a paramedic both praised the paper for publishing the photograph because they felt it worked to promote safety.

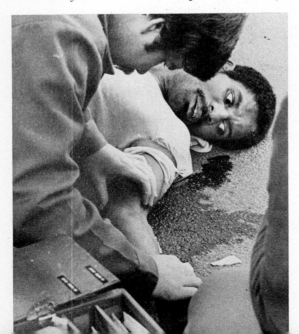

Figure 8.7 Photographs of people near death can elicit negative reader reaction, and editors must face the backlash of a critical public. (Photograph by Robert V. Niles, chief photographer, *Poughkeepsie Journal*)

Figure 8.8 This tightly composed photograph of an injured child, the child's distraught family and an incoming rescue helicopter generated only one negative complaint. The child was alive when the photograph was published but died a few days later. (Acey Harper photograph)

Figure 8.9, however, received a lot of complaints. The photograph, showing the body of a boy who died during one of the eruptions of the volcano in Mount St. Helens, Washington, in 1980, was labeled unimaginable, repulsive, callous, gross, cruel, tacky, in very poor taste. One of those who complained was the boy's grandmother who knew only that the boy, his brother and father were in the eruption area. Nobody knew their fate until the *Seattle Times* published the photograph on page 2 of its fourth section almost two days after it had been received on the wirephoto net.

Times executive editor James B. King said he approved the publication of the photograph because it showed a human victim of the volcano. Said *Times* day picture editor James C. Heckman: "Thousands of words about gas velocities, air temperatures and ash falls don't begin to tell the story of the violence and instant death as that one picture." All in all, those who defended publication wherever they were saw the photograph as news, as a graphic and poignant element in a larger tragedy. The photograph, by the way, was taken by a photographer from the *San Jose* (California) *Mercury*, which devoted approximately a third of its front page to the picture. The photographer was the same George Wedding mentioned earlier for receiving a world understanding award.

Figure 8.9 The human side of the eruption of the volcano at Mount St. Helens in Washington in 1980 came across in this photograph by George Wedding of the *San Jose* (Calif.) *Mercury.* (Copyright 1980 by George Wedding and *The San Jose Mercury News*)

Consider Figure 8.10, which shows a man screaming as firefighters pull him from his smashed van. He sustained two broken legs, which is why he is screaming as the firefighters lift him from the wreckage. The photographer, Thelma Robinson of the *Centre Daily Times*, State College, Pennsylvania, had to argue with her city editor just to get him to argue with his editor to publish the photograph. No one doubted it was a good photograph, but some of the editors were reluctant to publish such a photograph of a local person. What if he died after presstime? The editors solved their problem by calling the hospital, and, upon learning that the victim's condition was good, talking to him and getting his oral permission to publish the photograph. The newspaper did not need the victim's permission because the accident occurred on a public highway, which the courts recognize as fair game for newspaper coverage. By getting permission the editors stilled one potential source of criticism. (No one ever complained to the editor.)

A couple of weeks later the same editors had to decide on publishing a so-so photograph of a woman trapped in her wrecked automobile. They easily rejected the photograph. Unlike the first accident in which the man was not at fault, the driver in this case had been the subject of a police chase, had been in three minor accidents before her big crash, and was legally drunk. The police planned on pressing charges. The editors felt that by publishing the photograph they would be adding to the person's problems, so they chose to publish just a story. Publishing the photograph would not have served the public interest. It is not, however, an invasion of privacy to publish a photograph of a current accident that occurs in public. Publishing it months or years later, however, could be an invasion of privacy because the photograph is no longer news (*i.e.,* current).

More clear-cut examples of privacy invasion arise with non-newsworthy photographs shot at a distance with a telephoto lens, which enables the photographer to see something not visible to the eye of a passer-by. Clearly, such photographs are not ethically obtained. Publishing them compounds the sin. Long-distance photographs worth using might show illegal activities and thus have news value.

Editors supporting the publication of photographs later considered by some to be an invasion of privacy or tasteless defend the publication on the grounds that the photograph serves a greater good. When Stan Forman of the Boston *Herald-American* photographed a fire escape breaking away from a building and casting two people to the ground—one to her death—the resultant flurry included an inspection of all of the city's fire escapes. Some editors used that to defend publication of the sequence (which won a Pulitzer). Some editors use the same defense in publishing gory accident photographs. People will drive more carefully after seeing such photographs, the editors argue. That hasn't happened, perhaps because readers have become jaded from seeing so many accident photographs.

Figure 8.10 The local accident photograph raises ticklish problems for editors of small-town newspapers who live in the same small community as the injured people. Although the only questions an editor should worry about are quality and accuracy of the photography, the close-to-home issue must also be addressed. (Thelma Robinson photograph)

Other editors would argue that they're not in the social good business, just the news business. They would say they publish photographs because they are *news* and not because they might solve some social problem. They are right. If an editor publishes a photograph with a greater good in mind, might not the same editor withhold a photograph because it might represent a greater evil? Editors must avoid a child-care mentality when editing newspapers. The major criterion for any photograph is its inherent news value. A photograph of a body crumpled up after falling 10 stories lacks the news value of a photograph showing the body falling, unless the victim is newsworthy (a public official), in which case any photograph might be used. Case-by-case judgment arises in many decisions on the selection of news photographs.

In the early 1960s the Associated Press transmitted a photograph of a Vietnamese monk who had doused himself with gasoline and then lit a match. The photograph shows the monk in flames; he was protesting the repressive regime he had to endure. Some editors rejected the photograph because they published morning newspapers and they did not feel it appropriate for a breakfast audience. The same editors undoubtedly would not use it in an afternoon paper because it would offend the dinner crowd. Other editors used it because the act of self-immolation showed the emotion of protest in Vietnam at that time. That was its news value. It showed something people in the United States would never have understood in words alone.

A later Vietnam photograph, this one of a police chief executing a suspected Viet Cong officer with a pistol shot to the head, appeared on the front page of the *New York Times* and the *Washington Post*, among others. (The *Times* had rejected the monk photograph.) NBC showed footage of the execution but cut away when the footage showed the corpse and blood rushing from the head of the corpse. The NBC producer made a decision between news and gore; he edited out the gore and kept the news.

Some editors would argue that distance between the reader and the event makes the photograph easier to use. A newspaper would reject the photograph of a local woman's body lying on railroad tracks but might show the photograph of firefighters removing the body of a youngster—his face clearly showing—from the waters of a river where his school bus had plunged—in Spain.

Nudity presents another area where editors do not agree. A photograph of a nude 19-year-old French female being rescued from suicide lacks news value (Figure 8.11). But what if the photograph shows a waitress in a topless bar or a dancer in a male strip joint; that is, what if the nudity is part of the story? In such cases, editors use out-of-focus photographs or photographs that do not show genitalia. The sensationalistic tabloids aside, most editors feel they are publishing a family newspaper—one the entire family can read without embarrassment. Community standards help editors in such cases.

Figure 8.11 A suicide attempt by a nude woman produced this photograph—and raised the question of publishing such a picture. The woman was not newsworthy, but what if she had been a famous person? (United Press International photograph)

Overall, editors must ask themselves if any photograph, no matter the content, contains enough newsworthy elements, adds insight to a problem or puts a story into context to make it publishable. If the photograph has a voyeuristic value rather than a news value, the editor has good reason to reject it.

Picture Pages

Picture pages represent the essence of photojournalism, the melding of pictures and words to depict a spot news event or a feature. Although the length of the word story can vary, the best picture pages contain short word essays and rely mostly on the visual to give the message. Putting a limit on anything can backfire, but the best picture page usually contains no more than five or six photographs.

Some newspapers routinely fill up a page of unrelated photographs of news events and call that a picture page. But the picture pages that a photojournalist would want to produce and that tell a story stick to a single subject. Multi-topic picture pages lack the thematic unity so necessary to retaining a reader's attention. A picture page should be a visual essay, not a set of visuals.

The concept behind designing a picture page is the same as designing a front page—the page must have a lead. That does not mean, however, that the photograph in the upper left-hand corner is the lead or that the largest photograph on the page is the lead. Often, the lead (or dominant) photograph is the most striking in content, size or position, but is not necessarily the largest. For example, the lead photograph could be one column by 21 inches deep or six columns by three inches deep and not be the largest photograph on the page. The atypical size would make it stand out.

Those who lay out picture pages should forget column sizes and use a blank piece of paper for a dummy. In that way they are more apt to present the photographs in a visually better size than the standard column size might allow. Furthermore, a five-column photograph centered over six columns visually breaks from the traditional columns and frames the picture in a background of air. Note how pictures are floated in Figures 8.12. Also note how each major module on the page lines up with at least one other module. That helps give the page unity.

Most photographs on a picture page need a caption not because the photographs need the words but because captions guide the reader through the page. Caption-less picture pages or pages with one caption referring to all pictures on the page function like ships without rudders—they are aimless and the reader avoids them because of lack of time to figure out what's going on. Occasionally a self-explanatory photograph—especially one that is not central to telling the story—can appear without a caption.

For the most part, photographs look best in rectangular rather than square shapes. A picture page on bowling does not mean the pictures

Figure 8.12 A picture page need not be laid out according to the standard columns of a newspaper. Pictures can be floated between normal column dividers. Note how each module on this page lines up with at least one other module. (Copyright 1979, *The Sun.* All rights reserved)

must appear in the shape of bowling pins and bowling balls. Also to be avoided are mortises, cutouts and insets, all of which detract from photographs. Type on top of photographs can be overdone as can reverse type. Keep air to the outside; don't trap globs of empty space between pictures or in the middle of the page. In all, those who design picture pages should strive for clean presentations that do not mutilate the pictures and words on the page or the newspaper's reputation.

The Mechanics

The tools of photo sizing are the pica stick, proportional scale and two Ls, which are optional. The Ls are cut from very heavy paper or cardboard (so they can endure many handlings) and enable an editor to move them about the surface of a picture to see how it will appear if cropped a certain way. Other editors use pieces of paper, which is not as convenient or as durable.

The measuring area of the standard pica stick is 12 inches long and is broken into inches down one side and picas down the other. A pica is a printer's measure equal to approximately one-sixth of an inch. An inch contains six picas. A pica breaks down into points, of which there are 12 in one pica. The point, of course, is the same point used to measure type. Thus, a 36-point headline is three picas deep (36 divided by 12 equals 3). Six picas equal an inch or 72 points. In 12 inches, there are 72 picas (6 picas to the inch).

The proportional scale, more commonly known as the "wheel," has on its face two scales, both of which are marked off in inches. Ignore the inches and use them instead as picas. After all, the wheel is a *proportional* scale and the sizing of photographs is an exercise in changing proportions. It doesn't matter how the measurements are labelled.

To change the size of a photograph, an editor must first know its width and depth in picas. To change a photograph 30 picas wide and 42 picas deep to three columns (41 picas for this exercise) the editor would take the inside scale of the wheel (called **SIZE OF ORIGINAL**), find 30 and line it up with 41 on the outside scale (called **REPRODUCTION SIZE**). In the window appears the percentage the reproduction camera must be set at to create a photograph in the size wanted by the editor. The percentage must be marked on the photograph. To learn the new depth of the photograph, the editor goes to 42 on the inside scale and sees what it lines up with. That figure (57 in this example) is the photograph's new depth. The photograph would be marked 3x57. (When not dealing with standard column widths, an editor marks a picture size picas by picas.) A photograph can be reduced using this same method.

Cropping

The art photographer has time to pose pictures and produces work that seldom needs cropping. But the photojournalist takes pictures on the fly and often has to settle for a poor vantage point. Just because the action doesn't take place where the photographer is doesn't mean the editor won't expect a good photograph of the action. Don Black was quite a distance away when he took the photograph of Rockefeller (Figure 8.5) and he used only 20 percent of the negative to produce the final print.

Black, like most photographers, did his cropping in the darkroom. But often cropping is done on the desk, especially when an editor sees something in a photograph that the photographer did not crop out. Whatever, a photograph should not be cropped just to fit a hole on a page. Cropping should be done to make a picture better, much the way an editor removes words here and there to make a story better.

Examine Figure 8.13 for a moment. It shows a British soldier standing guard outside a clothing store in Belfast, Northern Ireland, while next to him two shoppers look in the window. To the left is a distracting reflection of nearby people. At the top of the photograph is something white that will no doubt wash out in reproduction and thus should be cropped out of the picture. The sidewalk, although it will reproduce adequately, is distracting foreground and should be cropped as close as possible to the people in the picture. That will bring the people closer to the reader. Likewise, the area to the right of the soldier adds nothing and should be trimmed away.

That leaves a photograph with three adults. Some editors might remove the female and her baby, leaving the two men—one of them with his eye on the photographer and the other with his eye on the manikin (Figure 8.14). Contrary to what you may be thinking, that is not dishonest cropping even though what remains is not the original photograph. What if the photographer had turned in the photograph of just the two men? Nobody would have been aware of what had been trimmed away, either in the taking of the photograph or in the darkroom. The photograph represents a slice of Belfast, not all of it. Any photograph is only part of a larger whole.

Cropping should remove that which distracts the reader from seeing the main point of a photograph. Beyond normal cropping (removing extraneous background and foreground) are tight and radical cropping, which offer the reader atypical perspectives. The typical radical crops are performed on mug shots. The Dubuque, Iowa, *Telegraph-Herald* tightly crops the mug shots that accompany its editorial page columns, usually cutting off the top of a writer's head right above the eyebrows and the chin from just below the lower lip. A pair of eyes, a nose and a mouth peer at the reader. Notice the tight cropping of Sen. Henry Jack-

Figure 8.13 and Figure 8.14 A photograph frequently needs cropping to improve it. In the photograph above a distracting reflection on the left and some grayish-white areas top and bottom can profitably be cut from this photograph. It can be done in several ways and still be effective. This cropped photograph (right) emphasizes the two men by eliminating previously mentioned distractions and the woman and child. (United Press International photograph)

son in Figure 8.15. Also notice the large size of the photograph, which was part of a multi-page series in the *Everett Herald*.

Inexperienced editors make many mistakes, especially if they lack a photographic background or an appreciation of the value of visual communication. Beginners tend to want to reduce photographs rather than crop them to the desired size. Too often a beginner will reduce an entire photograph rather than crop out of the photograph the uninteresting and the distracting. A reduced photograph means a reduced image and a loss of detail. Figure 8.16 shows how a single-column mug shot can be cropped from a larger photograph without losing detail. Some editors might use the photograph of former New York Congresswoman Bella Abzug in full—but reduced. The photograph, however, is not worth running full size because of the washed out background and out-of-focus foreground.

Figure 8.15 The lead photograph on this page shows tight cropping. (Copyright The Daily Herald Co.)

To tell the production department which part of a picture to crop out, an editor marks the sides of the photograph (Figure 8.17). An editor never marks on the surface of a picture because the editor may have a change of mind about the size and will need to remark the photograph. Pencil and ballpoint pen marks will not come off the surface of a photograph. Other than crop marks, all instructions to the production department usually get placed on the back of a photograph.

Figure 8.16 Although this photograph of former Congresswoman Bella Abzug might run in full, some editors would reduce it—at a loss in facial detail. Without reducing the photograph, however, an editor can crop out of it a standard-sized face shot that retains the detail of the original photo. (R. Thomas Berner photograph)

Figure 8.17 Crop marks are shown in the border of a photograph but never on it. (R. Thomas Berner photograph)

Caption Writing

A good caption with a photograph completes the thought the photograph starts or provides something the photograph doesn't, such as a name. The caption gives the photograph context and explains anything not immediately clear to the reader. Just like a story, a caption requires strong verbs, the kind that denote action not passivity. A caption is usually written in the present tense because it describes the photograph the reader is looking at. That immediacy best comes across in the present tense. Frequently, a time element does not appear in a caption, especially if a story accompanies the photograph. If a time element is needed, it does not appear with the present-tense verb. It appears in another sentence or in a subordinate clause.

The editor who writes a caption always has the photograph before her as she writes. Wise editors want to see what they are writing about and know they can avoid mistakes that come with writing about something they cannot see. A chief editor, for example, may crop a photograph and not advise the copy editor who then writes the caption from memory. The newspaper will look silly if the caption mentions someone or something cropped from the photograph.

Here is the caption that accompanied the wirephoto from Belfast (Figure 8.13):

> TIGHT SECURITY IN EFFECT
> BELFAST, N. IRELAND: Security forces throughout Northern Ireland were put on alert April 17 for possible reprisal attacks for the death of an IRA official and the 60th anniversary of the bloody Easter uprising. The current alert is in addition to the tight security measures put into effect in and around the city's shopping center last week. Here, an armed British soldier stands guard in front of a clothing store as two pedestrians check out the window. Protestant militants marched throughout Northern Ireland April 19 under the watch of the strong security forces seeking to prevent any violence.

The caption does not refer to the photograph until the third sentence. After the first sentence, though, the reader may assume that the wrong caption appears with the photograph and go on to reading something else. What that caption needs is an introductory sentence that is about the picture.

> A British soldier stands guard outside a store in Belfast, Northern Ireland, unnoticed by two shoppers and their child. The guard is one of the British security forces put on alert throughout Northern Ireland yesterday . . .

Now the first sentence tells about the photograph, and the rest of the caption provides the context. In essence, the wire service's sentences were reordered. Also, whoever would rewrite the original would reduce its length. A good caption does not make the reader linger but provides quick information and lets the reader continue. Three short sentences make a good caption length.

The success of a caption begins with its legend or lead-in. In the case of the preceding caption, a wire service editor provided the legend of **Tight Security in Effect.** Since that legend doesn't fit the picture, though, the copy editor who rewrote the caption would also create a more germane legend. For Figure 8.13, one of these legends might do: **On Guard, At the Ready, On Alert, Guarded Shoppers, Guarded Irish Shoppers.**

The legend (or its equivalent) should be as seductive as a headline. That's one reason names make terrible legends. The good legend sums up the photograph and entices the reader to read the caption. On a photograph of a woman being arrested for throwing an egg at a politician, a novice wrote: **Egg Thrower Arrest.** Well, that sums it up but it's hardly enticing. A possible replacement: **Egg On Her Face.** Among other things, the legend turns around a cliche and uses it as an appropriate metaphor. Make sure, though, that the metaphor is apt. A student editor wrote this legend—**Dog Days of War**—for a caption about heavy fighting. But "dog days" have nothing to do with war; they refer to the hottest time of the year, usually late July and early August.

Unfortunately, good legends do not abound. Good headline writers make good legend writers for they know their mission and they approach it with zeal. A dull headline writer usually produces dull legends.

Caption writing, like headline writing, has its own set of rules, some of which duplicate other aspects of newspaper production. For one, identify every recognizable face in a photograph. The standard form is to say *(from left to right)* but a more interesting way cites some form of action a person is taking: (smiling), (frowning), (walking away).

Second, a caption writer should not editorialize. Present the facts as neutrally as possible and let the reader make the judgments. Third, don't be cute when the photograph doesn't call for it. For example, the writer of a caption for the photograph of the nude French woman attempting suicide would have been wrong to say she was "in the buff" or "dressed in her birthday suit." (Besides being cute, that's obvious.)

Fourth, be honest about the source of a photograph. If the dictator of a country provides a photograph of his torture-free prison after having been accused of conducting torture in the prison, note that the dictator provided the photograph. It would probably be necessary in such a situation to state that the dictator would not allow news photographers inside the prison. Another time to reveal the source comes when the newspaper is using a file photograph. When the mug shot of an 85-year-old person who just died makes the person look 55, the newspaper should indicate the age of the photograph. That's usually done by noting the year the photograph was taken.

Fifth, a camera can lie and the perspective it provides might not be honest, especially if a telephoto lens (which makes subjects appear closer to each other than they are) or an extreme wide-angle lens (which distorts) is used. At the same time, when the staff photographer produces a work of art, do not tell the readers what f-stop and shutter speed the photographer used. The work of art arose in the eye of the photographer, not in the mechanics of the camera, and by providing mechanical information, the newspaper is contributing to the delinquency of amateur photographers who would rather imitate than create.

Finally, rewrite wirephoto captions. They are turned out rapidly and sometimes as an afterthought. A thoughtful copy editor who takes an extra minute to do the job well can always improve such a caption.

Experts say that people have become more visually aware and they cite the declining circulations of visually deficient newspapers as proof of their hypothesis. The fact of the matter is, people cannot help but sense the visual since the visual represents one of their five major senses. A good editor recognizes that the best stories are not told one dimensionally, but with as many dimensions as the editor can muster. Photographs represent one of those dimensions and deserve equal treatment with words.

Suggested Readings

Photojournalism: The Professionals' Approach, Kenneth Kobre, Curtin & London, Inc., 1980.

Moments: The Pulitzer Prize Photographs, Sheryle and John Leckley, ed., Crown Publishers, 1978.

CHAPTER NINE
Wire Services

The Two Major 'Wires' in the U.S.A.

The state, national and international news that appears in most of the newspapers in the United States come from two major wire services—United Press International and The Associated Press. These two wire services provide an estimated 70 percent of all the news heard or read in the United States. Larger newspapers and television and radio stations subscribe to both, which permits editors to choose the best story between the two or combine elements from both. Smaller news media, though, often rely on one service primarily because two would transmit more copy than any newspaper or station could print or broadcast.

The two services differ in structure and reputation. The United Press International (formed in 1958 with the merger of United Press and the International News Service) is intended to be a profit-making venture. It is owned by the E.W. Scripps Company and the Hearst Corporation. Both companies have subsidized UPI through many years of losses, and in the late 1970s the two owners tried unsuccessfully to sell it, thus fueling rumors that UPI might fold. The Associated Press, on the other hand, is a non-profit cooperative of member newspapers and broadcasters. Any budget surplus is used for development. Nobody receives stock dividends.

Both wire services, while covering much the same news, still exhibit differences. Substantive differences are difficult to describe because each service's reputation can vary from state to state and decade to decade.

At one time the UPI was known as "a writer's wire" because that service's stories were frequently more interestingly written while the AP's tended to follow the bland inverted-pyramid formula. AP has since shorn itself of its reputation for dullness. The quality of state government coverage varies from state to state, and editors subscribing to both services develop a feel for which service is better and then seldom check the other service for stories in the state government category. It's human nature to do that, but it's not good editing.

Both "wires" (as they are called) deserve a lot of credit for initiating the electronic revolution discussed in Chapter 1. Very early in the 1970s both realized they could meet deadlines faster and produce a more efficient report if they converted to electronic editing systems. The two continued the revolution by introducing high-speed service, higher quality wirephotos and satellite delivery of the news. Newspapers started changing over when they saw the benefits.

Newspapers that had never before purchased wirephotos acquired the service because its quality virtually matched photographs produced by the newspaper's photographer. With VDTs installed, newspapers dropped the turtle-like 66-words-a-minute service and went to high speed, which delivers the news at 1,200 words a minute and which allowed the wires to expand their coverage and upgrade their services. The high-speed service not only delivers faster, it also delivers better. Rather than waste time with new leads that member newspapers had to affix to earlier stories, high speed allows the wires to send a completely rewritten story (slugged "writethru") in seconds, thereby saving newspaper editors time in updating the day's edition. The high speed also enables newspaper groups and chains to set up their own delivery system by using an open channel in the wire services' trunk lines. Similarly, syndicates that provide feature and column material to newspapers use other channels to send their fare, thereby cutting down on mailing costs and reducing their reliance on sometimes unreliable mail service.

In addition to providing radio stations with printed news copy, both AP and UPI furnish full audio services. They include hourly national and international newscasts, special reports, sports, stock material information and live broadcasts. High speed capability has also allowed the AP to split its service to radio and television stations, which ended the sometime dichotomous problem of serving different media on one wire.

Organizational differences between the wires mean more to wire service employees than to users, so a detailed description is omitted here. Although both wires are headquartered in New York City, they have bureaus throughout the United States and the rest of the world. The bureaus within the United States are capable of taking over and distributing most of a day's reporting when equipment or electrical problems plague headquarters. In 1980 UPI opened a computer system in Dallas,

Texas, that not only backstopped New York but increased the delivery of news by a factor of 10.

The news of the world—filtered through bureaus—reaches the main distribution center of each wire service by entering a vast computer storage center for later retrieval and redistribution by the slot editor. That editor, who must stay on top of incoming stories and new leads, works with the news editor who decides which wire a story goes on (A, sports, financial, etc.) and what priority it receives. The news editor also assigns work to rewrite (copy) editors, who fix poor writing and remove local references from stories so they're fit for understanding by a larger audience. The news editor also checks the finished work of these rewrite editors. The file editor actually assigns the story to the designated wire after checking it. The supervisor, in the meantime, reads all major stories and puts together that day's digest or budget for members.

In deciding which stories rate budget treatment, the supervisor hears from the many bureaus around the world. Bureau editors who feel they have submitted excellent stories will lobby with the supervisors to get those stories listed on the budget. The newspaper analogy is the section editor who argues to get a particular story on Page One. It's a matter of pride to be represented on Page One. Daily the many editors meet to decide how to process the news flow. For these meetings, the bureaus are linked through telephones so bureau editors can participate. One person who attended such meetings said it is "like being at the center of the world."

The editors of one wire service, of course, are always scheming to beat the other wire service. No wire service editor likes to hear that the other service placed a certain story on the wires first. Even though the receiving newspaper may not go to press for four hours and the difference between the delivery of the two stories is three minutes, the wire editor who comes in second feels beaten. The wire editors believe that a newspaper that subscribes to both services will use the story it receives first. At the same time, it's a good selling point for a wire service bureau chief dealing with a potential client: "Look how many times we beat them." Every day wire service editors check metropolitan newspapers to see how the papers played major wire service stories. The editors keep a tally to see which service gets used the most.

In addition to having bureaus in foreign lands in order to get foreign news for U.S. newspapers, the wire services also provide news to foreign countries. The Latin American desk at the AP, for example, translates stories into Spanish and Portuguese. The UPI offers a Spanish code converter that provides stories in Spanish (right down to the punctuation peculiar to that language). The stories can be processed in electronic systems.

Domestically, the AP and UPI provide a variety of wires to fit the needs and budgets of large and small newspapers. The major wire—the one that gives the top news first—is called the A wire, offered in high and slow speed. It provides news faster and in more detail than smaller wires. Usually, only large newspapers need it or can afford it. Smaller newspapers subscribe to a state or regional wire. Depending on the area, the regional wire might serve three small states or just one. In larger states, the regional wire might be split into eastern and western or northern and southern divisions (called "legs") so the wire services can provide more localized news. In Pennsylvania, which has a split AP wire, "more localized news" means Philadelphia stories for subscribers on the eastern leg and Pittsburgh stories for the western leg.

A wire considered especially important to larger newspapers is the financial or stock wire, which moves the stock tables at high speed. The AP provides a wire that moves the stock tables at 9,600 words a minute, a boon to afternoon newspapers with special deadlines to get the day's stock report published on the same day. Another wire, this one especially useful to morning newspapers, is the sports wire, which provides individual game stories and statistics not found on a regional wire. Morning newspapers, known for having a heavy sports orientation, receive an abundance of sports stories not provided on smaller wires. The sports wire selection allows sports editors to present a package of stories bent to local interest rather than relying on the roundup stories a small wire provides. The roundup stories traditionally lead off with the big winners or the division leaders, meaning that a small-town fan whose big-city sports team is not doing well won't get depth coverage from a regional wire. After all, who wants to read about losers?

The presence of wire services is not without its drawbacks. As told so well by Timothy Crouse in *The Boys on the Bus*, reporters for major newspapers tend to write their stories to agree with the wire services' emphasis. Such a unity of emphasis makes a mockery of the Founding Fathers' intention for the First Amendment from which they hoped a multitude of conflicting ideas would arise. The pack mentality, of course, is not the fault of the wires. It's the fault of newspaper editors who are afraid to be different.

Some critics of the wire services suggest that they are nationally oriented, homogenized, often shallow and bland. Given the changing newspaper (see Chapter 10), the wire services will no doubt continue to upgrade their writing and try new writing styles and reporting approaches. In fact, the wires may have to lead in this category because newspapers outside the major cities tend to be conservative and slow to respond to trends. The "shallow" label will always be with the wires. Though they have attempted to provide more than spot-news coverage, their strength lies in quickly turning out information about today. Trends don't sit well with the wires, in part because such depth coverage requires money but does not come with the assurance that member newspapers or clients will use the stories. The AP's solution to this problem is the joint project in which member newspapers and wire service reporters work together on a topic. The AP then sends the results to all subscribers.

In a related service, participating newspapers feed electronic carbons of some stories with statewide interest from local computers over telephone lines to a central AP computer where they are redistributed to AP members. Because of the direct and quick link through computers, participating newspapers have increased their contribution to the daily wire report and editors believe that all-round AP coverage has improved.

The national orientation tag comes from both services' attempts to provide copy mutually interesting in California and Rhode Island. As a result, the services may avoid regional stories—say, about the Southwest or the Northeast—because such stories won't play uniformly well across the nation. Related to this issue is the wires' reliance on local newspapers to provide coverage of local events that might be of interest to a wider audience. Again, this is an uneven problem, but the result is the same. By relying on local news media to objectively cover a local event, the wires have yielded their responsibility to get the complete story. Local editors tend to want to protect their communities from outside harsh publicity. Once the wires realized the problem, they began sending reporters to cover major news events, although they still had to rely on local editors to tell them if the event was worth covering.

The two major wire services have also been criticized for stereotyped coverage of international events, of covering in detail spot news such as terrorism, flood, famine and pestilence but seldom bothering to cover in depth the many stories that would provide a U.S. citizen with a rounded view of the world. In addition, developed nations get better coverage than developing nations. Poor international coverage also reflects a cultural problem. Wire service editors know their audience and do not go against the tide of cultural ignorance and intellectual deficiency the audience represents. Larger newspapers supplement their international coverage by subscribing to foreign news services such as Agence France-Press, Reuters, Hsinhua, and Telegrafnoie Agentstvo Sovetskovo Soiuza (better known by its acronym, TASS).

Supplementary Wire

Newspapers that want to round out their wire coverage subscribe to supplementary wires. Newspapers that belong to chains or groups receive additional wires such as the KNT News Wire, the Gannett News Service, the Christian Science Monitor News & Photo Service or the Newhouse

News Service. Some of the supplementary wires operate as partnerships. The KNT News Wire comprises Knight-Ridder, the *Chicago Tribune* and the *New York Daily News.* Another partnership that also provides a wire for anyone who wants to buy it is the Los Angeles Times-Washington Post News Service. An individual wire service that rates highly with some editors is the New York Times New Service. The Register and Tribune Syndicate Inc. provides the Christian Science Monitor News & Photo Service. The Newhouse wire is available through the Field News Service, which also provides stories from the Chicago *Sun-Times* and the Baltimore *Sun.* The Reuters News Agency, which has an international clientele, has an exchange agreement with Canadian Press, a national news agency similar to AP and UPI.

The content of these many wire services varies, but with the exception of the British-based Reuters service, the idea behind them is the same—supplement major wire service coverage with columns, features and stories the wires don't provide. The supplementary wires do not try to compete with the AP and UPI; they try to complete them. New York Times News Service subscribers like not only the depth articles and analyses the service provides but also the editorial package—the *Times'* columnists who appear regularly on that newspaper's op-ed page. The KNT Wire, while covering Washington and other national and international news, boasts that it offers how-to stories, the kind that help readers. As the next chapter notes, such stories have increased in usefulness and popularity as newspapers have modified content to meet reader needs.

By combining the services of two or more newspapers, the supplementary wires increase their reach across the nation and the world. The Los Angeles Times-Washington Post service combines 50 bureaus and then adds contributions from *Newsday* and the *Dallas Times Herald,* Agence France-Press and the *Guardian* of London. *Newsday's* contribution includes a bureau in China.

Knight-Ridder established foreign bureaus both as a way of improving its international news coverage for the KNT wire and as a way of offering reporters of Knight-Ridder newspapers an opportunity for overseas assignments. Member newspapers provide correspondents to staff the bureaus. Also, Knight-Ridder, like other groups and chains, provides subscribers with stories from member newspapers. Such service increases the mix of any user's content.

In addition to the supplementary wires are many syndicates which provide a variety of copy (usually by mail) that ranges from astrology to youth. The crossword puzzle, horoscope, comics and some of the columnists on newspaper editorial and feature pages are provided by syndicates. Even the Smithsonian Institution has a syndicate that distributes monthly stories on art, history and research in the sciences.

Using the Wires

People just learning the skill of fielding a baseball are always told to charge a ground ball when it's hit toward them rather than waiting for the ball to get to them. "Play the ball; don't let the ball play you," the learners are told. The analogy applies to the wires—editors should use the wires to their best advantage rather than just stuffing wire stories throughout the paper wherever a convenient hole pops up.

No editor should thoughtlessly publish any wire story. Supposing the story has a local angle deep within it? The story should be rewritten so the local angle appears as the lead or near the beginning. And what if the two major wires offer nonduplicative stories on the same topic (*i.e.*, written from different angles)? A good editor would combine the best of both instead of rejecting one story outright. What if a wire story appears in such tortured shape that it needs rewriting? Either complain to the wire's editor or have a copy editor rewrite it, but don't publish as is because the critical reader will consider the story an error made by the newspaper, not by the wire service. And it is the newspaper's error.

Beginning desk editors should also guard against the bulletin mentality of both wire services, which in the heat of competition may offer something sensational that turns out to be a dud—after the presses are running. In the early 1970s, a wire service bulletin from Athens telling that air raid sirens could be heard over the telephone from Cairo presented the image of Israeli jets about to devastate the Egyptian city. The newspapers printing that bulletin, with all it implied, looked stupid when the wire service reported—after deadline—that the air raid sirens had sounded in error.

During the 1980 Republican convention, both wire services announced that Ronald Reagan had selected former president Gerald R. Ford as his running-mate—approximately an hour and a half before Reagan chose George Bush. Both services quoted by name people they considered reliable sources, but the sources were wrong and it speaks poorly of good journalists that they didn't query their sources deeper and harder. It was, said Louis D. Boccardi, vice president and executive editor of the AP, "a chaotic moment." For that reason, more caution should have been exercised. In a more tense event, freedom for 52 Americans held hostage for 444 days in Iran, both wire services announced the freedom of the hostages almost an hour before their planes took off from Iran. Because neither wire service was allowed to have correspondents in Iran, they had to rely on foreign journalists, who themselves were not permitted near the airport to witness the release of the hostages. Perhaps the release time would not have meant as much were it not for the fact that the United States was near the moment of inaugurating a new president and it was significant if Iran freed the hostages during the outgoing president's term or at the start of the new president's term. Those newspapers that published premature wire service reports on the hostages' release provided inaccurate information. (The wire services, by the way, announce bulletins with a ringing of bells on a teletype machine. In a VDT system, which supplants the teletype, a message appears on the screen to advise a wire editor that a bulletin is coming in.)

Spot news no longer sells newspapers the way it once did. Radio long ago replaced newspapers in the spot news service. In fact, radio, because it provides only a headline service, requires newspapers to provide more than bulletins. Modern editors realize that their strength lies in providing well researched, detailed stories—the stories behind the hasty headlines of another medium.

Wire service editors would be embarrassed to hear some local editor tell of locally misused wire stories. Those wire editors do not send their reports because they expect local editors to unquestioningly publish everything. When asked, wire editors shrink from providing advice they sense would replace local judgment. Wire editors expect creative use of their reports. In fact, local editors may freely rewrite—without credit—any wire story they want. Some newspapers do that to an unethical fault, going so far as to not even thinly disguise the rewrite and then putting a local byline on the "rewrite" and representing it as staff work. The remainder of this chapter provides future editors with advice on how to use the wires properly.

What the Symbols Mean

The wire services use many symbols as a shorthand method of telling editors a lot of information about stories. Most of the symbols used by the AP, UPI and many of the supplementary wires are the same because of the American Newspaper Publishers Association, which urged standardization for the sake of multiple-wire users and users with automatic story sorting systems.

Two standardized symbols are the priority code and the category code. On hard copy (paper copy from a teletype machine), they can be found on the line that follows a story's transmission number. On a VDT, the transmission number and the priority and category codes appear together on a single line. Editors using VDTs must know the codes so they can spot high priority or special section stories merely by examining a directory (see Figure 9.1)—that is, without having to consume a great deal of time by opening every story and reading the lead to see if the story is high priority and to what page editor it should be sent. Systems that automatically sort stories, of course, route the story for the editor. The priority codes are:

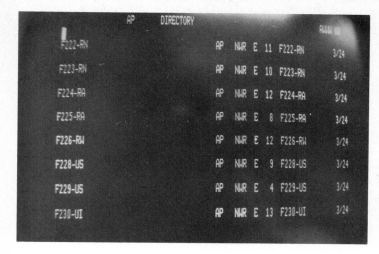

Figure 9.1 A simple wire service directory called up on a video display terminal. (R. Thomas Berner photograph)

f—flash r—regular
b—bulletin d—deferred
u—urgent a—advance for weekday use
s—advance for weekend use

The wires seldom use the flash code, which would interrupt any story as it is running. Flashes have appeared on stories ranging from the safe landing of astronauts to the assassination of a president to the nomination of a candidate to the death of a pope to the release of 52 Americans held hostage in a foreign country. The bulletin code appears on stories of bulletin importance or advisories that need quick attention. The urgent code apears on prime news and corrections. The regular priority code appears on scheduled stories—most of the stories on the wire. The deferred code, when used, appears on stories of secondary importance. Stories containing **a** or **s** code are sent "hold for release (date)."

In addition to the priority code, each type of story has a code by which a computer can sort and route to a particular queue. They are:

a—any domestic news not from Washington
b—special events
c—regular features
e—entertainment or cultural
f—financial
i—international (including the United Nations)
k—commentary
l—lifestyle
n—regional (such as a state wire)
p—national politics
q—result or period score of a single sports event
s—sports
t—travel
v—advisories
w—Washington
y—for internal routing among wire bureaus or for reruns

Thus, a copy editor looking at an AP directory of stories on a VDT and seeing this computer-generated transmission number from the A wire—**a056-uw**—would know it belongs to an urgent Washington story. The story might already be in a Washington file created by the newspaper and fed by an automatic sorter that would direct any w-designated story to it. A sports editor seeing a **114-uq** would know it's probably a single-line final score (Iowa 61, Georgetown 60); the computer (if programmed for this) knows to put all q-designated information together to compile a list of scores.

The next line of importance is the keyboard slug line which starts out with one of three cycle designators, **AM, PM,** or **BC**—codes that respectively indicate stories for morning newspapers, afternoon newspapers or both cycles. Next comes the keyword, the story's slug in 21 or fewer characters. During the Olympics of 1980, however, the AP inserted between the cycle designator and the key word a special identifying slug (OLY) to enable automatic sorting systems to route all Olympic stories to one directory. On a daily basis entertainment features from AP carry and ENT code. The keyword slug is important because it remains the same on all new leads, adds, inserts and substitutes. Following the slug is a word count that exceeds no more than 450 a take.

On top of that, the wires also tell if the story is budgeted by designating it **Bjt** (AP) or **sked** (UPI) and how many takes the story is by following **Bjt** with, for example, **2 takes.** The word count follows in a cumulative set-up—**450–675**—to tell the editor the total number of words in the first take and the total number of words in the story. A first add to such a story includes **Bjt–1st add,225.** Starting with a number, here is a regular sports story for an afternoon newspaper, from the budget, two takes long.

> **a041-rs**
> **PM-Cowboys,Bjt,450-600**

The second take (also called the first add):

> **a042-rs**
> **PM-Cowboys,Bjt-1stAdd,150**

During the morning the wire service sends a new lead and to make the lead easy for identification, the wire editor uses not only the exact slug of the original story, the editor also provides the number of the story, called now the reference number. Thus:

> **a102-us**
> **PM-Cowboys,1stLd,a041,200**

Instead of **Bjt,** that section of a wire story could contain any of these phrases: **Advisory, KILL, WITHHOLD, ELIMINATION, Insert, Sub** (for substitute), **Correction, Writethru** (for write through, meaning an earlier story has been completely rewritten), and **Box** (for boxscore).

Stories that are two or more takes long contain special instructions at the end of the first take and the beginning of the second. Figure 9.2 shows part of a two-take story. Notice how the second take includes the dateline and repeats the last two words of the first take. In those circumstances when the words do not match up, it usually means the end of the first take was not fully transmitted.

```
f208                              f209
     r s lbylczzcryyr                 r s lbylczzcqyy
                  406                              407
AM-BBN--Phillies-McBride, Bjt-   AM-BBN--Phillies-McBride, Bjt-
2 Takes, 420-up                  1st Add,250
Laserphoto                       CLEARWATER, Fla.: ABOUT IT."
   By RALPH BERNSTEIN             McBride claims that he has
      AP Sports Writer           yet to reach his potential as a . . .
  CLEARWATER, Fla, AP -
Bake McBride spent the kind of
winter during which reading a
good book was his only peace
of mind.

             . . .
 . . . "I even played when I
messed my knee up, some 40
games. That's just the way it
is. There isn't anything I can
do ABOUT IT."
   MORE
      _____
03-10-80 01.40pes
```

Figure 9.2 A two-take story carries similar or related information at the start and end of take one and the start of take two to make merging the two takes easier.

Wirephotos typically begin with the initials of the originating station followed by a number that designates which number wirephoto the station has sent that day. Next comes the dateline (which, unlike a story, contains the date) and then the caption. AP introduces captions with an all-caps legend it calls an overline. ("Use verbs in overlines, avoid labels and lifeless phrases," the stylebook correctly advises.) The end of the caption includes a credit, the initials of the caption writer, and, for AP, the day of the week the caption was written (1 equals Sunday and so on) and the time the caption was written. Following that is the source of the photograph (such as **stf** for staff or **mbr** for member and the name) and finally the year of transmission. Figure 9.3 shows AP and UPI captions.

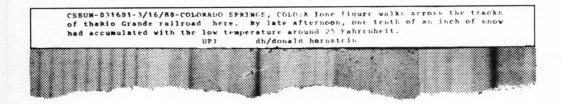

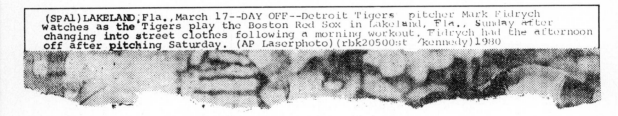

Figure 9.3 Captions from United Press International and Associated Press wirephotos.

Budgets, Directories, Advisories

The wire services announce their wares early in the a.m. and p.m. cycles by sending a list of top stories and photographs. These lists are commonly referred to as budgets, digests, directories or schedules. Whatever they are called, they are broken down by topics, they give a story's slug, and they tell briefly what the stories are about and how long each one is (see Figure 9.4). Wirephoto directories are not always as detailed, although some include the information on whether a photograph will be horizontal or vertical.

Some of the words common to these directories include **developing, will stand, should stand, with separate. Developing** means a continuing story, one the wires expect will provide new information and new leads (if not writethrus) during the cycle. A local editor handling an early version of a developing story would not bother to edit the story because a new version might replace it and make the editing unnecessary. Similarly, an editor does not dummy a developing story on an early page (a page that is made up early and cannot be changed later).

Ripe, though, for early page use are those stories marked **will stand.** That means the wire service editors are not planning to update the story, have not even assigned a reporter to keep up with the story. A **should stand** story means the wires don't expect an updating, but anything can happen. In fact, the people who assign such pieces of advice to

a200
   r v ssbylczcczc
am—sked 3-10
Editors:
The UPI report for Tuesday
morning papers:

IRAN

   IRAN Tehran, Iran —
Revolutionary council decides
against handover of hostages;
Ayatollah Khomeini says U.N.
commission must first issue
report on crimes of deposed
shah before being allowed to
see American captives. 600

POLITICS

   P R I M A R I E S Undated —
Florida, Georgia and Alambama
hold primaries Tuesday in what
looks to be big day for Ronald
Reagan and George Bush. At
stake are 208 Democratic and
114 R e p u b l i c a n
delegates. Wrapup, 600, with
sidebars on individual states
and candidates as warranted.

NUCLEAR

   TREATY Washington —
Monday is deadline for countries who buy enriched uranium
from U.S. to either wign treaty
denouncing nuclear weapons or
open up atomic plants for
inspection. India has done
neither. 350

   THREEMILE Middletown,
Pa. — Disabled Three Mile
Island nuclear plant to vent
small amount of radioactive
krypton into the atmosphere.
400.

   RADIATION Washington —
Scientists say it will be
difficult to estimate precise
risks of very low radiation
exposures common in today's
society. 400.

WASHINGTON

   Budget Washington —
Only a week ago Congressional
Budget Office said budget
deficit would reach $20
billion; today it ups that
figure to a possible $25
billion. 400.

   TURKAID Washington —
Report to Congress says Turkey
can no long fulfill NATO
responsibilities; faces danger
of military coup. 400.

DOMESTIC

   Schools Detroit — Teachers
at four suburban school
districts go on strike, idling
24,000 students. 300.

   GACY Chicago—Lawyers plow
through final stages of mass
murder trial of John Wayne
Gacy; expect case to go to
jury this week.

   PINTO Winamac Ind. —
Prosecutor in reckless homicide
trial of Ford Motor Co., urges
jury to set national standard
for production of safe cars.
400.

   BOYS Denver—Investigators
puzzled by fatal shooting of
two young boys abducted while
walking to store for ice cream.
300.

   TREEN Baton Rouge, La. —
David Treen, who broke century-
old Democratic stranglehold on
Louisiana governor's mansion,
takes oath, 350.

f029
   r s czzclbylqyy
                     112
PM—Digest,
   AP Sports PMs Digest
      Monday PMs
   INDIANAPOLIS — UCLA

Coach Larry Brown, analyzing
tonight's title game against
Louisville in the NCAA basketball tournament, made a public
announcement that he doesn't
trust guys who wear white
shoes in the winter, pour ket-
chup on eggs and put their and
sneakers on before their pants.
It's good to see fun returning
to the game. By WILL GRIMSLEY.
PM—Grimsley's World.

   INDIANAPOLIS — UCLA, the
Cinderella team of the NCAA
has one more All American
hurdle to clear before it can
go to the ball — Louisville's
Darrell Griffith. By ALEX
SACHARE. PM—BKC—NCAA General.

   PONTE VEDRA BEACH, Fla.—The
Tournament Players Championship
developed into one of the most
pressure-packed events in
recent history, and Lee
Trevino won it, leaving in his
wake the likes of Jack
Nicklaus, Gary Player and Ben
Crenshaw—but not in that order.
By BOB GREEN. PM—TPC Golf.

   NEW YORK—Tracy Austin
returns to her Rolling Hills,
Calif. high school to be just
one of the kids again. The only
difference is she's $100,000
richer after beating Martina
Navratilova in the finals of
the women's indeer tennis
championship. By BOB GREENE.
PM—Women's Tennis.

03-24-80 03.01aes

Figure 9.4 Whatever their names—digests, skeds or budgets—the collections
of the top stories of the day enable newspaper editors to plan their package.

directories cannot predict the future and any story can become the opposite of a wire editor's expectation. For example, a reporter sent to cover a natural disaster (marked **developing**) might not be able to get new information to a bureau because of a lack of communications facilities. The best editors expect the unexpected and do not fret when the unexpected happens.

With separate means the story includes a sidebar. A **roundup** usually covers all aspects of a major topic, although most of the aspects get brief coverage as in a roundup of all professional football games played on a Sunday. One game is highlighted; all others get a subhead and a paragraph. The wires also provide **analysis** and **commentary**; stories so marked should receive the same designation in print so readers don't think they're getting straight news.

The wires use advisories for various reasons, from alerting editors to additional potential stories to giving directions on how to obtain press passes for special events. Some advisories announce the travel plans of presidents and those who would be president. Advisories tell editors of news conferences that may produce stories for their editions or of court decisions that may come down on time for today's paper.

Budgets, directories and advisories are useful tools to any local editor. But how they appear now and what they will look like in the future will most certainly change. Already done experimentally at some newspapers, the wires provide only digests or abstracts of all stories and the local editor decides which stories to order for the day. The editor summons the stories from the wire service's central computer, which reduces individual newspaper storage needs as well as transmission costs. The newspaper pays an annual fee and then so much for each story called from the central computer.

But this cafeteria approach could have pitfalls that future editors must remain cautious of. If, for example, the abstracts are only leads, wire service reporters might overstate their stories in the lead just to get them selected locally. Another problem may develop with feature stories that have engaging leads (as they all should) but might not get chosen because the local editor lacks enough information to decide if the story suits local readers. If the editor summons the story, the newspaper pays for it even if the editor decides not to use it. Whatever the pitfalls, such a system will not replace present wire service distribution until every wire service user has an electronic editing system. That day is not far off.

New Leads

A new lead updates a story already on file and presumably places the most current important information at the beginning (or "top") of the story. New leads appear in sequence, beginning with **1stld** (for "first lead") and continuing through the number until the end of a cycle when new stories are written. New leads are necessary for stories written in advance of an event (the announcing of economic statistics, for example) because they provide background or context that fleshes out the newer information. When wire editors anticipate a new lead, they will say so in their budgets or advise at the top of the stories they expect to put new leads on. Such stories are marked **may be topped.**

New leads, as noted before, carry the same slug and provide the number of the story they go with. A new lead gives pick-up instructions at the end, telling the local editor where the old and new should be joined. As a double check, the wire story also provides the first two or three words of the pick-up paragraph (see Figure 9.5).

Sometimes the new lead for, say a Washington-datelined story comes from some place else. A story about the president embarking on a seven-nation tour would begin with a Washington dateline. When the president reaches the first country (Cuba, perhaps), the wires would send a new lead telling of the president's arrival. The new lead would have a

```
a080
      r i sscxcryrc zc
pm-lebanon 1stld-writethru 4-8
  Lebanese militiamen promise
release of captured Irish
soldiers
  BEIRUT, Lebanon UPI -
Lebanese renegade MaJ. Saad
Haddad's militias promised the
gradual release of 10 Irish
privates from the U.N. peace-
keeping troops held since
Monday and said the first three
are likely to be released soon,
a U.N. spokesman said today.
  The spokesman denied reports
that four of the soldiers had
been released earlier in the
day.
  The soldiers were captured
Monday by Haddad's militiamen
after a clash between two sides
around the strategic bridge of
At Tiri on the Lebanese
frontier, during which one
Irish private was seriously
wounded and taken to a hospital
in the Israeli town of
Haifa. . . .
```

```
a090
      r i sscxciycc zc
pm-lebanon 2ndld-PICKUP3RDGR-
af 4-8
  Militiamen free three Irsh
soldiers, threaten to kill
others
  BEIRUT, Lebanon UPI - Lebanese
renegade MaJ. Saad Haddad's
m i l t i a s released three
Irish privates of the U.N.
peace-keeping force today but
kept six others in captivity
and threatened to kill them if
the Irish Battalion does not
leave the border village of
Al Tiri, a U.N. spokesman said.
                    . . .
  He said the militia opened
fire a few minutes after the
release of the three privates.
pickup 3rd graf: The soldiers
      upi 04-08 10:58 aes
```

Figure 9.5 A story and its new lead with pick-up instructions.

different dateline (Havana, in this case). To avoid confusion, the wires would include the following phrase on the new lead—**precede Washington**. That tells local editors that the original story carried a Washington dateline, not a Havana dateline.

Editors using electronic systems find that processing new leads is simple. Rather than fumbling around with two parts of a story—one of them the original in type in the production department—an editor can summon a copy of the original story and affix the new lead then send the new version to the shop with instructions to kill the original. The speed of electronic printing equipment makes that process simpler and faster than it had been when stories were sent on 66-word-a-minute teletypes and type was set on a Linotype machine (the laborious metal creature—mentioned in Chapter 1—that inhabited pre-electronic production departments).

New leads can create problems for sleepy editors who do not reread stories after a new lead has been affixed. Editors should reread to ensure that in writing a new lead, the wire reporter did not repeat information from the earlier story, information that may appear late in the story. Typically, a person's full name and identification are repeated. In such cases, the alert editor deletes the information from the original story because it is needed early in the story.

Developing Stories

Stories in which developments change throughout a news cycle become developing stories—marked by new leads, inserts, subs, writethrus and hold-for-release leads. Inserts are used to add secondary or clarifying information to a story. Substitutes clarify information or update stories, such as the disaster story cited in Chapter 3 in which authorities identified six dead people and speculated on the identity of the seventh body. Once the seventh person's identity was known, the wire service sent a substitute paragraph to replace the one containing the speculation. As figure 9.6 shows, inserts and substitutes carry information telling local editors which paragraph precedes and follows and which paragraphs an editor should delete. Corrections carry the same directions.

As more newspapers acquire electronic systems and highspeed wire input, writethrus will become more common and new leads will appear less frequently. That will happen because wire service reporters and editors can more easily and speedily redo a story and send it without delay on a 1,200-word-a-minute circuit than they can on a 66-word-a-minute circuit. Thus, the wires will remove the inconvenience noted under "New Leads" of dealing with pieces of a story. Instead, a complete story will replace the original. Figure 9.7 shows an original story side by side with a writethru.

a084

    r a sec zcryru v
pm-rig 2ndid—writethru 3-24
  two confirmed dead; late
details
  GALVESTON, Texas UPI
— An offshore gas drilling
platform about 100 miles off
the Texas coast blew out and
burst into flames early today,
forcing its 42-man crew to
evacuate. The Coast Guard said
two men were killed and at
least three others were
missing.
  Many of the injured, numbering
as many as 22, suffered severe
burns and were taken by helicopter to Galveston hospitals.
More than a dozen other workers
were rescued unhurt by two
crewboats anchored overnight
alongside the platform.

  "When they evacuated the
platform, most of the people
got into the evacuation
capsules and were lowered into
the water and then were
picked up into the two boats
and then taken to a nearby
platform and treated m e d i-
c a l l y," said Harper.
  Pennzoil operated the platform for Pool Offshore Co. of
Harvey, La., but had only one
worker aboard. The other 41
workers were contracted by
Pool, Harper said. The platform was located in the Golf
of Mexico 95 miles southeast of
Galveston in 310 feet of water.
  The Coast Guard used heli-
copters, planes and a cutter
to search for the missing.
    upi 03-24 10:31 aes

a096

    r a ssc zciyccyn
pm-rig 2ndld—sub7thgraf—pick-
up8thgraf 3-24
  clarifying operator—ownership
x x x said harper.
  Pennzoil operated the platform for itself and other
companies sharing the explora-
tion lease for that area of the
Gulf of Mexico. Pool Offshore
Co. of Harvey, La., was the
drilling contractor and em-
ployed 41 of the 42 people on
the rig. The other was a
Pennzoil employee, Harper said.
  The platform was located 95
miles southeast of Galveston in
310 feet of water.
pickup 8th graf: the coast
    upi 03-24 11:39 aes

Figure 9.6 Information that will replace other information in a story comes
to the newspaper marked "sub" (for substitute).

Hold-for-release leads appear on developing stories when the wire
editor is fairly certain of what development will occur next in the ongo-
ing saga. A typical example of the 1960s and 1970s was the U.S. space
program in which the wires would write leads based on what was scheduled to happen. (NASA had every moon trip timed to the second, it
seemed.) Such leads would be marked **Hold for release, expected release time 1:30 p.m.** For the editor with a 1 p.m. lock-up (meaning all
pages are finished and headed for the press; no changes can be made),
the temptation to use a 1:30 lead and thus publish as fresh a story as
possible was overwhelming. But the editors who, for example, used the
hold-for-release lead that said the United States and Russia had linked
in space were confounded when the hook-up did not go smoothly and the
wires killed the advance leads and substituted different leads. At the Republican National Convention in 1980, the UPI sent a lead declaring Reagan had picked Ford but told subscribers not to release it until after
midnight. One daily went to press 15 minutes before midnight—with
erroneous news. The rule of thumb: Don't use leads designated for release after the newspaper's deadline.

```
a070
    r a ssczcbsac zc
pm-paintings 3-24
Picasso, Dali works stolen from
apartment
  NEW YORK UPI — A burglar
broke into a Manhattan brown-
stone early today and stole
more than $200,000 worth of
artworks by Pablo Picasso and
Salvador Dali, police said.
  A Police Department spokesman
said Tom DeMaio, identified
only as a Broadway producer,
left his first-floor apartment
about 10 p.m. Sunday night and
returned home about 2:30 a.m.
to find a front window smasked.
  Missing from his art collec-
tion were a Picasso painting
and a sketch and a painting by
Dali, police said. The pieces
were not immediately iden-
tified.
        upi 03-24 08:56 aes
```

```
a082
    r a ssczcryrbyl
pm-paintings 1stld-writethru 3-
24
  increased value, works iden-
tified
  NEW YORK UPI — A burglar
broke into a Manhattan brown-
stone early today and stole
some $400,000 worth of art-
works by Pablo Picasso and
Salvador Dali, police said.
  A Police Department spokesman
said Tom DeMaio, described as
a B r o a d w a y producer,
left his first-floor apartment
late Sunday and returned a few
hours later to find a front
window smashed.
  Missing from his art collec-
tion were Picasso's "The
Clown," v a l u e d at some
$300,000 and two works by Dali,
"Dying Woman" and "Zodiac,"
police said.
        upi 03-24 10:17 aes
```

Figure 9.7 A rewritten story is called a "writethru." Shown here are an original and a writethru. Writethrus, of course, are often much longer.

Advances

The typical advance story is a column or feature article sent on, say, Tuesday for use on Wednesday. The wires send advances so newspapers have stories for earlier pages, including those pages made up a day in advance. More importantly, sending stories in advance helps the wires cut down on jams on slower circuits. Another type of advance story comes on a special Sunday feature filing and its day and cycle of release are marked. A story for use in a Wednesday afternoon newspaper would say **For Release PMs Wed., March 10.** A newspaper published the following morning (March 11) could also use the story, but the PM paper gets first crack. Wirephotos accompanying advances are clearly marked, giving not only the date of release but the byline and the slug on the story.

Another type of advance is a story sent early in a cycle for release later in the same cycle. The story gets advance status because some or all of the story is based on something that is scheduled to occur later in the cycle. For example, someone who will appear before a congressional hearing might provide reporters with an advance copy of a statement prepared for the hearing. The wire service reporters write a story based on the statement and, then, once the statement is given, a wire editor will send a bulletin clearing the story for use.

A related type of advance includes the caution **For release at 1:30 p.m. EST—time set by source.** The source could be investigators for the Nuclear Regulatory Commisson who have not yet reported to their superiors. Since early promulgation of the information might result in a more accurate and understandable story, the source provides copies, but on the condition that the public not get the news until a certain time. When the information seems absolutely newsworthy, some newspapers might violate the advance status by rewriting the story in the conditional mood.

> Investigators hired by the Nuclear Regulatory Commission were prepared today to warn that nuclear accidents like the one at Three Mile Island "could have happened in a lot of places."

That approach is fraught with ethical and practical problems, especially if the scheduled story doesn't come off. Same-day advances—like hold-for-release leads—deserve cautious treatment, and smart editors use no advance whose release time has not yet come.

Combining Stories

Equipped with a VDT that can display two stories at the same time, an editor has the opportunity to compare competitive wire service stories and combine their best aspects into one story. In some cases, combining stories leads to a complete rewriting, a job handled by a copy editor, not a reporter. In other cases, combining stories means inserting paragraphs of one wire service into the other wire service's story. The copy editor must create transition so the story does not come off as a collection of unrelated paragraphs.

Another form of combining is really the insertion of a parenthetical paragraph that might point out a discrepancy between two stories. For example, the UPI says 15 people were injured in an airplane crash and the editor has decided to use the UPI's story. But if AP's account says 13 people were injured, the editor might insert in the appropriate place in the UPI story: (The Associated Press reported 13 people injured.) If the two stories contain many discrepancies, it's best to query both services for an explanation.

When an editor combines two stories, he or she must decide how to handle the byline and dateline. Combined stories should no longer carry the names of the individual wire service reporters because they did not produce the final story. Usually, a newspaper will change the byline to "From our wire services" or "By the Associated Press and United Press International" or "Combined from wire reports." The parenthetical credit in the dateline is removed.

Combined stories require extra special checking against repeated facts and names, names without identification, and inconsistent spelling and style. Neither wire service presents style-perfect copy and the copy editor must watch for inconsistencies between the two. Another caution arises with copyrighted stories from supplementary wires. The copyright covers the form the news takes, not the news itself, so a copy editor combining such stories may freely rewrite but may not reproduce verbatim without credit.

Creating Summaries

Although newspapers are usually thought of as publishing long stories about the news, many newspapers distill less important news into summaries. Readers don't have to have all their news in great detail every day and not every newspaper always has a great amount of space to print the news in detail.

The writing of summaries falls to the copy desk. The job may require rewriting two wire stories into one or it may require condensing just one wire service's account. Whatever, a summary is not created merely by using the first two paragraphs of a collection of stories and throwing the rest away. A good summary captures the essence of the story, giving the reader 10 inches of feeling in 2 inches of type.

The model of good summary writing is *The Wall Street Journal*, whose inside page editors daily write a Page One column called "What's News—." Half of the column is an index to stories inside while the rest is a summary of major news stories. The major news stories get no further detail inside.

Here is the beginning of a *Wall Street Journal* story that appeared inside:

> CHICAGO—International Harvester Co. is approaching a critical point this week as it seeks to pull off one of the biggest financial juggling acts in corporate history.
>
> The maker of trucks, farm machinery and construction equipment is scheduled to meet here Thursday with more than 200 bankers, and many people think the company's survival is at stake. The bankers, all of whom have lent the company money, will hear details of Harvester's recently an-

nounced plan of debt restructuring and will have their first chance to haggle about the proposal.

The restructuring promises to be arduous and explosive. Harvester wants a $4.7 billion financing package in place by May 15, replacing hundreds of short-term bank credit arrangements with three "umbrella" agreements—one for Harvester, one for its credit corporation and a pact to sell $1.5 billion in receivables to some of the larger banks.

This is how an editor condensed that for Page One:

International Harvester will present a $4.7 billion debt restructuring plan to its lenders Thursday. Harvester wants to replace myriad short-term agreements with three major ones for the parent, its credit unit and the sale of $1.5 billion in receivables.
(Story on Page 2)

Note how tightly written, how to the point, the summary is. The editor who wrote it and others like it did not zip through the chore. According to the authors of *What's News—Dow Jones Story of The Wall Street Journal*, the *Journal's* front-page column takes six or seven minutes to read but is written over a 16-hour period each day. "It's written to be easy to read, not a word wasted," the book's authors say.

No beginning editor should assume writing such a summary is easy. The beginner should expect to spend a lot of time learning the art of summary writing.

Localizing Stories

If the federal government announces a series of grants for 15 states, the wire services are not going to put the state of local interest in the lead. That's up to local editors. The process is known as localizing, that is, giving the national story a local angle. A local angle could also be something more specific, such as a grant for a local organization or person.

Disaster stories provide opportunities for localizing. Supposing a plane crashes and 200 people die, including five from, say, Nebraska. Nebraska newspapers using the story would insert in the lead that five of the dead were Nebraskans.

The first Chinese excursion plane to fly the route of the Long March crashed today. All 200 people on board—including five from Nebraska—were killed, Hsinhua, the New China News Agency, reported.

Another editor, however, might want the lead rewritten for better local emphasis.

Five Nebraskans were among 200 persons killed when the first Chinese excursion plane to fly the route of the Long March crashed today, Hsinhua, the New China News Agency, reported.

In addition to changing the lead, the local editor would also ensure that the names of the five Nebraskans appeared early in the story, probably in the second paragraph.

Localizing state stories might mean rewriting to get the name of a local person or organization on top. It would also mean calling that person or organization for more details, an assignment that could go to a reporter or a copy editor.

Any story can be over-localized, such as reporting the injury of a local person in an accident in which 50 people died and not mentioning the deaths until the third or fourth paragraph. One newspaper supposedly localized a story about President Kennedy flying from Washington to the U.S. Air Force Academy in Colorado with a headline that went something like this: **Kennedy to speak at Academy; will fly over Iowa en route.**

Another type of localizing occurs when newspapers use wire service stories as pegs for local stories, sometimes generating a complete local story and other times just rewriting the top. Alert copy editors watch for wire stories with potential local angles. For example, a story that says people who paid in advance to go to the Olympics in Moscow might not get their money back raises the question—Any from my town? Call local travel agencies and then follow up with calls to the affected people. What does an increase in the prime lending rate mean to local banks? How are local farmers affected by changes in grain futures? Will a cut in the defense budget affect the nearby Army base?

The possibilities are endless. What every good editor remembers is that the wires provide not only state, national and international news but also an opportunity for local journalists to show their reportorial skills. Good editors know that the wires are their servants, not their masters, and they use the wire reports accordingly.

CHAPTER TEN

Newspapers Under Fire

The Decline in Readership

Those who thought television had devastated magazines and had taken large bites out of newspapers in the 1960s learned in the 1970s that newspapers were in worse condition than first believed. Reborn as speciality publications, magazines made a comeback, but daily newspapers—as reflected by their circulation figures—stood pat. The population of the country grew but daily newspaper circulation failed to keep pace, a shortfall with roots in the late 1950s. It was not until 1980 that circulation reached the level of the 1960s—approximately 62 million a day.

For some newspapers—especially in metropolitan areas—the decline was cataclysmic. Some went out of business while others suffered from a weakened financial base infected by 10 to 25 percent circulation declines. The advertiser, among others, was not happy. But advertisers were not the only ones who complained; editors began to realize that the slipping base of readership detracted as much from the editorial product as it did from the advertising product and that the two had to survive together. Publishers initiated countless studies to find out what had happened to the readers. Editors soon found they had to stop blaming television for the decline in readership.

Various researchers learned that among the young, newspaper editors had the image of cigar-smoking, middle-aged, isolated people who were more interested in protecting the status quo than challenging their readers. The image prospered at the tail end of the Vietnam war and the Watergate scandal, both of which triggered mistrust in public institu-

tions. Television, of course, deserved some of the blame for the readership decline, but not the proportion editors attributed to it. Some studies
suggested that people who rely on television for news rely as much on
newspapers. If anything, television should have helped readership. Of
course, television implanted in society a visual awareness that was not
satisfied by dull-looking newspapers of gray columns of type and small
photographs. In that regard, television affected readership.

Leisure time eroded reading time and editors soon realized that
anything people could do with their free time competed with newspaper
reading. Yes, television was a competitor and so was radio and so were
the many speciality magazines. But so was free time—the opportunity to
garden or work at a hobby. Who wants to read a newspaper delivered in
the late afternoon as the last few good rays of sun remain for weeding or
raking or just relaxing? The product was no longer relevant.

Readers also sensed an alienation—that the newspaper was not a
member of the same community. Words like "uncaring," "unresponsive,"
"inhuman," "out of touch" appeared regularly when researchers asked
people why they didn't like their daily newspaper. The readers sensed
that newspaper editors didn't care much for the reader beyond making
the reader a statistic in the circulation manager's book. Such a feeling
came naturally as the consumer movement grew and editors ignored or
played down the issues the movement raised. "Why shouldn't they?" a
cynic asked; "they want to protect their advertisers." Editors were seen
as taking care of their advertisers at the expense of the consumer—the
person who bought the newspaper. The same feeling prevailed among
readers whose newspapers faintly covered local government by relying
on handouts from politicians or by failing to examine deeply the empty
words of some leaders. Against the groundswell of alienation and declining readership and circulation, newspaper editors entered the 1980s with
a new attitude and a new desire to create something the readers would
buy—and read.

The Medium Reacts

One startling thing editors learned from readership and reader attitude
studies was that the reader spent a certain amount of time each day with
the news media—and that was it. The image of someone reading a newspaper for an hour no longer held up. Twenty minutes became the accepted maximum time—and some researchers suggested half that time.
Thus, if the newspaper did not arrive at the time the reader usually set
aside to read it, the newspaper might go unread while a television or
radio station or magazine might get more attention. What editors had to
do was design a product that would make the readers want to read. One
successful method of getting back readers has been the mini-newspaper,

which takes the concept of a zoned newspaper one step further by creating within the main newspaper a second newspaper designed only for a segment of the readership. In Chicago, the *Tribune* competes against the many suburban dailies and weeklies with its own *Surburban Trib*, actually 10 different tabloid-sized newspapers stuffed inside the *Tribune*. In Yakima, Washington, two newspapers containing minutiae from geographical areas in the valley there appear weekly in the *Herald-Republic*. In Washington, D.C., *The Star* provided five weekday local editions, each a section of news, features and advertisements devoted to a specific area around the nation's capital. Weekly the *Louisville Times* and *Courier-Journal* publish a special section geared to geographical areas of those two newspapers' home county (see Figure 10.1). All of those special newspapers carry information that the larger publication does not have room to publish because the information would be too local or specialized for the large market.

Figure 10.1 Zeroing in on a specific locale with in their circulation area, *The Louisville Times* and *The Courier-Journal* publish special sections called "Neighborhoods." (Copyright 1980 *The Louisville Times* and *The Courier-Journal*)

Other responses have included new feature items or a greater stress on good writing. Stories about the self sprung up during the so-called "me generation" of the 1970s, not only because readers were self-centered but also because they wanted information that helped them cope with life. Newspaper attempts to become a bigger part of readers' lives included expanded letter-to-the-editor columns and other forums that invited reader comment. Taking a hint from the speciality magazines, some newspapers enlarged their coverage of leisure activities so readers needed the newspaper to learn what they could do with their leisure time. More consumer-oriented stories filled newspapers and suddenly readers found they needed their local daily. The Norfolk, Virginia *Ledger-Star* began publishing "The Daily Break" (Figure 10.2), a leisure activities page aimed at the 18-35 age group. The paper claims to have lowered the median age of its readers from 46 to 42 and to have reversed circulation losses.

Figure 10.2 Special sections or pages devoted to leisure time and entertainment have helped some newspapers gain young readers.

Other changes came about. Newspapers started looking better as graphic artists became as important as editors. Some newspapers added special sections while others redesigned their packages. Color became more prominent. To recapture the young, some newspapers created their own tabloids or added syndicated tabloids. *The Mini-Page* (Figure 10.3) aims for young school children; *Youth Beat* seeks teenage readers. Such efforts have been made in the past, but in recent times the efforts have increased and become more systematic.

None of these changes came without their critics, who saw the newspaper turning away from its First Amendment obligation to inform the public and toward a soft-news approach of pablum—a *People* magazine orientation of personalities, personalities, personalities—and no news. Some critics called the changing newspaper mush and said it was edited for people whose brains were equally soft. Mediocrity, not excellence, became the byword of journalism, the critics charged, and some complained that newspapers—tuned through market research to what their audiences wanted—had softened their editorial bites so as not to offend anyone. Whatever happened, a new approach to newspaper publishing had occurred. Little was left to chance.

Readership Surveys

Not so very long ago, editors prided themselves on the fact that they had their finger on the pulse of the community. "I know what my readers want," the pompous editors would say, backing up their claims with nothing but more hot air. The decline in readership proved that many editors had no idea what their readers wanted.

More interestingly, the readership and reader attitude surveys that evolved out of the readership decline showed that the results of the intuitive approach to editing newspapers was often far from what readers wanted. The only place editors and readers agreed was the need for local news, although no researcher to date has determined just what local news is. (Is it a report on local government or a blurb on some 6-year-old's birthday party?) Depending on which survey you read, one area that doesn't interest a lot of readers but does interest a lot of editors is sports. The surveys that learned such information don't take into account that many editors once worked the sports beat, that being the route to the top in the newspaper for some years. The editor was in sports; therefore, sports were important. Those sports pages that took a turn for the best also covered participatory sports—the kind readers could appreciate because they could be part of it.

Newspapers were the last medium to make use of scientific surveys and other kinds of research. Magazines, for example, not only rely on surveys but some have their own research departments, which work with

all other departments in the magazine, not just editorial. Magazine surveys take various forms, including the insertion of questionnaires which ask the reader if certain articles in that issue were helpful or not. Some magazines send issues to selected readers for evaluation and others rely on personal interviews. Television and radio have long relied on surveys to determine content. Market-savvy radio station owners learned in the 1960s that intuition was a poor way to sell a product and turned to surveys to see what kind of format (*i.e.*, rock, country and western, all news) appealed.

Now newspapers have joined the list of those media relying on surveys, although the newspapers often use what they learn not so much to change the product but to retune or fine tune it or justify what is already being done. Readership surveys pinpoint problems; they do not provide answers. When a particular type of coverage receives much criticism, an editor evaluates it not with an eye to getting rid of it but with an eye to improving it. Research tells editors not where to go but how to get where they want to go. City council meetings will always be part of a newspaper's local fare, but how the newspaper reports the meeting (more graphs and sidebars, perhaps) may change because of reader unhappiness learned in a survey. The Dubuque *Telegraph-Herald* has conducted a series of surveys on each section of the paper to see how well each section communicates. The paper has its own research department.

Readership surveys have already uncovered some interesting problems. Readers believe that local news leans too much on governmental and political events, which are easy to cover but which can lack the importance more grassroots or depth coverage might turn up. Readers believe that newspapers lack positive news about the community and others say newspapers are written for journalists and government officials, not for readers. Some believe editors are out of touch, a remark some editors would disagree with by pointing to their membership in the local country club as proof they are "in touch." Readers also sense that the pontificating newspaper that yells loudly about other people's mistakes is slow—if not reluctant—to correct its own errors. Similarly, the individual senses discourteous treatement when calling the newspaper, while others shy away from any contact because they know of the paper's ability to hurt people.

No editor learned that kind of information on intuition, but once apprised of it, good editors responded positively. Some editors routinely send questionnaires to people named in news stories as a way of checking the accuracy of stories. Other papers solicit reader opinion on a broader scale and others have hired in-house critics (called "ombudsmen") to evaluate the newspaper's work and, in some cases, report to the readers in columns published in the newspapers. Some editors have kept their finger on the pulse of the community by regularly walking the streets of their town and soliciting face-to-face reader opinion. Other editors have formed readership and focus groups to regularly critique the newspaper's work.

Marketing

Readership surveys have shown editors they don't know that much about their readers. The readers, the surveys show, come from all walks of life and often change during the day—the businessperson going to work in the morning wants stock tables but going home that night might want information on gardening or lawn care. Making the news product appeal to such a person requires marketing a product whose content has first been shaped by editors who know what their readers want.

Marketing takes several forms, including the weekly meeting of editors and circulation department personnel to delve into reasons readers give for discontinuing their papers. Another approach personalizes reporters and photographers, but that runs the risk of creating a "star" system in which the reporter or photographer rather than the news is important. Such hype smacks of an image orientation rather than an information orientation.

Some newspapers promote heavily, touting in Monday's paper what special features will appear the next day and throughout the week. Figure 10.4 shows a promotion from the *Fort Worth* (Texas) *Star-Telegram.* Some newspapers use radio and television to promote themselves, something they would have never done when those two media were in their infancy and considered beneath newspapers.

The good marketing newspaper keeps readers attuned to what changes the newspaper might be making. When a newspaper builds a new plant or installs a new press or switches from afternoon to morning publication, the newspaper heavily promotes the changes so the reader knows what is going on and feels a part of it.

That type of promotion aside, editors have segmented their markets various ways to find new readers and regain lost ones. The segmentation breaks the market along geographic, demographic and psychographic lines.

Geographics.   Dividing the audience according to where its members live is nothing new. Magazines have been delivering audiences to advertisers like this for years and newspapers have taken up the form through zoned editions—that is, editions in which part of the product is devoted only to one zone out of many. Newspapers in cities with large Hispanic populations publish editions in Spanish. The *Evansville Courier* and the *Evansville Press,* sister publications in Indiana, publish special news tabloids geared to one of two counties around Evansville. Even non-subscri-

Figure 10.4 Self-promotion enables a newspaper to alert readers to stories planned for later issues.

bers receive the paper on its one-day-a-week appearance.

The aforementioned mini-newspapers represent another geographic approach and the future holds promise for more newspapers of that type because of the electronic equipment which makes storing and reusing stories so easy. Editors can easily package and repackage great quantities of news merely by pushing buttons on VDTs.

Demographics. The magazine industry, with its many specialty publications, has shown newspapers that there's more than one way to sell a product. Newspapers—especially in competitive markets—no longer think of themselves as aimed for a mass audience but instead tailor themselves to a coalition of certain groups within the mass. Special editions appear only when those groups are active: The newspaper carrying stock tables in the morning for business people may market itself for leisure time activity when it attempts to appeal to those same people as they're homeward bound at night. The working woman, unlike her housewife predecessor, wants a much different newspaper to serve her. The *Yakima Herald-Republic* has opted for a page called "Femme," which has a working female orientation (see Figure 10.5). Senior citizens represent still another news-market segment.

Entire products have been reformatted on the basis of demographics. One of the more notable is the *Los Angeles Herald Examiner*, which shucked its blue-collar audience for a young reader with more money to spend. That approach shows marketing gone amuck as a newspaper throws aside some of its audience because it doesn't have enough money and, perhaps, won't frequent the elegant advertisers. The newspaper that ceases to cover that part of the community which does not subscribe leaves that community without a voice.

Psychographics. Still another marketing technique is to peg a newspaper's appeal to distinctions in lifestyles and personalities. Such an approach accounts for the success of speciality magazines and points the way some newspapers might go. The major experiment in this area was *Consumer Extra*, an adless, separately sold tabloid published by the *Courier-Journal* and *Louisville Times* in 1979. The consumer-oriented newspaper fell short of its 18,000 break-even circulation goal so its creators folded it. But the possibility of creating similar magazines and selling the main newspaper to those individuals who would also subscribe to preferred special supplements for an additional fee is not that far off.

Format Changes

The newspaper industry, generally conservative, responded to the decline in readership in several ways once considered radical. Readership surveys aside, other approaches took hold as newspapers sought ways to shake themselves from the readership doldrums. Format changes spelled the difference for some.

Probably the most radical of changes occurred with afternoon metropolitan newspapers, which, feeling the loss of readership more than their a.m. competitors, began publishing morning editons. That schedule put the afternoon papers into direct competition with the morning papers. Afternoon newspapers that began a.m. editions include the *Washington Star*, the *Detroit News*, the *Dallas Times Herald*, the *Oakland Tribune*, and the Philadelphia *Bulletin*. The effort did not help the *Star*, which died on August 7, 1981. Thriving dailies have started Sunday editions to keep out city newspapers and some papers have switched from p.m. to a.m. publication only on Saturdays to get away from trying to hook readers during the dead period of Saturday afternoon—a leisure time in many U.S. homes.

Other format changes include special sections or columns on recreational sports, celebrities, medicine, food and fashion, consumerism, teenagers, leisure and love, gardening and grooming, television and travel, pet care and home repair, investments and hobbies, and the inclusion of comprehensive calendars on cultural and leisure activities. News about religion has been increased; reviews of books have (unfortunately) been cut back. Additional sports columns and news features have found their way into print and most newspapers that weren't six columns took on the eye-appealing format. Section logos were created to help the reader find the news faster and photographs and graphics received better display, sometimes through the use of color.

From p.m. to a.m.

A wire service story written at 8 a.m. for use in a newspaper that would publish at 2 p.m. and be read at 6 p.m. might begin this way: "Theodore Rand's second murder trial today was in the hands of the jury." Unsure what would develop between 8 a.m. and 6 p.m., the writer had to use past tense to describe an event that was continuing all day. The same writer writing for a morning newspaper would be writing the story at the end of the day—when the news cycle is usually spent—and would not have faced the problem of how to cover an event that could be superseded.

The one major problem afternoon newspapers face is timeliness. News often breaks in the afternoon—in time for the 6 o'clock news on television but not in time for the 2 p.m. press run. Thus, many afternoon newspapers—no matter how disguised—read like rewritten morning newspapers. The readers learn from their afternoon newspapers what they could have read in the morning or seen on television the night before. Why buy a rehash?

Many reasons for converting from an afternoon to a morning publication exists. Those who have studied a.m. and p.m. markets say that a.m. papers have been more successful. Traffic jams that delay the delivery of evening newspapers don't occur in the middle of the night when morning papers are delivered. Energy is saved when presses are run at other than peak hours (such as 2 a.m.). Morning readership doesn't face the competition for time that evening readership does. Advertisers in a morning paper can anticipate same-day response because readers can see an advertisement in the morning and buy that day, rather than waiting—and maybe forgetting—overnight. An advertisement published in the morning is assured a longer shelf life, which enhances its sales ability. The freshness of news in a morning paper makes it more attractive to readers.

Papers that have switched to a.m. find they can package better and that the quality of writing must be better. The reader has no time for long stories, all of which requires reporters to break their once long reports into brightly written sidebars to allow the morning reader to pick and choose among the issues.

Some papers have not gone all the way in converting to a.m. The *Rochester Times-Union,* which has a sister publication in the morning, the *Democrat and Chronicle,* converted only on Saturdays by becoming a magazine inserted in the morning *Democrat and Chronicle. Times-Union* officials killed off the Saturday afternoon edition because of declining reader and advertiser interest.

What Lies Ahead?

Trying to predict the future provides more than its share of work for some people, including those in marketing, especially any form of marketing that relates to newspapers. Some of what they foresee is obvious— more working women and more senior citizens were evident in the 1970s. More working women means, among other things, a rise in an interest in business news because working women will probably also invest in the marketplace. Working women, too, are expected to read more newspapers and watch less television and to be more interested in a variety of topics, from consumer safety to the environment. Newspaper advertising that does not stereotype women as housewives will appeal more to working women.

With the teenage population declining in the United States, all news media will have to serve a more mature audience. The 1970s' interest in young readers will probably lessen as the young represent less and less of the overall market and audience. Service industries will have to expand to care for the more adult population and the increase in the workforce suggests more leisure time—trends that newspapers must keep abreast of if they intend to improve circulation. Minorities will not only increase but will fill long-overdue jobs of importance. As an economic force, they will have to be catered to.

Experts expect a growth in religion during the 1980s, and church pages as newspapers of the 1970s published them may have to expand to cover less traditional sects and movements. Religion editors will need to sense undercurrents and report on them. Reporters with only a journalism degree will find themselves less marketable than reporters with a background in a second field. The computer, of course, will grow in importance and newspapers will need to satisfy the participants in what is likely to become a major leisure activity—the home computer.

The technological advances reflected in the general interest in computers will mean a more educated audience. Newspaper readers will want education and newspapers can help provide it. In fact, those same technological advances—as mentioned earlier—can mean a tailor-made newspaper. Any reader can buy a main section with an index, select from the index additional sections or more details on an event and purchase those—from the living room computer. Newspapers may be thinner and more compact, but the many tabloid (or whatever the size) inserts available on a cafeteria-style basis will ensure a newspaper that lives longer because its usefulness will extend beyond hard news. In other words, a newspaper's temporary permanence will grow.

Part of the growth has begun with the changes to a.m. publication schedules. Editors will package better, creating a more usable, functional product. A newspaper published in the morning might contain four sections, with two of them filled with hard news (including sports) that the reader will absorb at the breakfast table. The other two sections will contain soft news—features, advice columns, opinion—which the reader can put off reading until later in the day. Thus, the newspaper will be useful to the reader at more than one time and for different reasons. The concept is not new—it exists already in the typical Sunday newspaper which not only packages for reading that day but for days later. The magazine supplement of any Sunday newspaper can be put aside for reading later in the week and the reader gets the bonus of mid-week reading. That's extending the life of the Sunday paper—and it will happen to dailies too.

Naturally, newspapers will face competition, both from the usual and unusual sources. The newspapers will change to meet changing reader needs and new societal concerns. Radio adapted to television and newspapers and television must adapt to a technology that challenges both. Look for more local news on television and more analytical and specialized news in newspapers. The exciting thing is that editors burned by the declining readership of the 1970s are more alert and more able to spot the trends and less likely to scoff when reader attitudes change. Intuitive editing will disappear. The reader should gain the most.

APPENDIX A
Editing Symbols

When relying on paper and pencil instead of a VDT, journalists use various editing symbols to tell printers what to do. The following shows the symbols and their functions.

The circle indicates:

A word should be abbreviated: The (October) 12, 1984, meeting

An abbreviation should be spelled out: the (Oct.) 1984 meeting

A number should be a figure: (two hundred thirty-nine)

A figure should be spelled out: (2)

The caret shows insertion in the following ways:

A word: a ∧rainy day in May

A hyphen: loose ∧ fitting clothes

A dash: The meeting ∧ predicted to be volatile ∧ turned out to be short and quiet.

A comma: The meeting ∧ scheduled for later this month ∧ will be good.

Quotation marks: ∧I blame you, ∧ the speaker said.

Apostrophe: Those were the speaker ∧s words.

Single and double lines connect this way:

When a word is ~~cut out~~ deleted and you want the line closed up but with one space between words.

When letters are deleted with~~xx~~in a word and you want the word closed up to appear as it normally would.

The transposition marker switches letters and words.

Sometimes letters within a word or within a sentence words are transposed and the copy editor has to show the correct order.

Letters to be capitalized are marked
tillie may williams

Letters to be lowercased are marked:
The Wind in the Trees

A period is inserted this way:
P⊗T⊗ Barnum

A new paragraph indention is marked:

that ⌊If you decide∧ a two-sentence paragraph should be two paragraphs, use the paragraph indicator. ⌊Such a mark is not necessary, however, when the writer has correctly indented.

If a paragraph is not wanted, connect the indented sentence to the preceding sentence:

Thus, you have the end of a paragraph and the start of a new one. But later you change your mind and want the new paragraph to be part of the old. Connect the paragraphs with the line hook.

Other symbols:
R or Rom: Roman type
I or Ital: Italic type
bf: bold face
bfc: bold face caps (all letters capitalized)
center, as in a byline:

⌐ By T.T. Jones ⌐
⌐ Journal Writer ⌐

flush left

⌐ By T.T. Jones

flush right:

Journal Writer ⌐

APPENDIX B
A Condensed Stylebook

This newspaper stylebook is based on the stylebook jointly developed by the Associated Press and United Press International, which you are encouraged to consult. The author's own style rules are so marked.

abbreviations Some titles before names are abbreviated, unless they appear in direct quotations. Abbreviate *Dr., Gov., Lt. Gov., Rep., the Rev., Sen.* and most military titles such as *Gen., Col., Capt., Lt., Adm., Cmdr.* When courtesy titles are necessary, use *Mr., Mrs., Ms.* (see courtesy titles).

Using the first three letters, abbreviate the months of the year (except May, June, Sept.) only when used in dates, such as Oct. 12 or Oct. 12, 1984, but October 1984.

Abbreviate the names of states in city-state combinations (Joplin, Mo.) with the exception of Alaska, Hawaii, Idaho, Iowa, Maine, Ohio, Texas and Utah. (see state names).

addresses Abbreviate in numbered addresses (326 W. Broad St.) *avenue, boulevard* and *street* but not *alley, drive, road, terrace* and others. Spell out when no number is given (West Broad Street).

Always uses figures such as *8 Pilsdon Lane* rather than *Eight Pilsdon Lane.*

Numbers used as street names are spelled our *First* through *Ninth;* above *ninth* uses figures (15th Street).

Directions that are part of an address are abbreviated (1015 S. Terrace Ave.) but are spelled out if no number is given (South Terrace Avenue).

ages Use figures at all times, even if the age is a single digit (Tommy Thompson, 5, eats an ice cream cone for photographers . . .)

a.m., p.m. Always use lowercase letters.

Since *a.m.* means *morning* and *p.m.* means *afternoon* or *tonight*, avoid redundances such as *9 a.m. this morning, 2 p.m. Wednesday afternoon, 10 p.m. tomorrow night.*

Bible When referring to the Christian Bible, always capitalize. In other references, lower case, such as: *The wire services' stylebooks are the bible at this newspaper.*

Never capitalize *biblical.*

capitalization In general, follow a downstyle approach in which only proper nouns, names and formal titles before names are capitalized. Titles after names or standing alone without a name are never capitalized.

Work titles or job descriptions are not capitalized: *At the game's end, quarterback Fran Tarkenton threw a touchdown pass to wide receiver Ahmad Rashad.*

Common nouns that are part of proper nouns but are being used in subsequent references are lower case: *The Republican Party* but *the party.*

century Always lowercase (21st century). Spell out *first* through *ninth* and use figures thereafter.

The 21st century, by the way, begins in 2001, not 2000, which is the final year of the 20th century.

city council/governmental bodies/legislature Capitalize full names such as *Houston City Council, the Tucson Fire Department, the Iowa Legislature* and capitalize second references to them when it is clear what is being referred to. *Houston City Council* becomes *the City Council, the Tucson Fire Department* becomes *the Fire Department* and *the Iowa Legislature* becomes *the Legislature.*

Condensed further, though, it is *the council, the department.*

congress When referring to the *U.S. Senate* and *House of Representatives* or to a foreign body that includes *congress* in its name, capitalize. Lowercase *congress* when it is not part of an organization's name or when used as a second reference to a group or as a substitute for *convention.*

congressional districts Always use figures and capitalize: *the 3rd Congressional District, the 23rd Congressional District.* But use lowercase in subsequent references: *district.*

congressman, congresswoman De-sexed references include: *House member, senator,* but not *congressperson.* (author's entry)

constitution Capitalize whenever referring to *the U.S. Constitution.* When referring to other state's or nation's constitutions, capitalize only with the state or nation's name: *the Oregon Constitution, the French Constitution.*

An organization's constitution is always lowercase.

constitutional Always lowercase.

county Capitalize in names of counties and county government units: *Schuylkill County, the Clive County Sheriff's Department.* Subsequent references in a clear context always take capital letters: *County Sheriff's Department.*

Lowercase *county* when it stands alone or as a subsequent reference to a proper name.

courtesy titles Avoid courtesy titles. A person's sex or marital status has nothing to do with that person's newsworthiness. However, apply courtesy titles to situations where confusion might result, such as when writing about a married couple and referring to one of them. Does the reference to *Jones* mean *Mr. Jones* or *Mrs. Jones* (or, if preferred, Ms. Jones)? Then a courtesy title is needed. (author's preference)

datelines Newspapers use datelines only on stories from outside the newspaper's immediate circulation area.

Generally datelines consist of a city name followed by the state (abbreviated per style): *Laramie, Wyo.* Well known cities do not need a state.

State names are not used in newspapers published in that state unless the city name by itself might cause confusion: *Washington, Pa.; Cairo, Ill.*

In roundup stories, state names might be necessary within the story proper to make references clear: *Altoona, Iowa,* and *Altoona, Pa.*

(Datelines are so called because at one time they included the date the action in the story took place. The two major wire services now put the time element in the lead, but some newspapers still use datelines.)

dimensions/weights Always use figures, but spell out *feet, inches, yards, meters, pounds, grams, ounces. The newborn baby weighs 8 pounds, 7 ounces and was 21 inches long.*

The only exception to metric abbreviations comes with *millimeter* (use *mm*) when used in reference to film widths (35 mm) or weapons (50 mm).

directions/regions Lowercase compass points when standing alone.

Capitalize regions known specifically by direction, such as *the West, the South, the Middle West, the East, the Northeast, the Southwest.*

Lowercase general directions when part of a proper name, such as *southern Texas,* unless the section is well known, such as *South Philadelphia* and *Southern California.*

distances Follow the general number rule: Spell out *one* through *nine* and use figures for *10* and above. *The proud parents of the 8-pound, 7-ounce, 21-inch baby took their child on her first trip—a five-mile drive to Grandma's.*

fractions Below *1,* spell out; above, use figures or convert to decimals. To convert 3¼ into a decimal, divide the 4 of ¼ into the 1 and affix the answer with a decimal point to the whole number: *3.25.*

hurricane Capitalize when part of a storm's name.

A storm is not a hurricane unless the sustained wind speed is 74 miles an hour. Lesser blowing attempts are called *tropical storms.*

Although hurricanes have female and male names, all subsequent references to them are made with the neutral pronoun *it.*

incorporated Although seldom needed in a corporation's name, when used *incorporated* is abbreviated and capitalized *Inc.* Do not set off with commas: *NL Industries Inc.*

initials When a person chooses to be known by his or her initials, respect that usage. Use periods but do not space between initials because video display terminals and typesetters use space codes as guides in justifying lines and a space between initials could place them on separate lines.

it/she Modern usage does not use gender pronouns to refer to neutral objects. Ships, nations and hurricanes are *it* not *she.*

names/nicknames Refer to people as they prefer to be known, such as J. Edgar Hoover and Jimmy Carter (whose full name is James Earl Carter Jr.).

The same guideline applies to nicknames, except when the nickname is intended as deragatory ("Fats" Olson).

Some people acquire nicknames because their given names are uncommon. Thus, *Amandus Lutz* was always known as *"Bud,"* which he preferred.

Nicknames are set off with quotation marks except on the sports pages, where nothing is used.

No. Always the abbreviation for number when referring to rankings. *The No. 1 ranked football team in the pre-season poll finished No. 19.*

numbers Generally, spell out *one* through *nine* and use figures for *10* and above.

Numbers at the start of a sentence are spelled out if the result is not ungainly, such as: *One thousand six hundred fifty-two students col-*

lected money to help fight cancer last year. The sentence works better this way: *A total of 1,652 students . . .* However, don't carry that rule to extremes. It's all right to begin a sentence *Five people . . . A total of five* wastes words.

For exceptions to the general numbers rule, see **addresses, ages, century, congressional district, dimensions/weights, fractions, No., temperatures.**

party affiliation Three possible approaches form the basic application of this guideline:

Republican Sen. Barry Goldwater of Arizona said . .

Sen. Barry Goldwater, R-Ariz., said . . . (note punctuation and abbreviation)

Sen. Barry Goldwater said . . . The Arizona Republican also said . . .

The choice often seems based on what goes best with the rhythm of the sentence.

pope/pontiff Capitalize *pope* only in a formal title, but never when used alone. *Pope John Paul II visited . . . The pope saw several . . . Pontiff* is not a formal title and is always lowercase.

post office Do not capitalize; the correct name is *U.S. Postal Service* although *post office* may be used when referring to the building where mail is distributed from.

president Capitalize only when part of a title, such as *President Lincoln.* When standing alone, lowercase.

quotations Clean up a speaker's bad grammar and word abuse and do not use unusual spellings to indicate colloquial speaking unless necessary to convey a particular sense, as in a feature story.

seasons Unless part of a proper name, the seasons of the year are always lowercase.

slang Don't use.

People may use slang when they talk, but when they read, they expect precision, not flippancy, in the words they read. Given the generational differences among many slang words, their use impairs communication.

spouse When referring to marriage partners in general, use *spouse* to avoid the implication that only men occupy work roles and women are only housewives.

state names Always spell out state names when they stand alone, but, with the exception of eight, abbreviate when used with town and city names in datelines and stories. Accepted abbreviations are: **Ala.,**

Ariz., Ark., Calif., Colo., Conn., Del., Fla., Ga., Ill., Ind., Kan., Ky., La., Md., Mass., Mich., Minn., Miss., Mo., Mont., Neb., Nev., N.H., N.J., N.M., N.Y., N.C., N.D., Okla., Ore., Pa., R.I., S.C., Tenn., Vt., Va., Wash., W.Va., Wis., Wyo. (Do not use U.S. Postal Service abbreviations; they are confusing.)

temperatures Except for *zero,* all temperatures are given as figures. Use the words *minus* or *below zero* to report such temperatures. Do not use a minus sign.

time element Except when referring to the current day (the day of publication) use the day of the week. Thus, a Thursday newspaper would refer to *Wednesday* and *Friday* where appropriate, not *yesterday* and *tomorrow.*

TV *Television* is more acceptable, especially in noun usages.

United Nations/U.N. Use *United Nations* as a noun; use *U.N.* as a modifier. *The United Nations met today to debate a U.N. resolution.*

United States/U.S. Use *United States* as a noun; use *U.S.* as a modifier. *The United States sends many U.S. products overseas.*

vice president As a formal title, capitalize; standing alone, lowercase.

women/men The two sexes are equal and should be treated as such. Copy should not assume a group of people is all male or female; copy should not refer to a woman's physical appearance (attractive) or a man's (muscular); copy should not use a woman's family relationship (mother of five).

In other words, treat men and women with equal respect and with a total lack of condescension and stereotyping.

APPENDIX C

Glossary

A wire the main or major wire of a wire service, it provides the best news fastest.

advance a story written and made available to an editor days before its publication date. Typically, such stories are features that do not have to appear immediately.

advertising the solicited and paid-for sales pitches that appear in a newspaper. The revenue from advertising pays the bills but the work of the editorial department attracts the audience for the advertiser.

agate five and a half point type. Frequently any small type, such as boxscores, is called agate, although the type may be slightly larger.

air white space intentionally placed on a page. It regularly appears around headlines and captions and between lines of type in addition to other places according to the page designer's choice.

art any graphic element on a page, including line drawings and photographs.

Associated Press, The a news-gathering cooperative.

attribution the source of information in a story.

access in computer language, a verb meaning to locate and process.

banner headline a headline that runs from one side of the page to the other.

ben day a type of border used in boxes; a ben day border is a pattern of dots.

brite a light-hearted or humorous story.

broadsheet   the format/size of a standard newspaper.

body type   type sizes used exclusively for stories; sometimes called "text type." Traditional sizes range from 8 through 10 point.

box   a border surrounding a story.

budget   a list of top stories. Also called "directory," "digest" or "schedule."

bullet   a dot used at the beginning of each paragraph that is part of a list. Some editors use dashes.

bulletin   a rapidly sent blurb that tells of a usually significant or dramatic change in a story.

bureau   a subordinate office of the main newspaper office.

butcher   a pejorative term used to describe a copy editor who does graceless work and makes stories worse rather than better.

byline   at the beginning of a story the name of the reporter who wrote the story or of the wire service that provided the story.

caption   the words used to complement a photograph.

char del   a VDT command for "character delete."

circulation   the number of newspapers sold, usually discussed in terms of number of newspapers sold in a day. Advertisers are charged rates according to a newspaper's circulation and one with a high circulation can charge more for an advertisement than a low-circulation newspaper can.

cliche   a phrase used so many times it has lost the warmth and glow of originality. Avoided in good writing; removed in good editing.

close   a VDT command that tells the computer a reporter has completed a story.

cold type   the reproduction of type through photographic means. So called because the process does not require the melting of lead and the attendant heat found in "hot type" methods.

column   (a) a row of type, any length. (b) a short essay usually expressing a viewpoint.

column rule   dark, vertical lines used to separate columns of type. Passe.

commands   functions built in to a VDT system and usually executed by pushing only one key.

computer   a piece of equipment capable of storing millions of pieces of information and processing that information speedily upon command.

computer printout   information computer-transcribed from the computer to a printer, often called a hard copy printer.

copy   (a) a VDT command that means "duplicate." (b) newsroom jargon for "story."

copy schedule   an editor's listing of stories assigned for use in that day's issue.

crash the phrase used to describe computer breakdown.

credit line the words at the end of a caption which give the source of the photograph. On wirephotos the credit line is no more than the name of the wire service providing the photograph.

crop the process of marking any art to show which parts are to be reproduced and which parts are to be cut (cropped).

cursor a blinking rectangular light that shows a VDT user's place on the screen. For example, a letter to be removed must appear under the cursor before the computer will delete that letter on command. The cursor moves in the four basic directions.

Datanews UPI's high-speed news service.

Datastream AP's high-speed news service.

deadline the final moment after which productive, economical work can no longer be accomplished.

dedicated a computer term meaning a piece of equipment can do only what it has been built to do. Some VDT systems are dedicated only to processing text.

discretionary time periods of freedom when readers can do as they please; generally considered competition for newspapers.

down style capitalizing only the first word and all proper nouns in a headline.

drop headline a subordinate or secondary headline that appears below the main line of a headline. A drop headline can be used when two stories appear under a main headline. The separate headlines on the stories are drop headlines.

dummy a hand-drawn schematic of what an editor wants a page to look like when in print.

edition a press run's worth of newspapers, not a day's worth. An edition is usually focused on a particular locale (city edition) or time of day (early edition). see **zoned edition**

evergreen a virtually timeless story.

face the type design; "face" is often preceded by a word telling which type of face it is, such as Caslon.

feature a human interest or soft news story written in a narrative or other non-newspaper style.

filler short items used to take up space when a longer story comes up short.

floppy disk a phonograph record-like disk on which computer programs or newsroom-generated information are stored for later accessing. More typically found in small newspapers.

focus group a gathering of newspaper readers brought together in an unsystematic fashion by a researcher looking for subjective analysis of a particular newspaper and for questions around which to build a readership survey.

folio   found at the top of a page, it contains the newspaper's name, the publishing date and the page number. Often incorporated into the section flag.

format   the shape or form of the newspaper's contents.

formatting   specifying through a VDT keyboard particular typographic requirements.

front end system   a computerized text-processing and type-generating system in which input is made at the initial point in the system (the VDT) and controlled from there.

graphic   a visual element designed to enhance the communication of a story. Drawings more than photographs qualify as graphics, although when editors refer to "graphic elements," they include photographs.

gutter   the vertical white space between columns.

hard news   news that occurs and is reported within a 24-hour or shorter cycle; information that is timely. (see **soft news**)

hairline   the thinest rule available for boxes. The next larger size is one point.

hammer headline   an all-caps word or short phrase appearing above a headline where a kicker normally appears.

header   a piece of information that normally appears on command at the beginning of VDT stories. The header might include space for a copy editor to indicate what edition the story goes in, which page it goes on, what size headline it gets.

headline   the larger type appearing (usually) above a story and telling what the story is about.

headline count   the maximum number of units a certain size headline will fill.

headlinese   slang or language abuse in headlines.

hellbox   a metal container in which printers threw lead to be melted down and recycled; a relic.

home   a VDT command that returns the cursor to the top left-hand corner of the screen.

index   a listing of stories and features in a newspaper issue.

insert   a VDT command that allows a user to insert a word or letter without erasing other words or letters. When not in the insert mode, a VDT is in the overstrike mode.

International Typographical Union   the union that represents members of the production department; at some newspapers the ITU also represents members of the editorial staff.

journalese   the jargon of journalism; not fit to print.

jump as a verb, the process of continuing a story from one page to another; as a noun, the continued matter.

justify a computer command that reformats a story on a VDT screen to show how the story will appear in type. Justifying a story will show where the hyphens are going to appear, enabling an editor to check for incorrect hyphenation.

kicker a smaller headline that appears above the main line of a headline.

label headline a verbless headline that gives the topic of a story but not the news.

lead the beginning of a story; usually only the first paragraph.

legend the (usually) all caps beginning of a caption; also called a "lead in." The legend can also appear in headline type to the side of or above a caption.

legibility the clarity of appearance of type.

library a newspaper's collection of reference works and the newspaper's own stories. Older journalists call it the "morgue."

libel anything published or broadcast that cast apersions on a person's good name.

localize the process of rewriting or editing a wire story so the angle of interest to the newspaper's audience appears at the beginning of the story.

marketing the various strategies devised to sell a product.

module a rectangle of any dimension in which a story or photograph or story and photograph is contained.

nameplate the name of the newspaper and other publishing information found at or near the top of Page One. Also called a flag.

new lead fresh information transmitted by a wire service to replace the beginning of an earlier story.

news the timely content of a newspaper.

Newspaper Fund a non-profit foundation supported by various newspapers and news organizations and dedicated to encouraging young people to consider careers in journalism. Two major programs provide internships for minorities and students interested in copy editing.

Newspaper Guild a union whose members include journalists.

newsprint the paper on which a newspaper is printed.

obit journalese for "obituary." An obituary is an account of a person's death and facts about the person's life.

ombudsman a member of the newspaper staff whose main function is to process reader complaints against the newspaper and to serve as an in-house critic of the newspaper.

open   a typical VDT operation which commands a computer to produce a story from its files.

package   the practice of putting related news items together for reader ease in finding them.

page   a VDT screen full of type. A page equals approximately 20 lines, or what a reporter would normally type on one sheet of 8½ × 11 inch paper.

pagination   the video-computer process of designing newspaper pages.

para   a VDT command given at the end of a paragraph so that the following paragraph will be indented.

para del   a VDT command for "paragraph delete."

peg   a story's *raison d'etre*; the main point on which the story hangs.

photojournalism   the melding of words and pictures into a coherent story told mostly with photographs.

pica   a printer's measure of type 12 points; approximately one-sixth of an inch long. Pica measurements are applied to column widths and photograph sizes.

pica stick   a printer's ruler.

point   the smallest measure of type; an inch contains 72 points. Point sizes are applied to borders, type and spaces or any other small area.

production   see **shop.**

proportional scale   a wheel-shaped device used for determining changes in photograph sizes.

publisher   the chief officer of a newspaper. The publisher oversees all phases of the newspaper, although he does not get involved in day-to-day decisions in any one department.

Pulitzer prize   journalism's most prestigious honor bestowed annually on the best journalists and newspapers (and plays and books).

queue   a dedicated space in the computer, set aside for a reporter to write a story or for wire service input or for copy editing.

ragged right   type with an uneven right-hand side; sometimes called "unjustified right."

RAM   a computer memory device that allows a user to access information from any point without regard for where the information appears in the computer. Abbreviation for "random access memory."

readability   the clarity of the written word.

readership survey   a systematic study of audience feeling toward the content of a newspaper or magazine.

refer   type within a story that refers the reader to a related story or photograph.

regional wire   a wire devoted to serving a particular area, such as a state, half a state, or many small states.

reverse type   any type that is reversed from black on white to white on black through production techniques.

ROM   a dedicated program that allows read-only memory. A user must always start at the beginning of the disk and search through to reach desired information. Very time consuming.

scratch pad   a queue in which reporters write stories.

screamer headline   a sensationalistic headline that overstates the story and appears in an extra-large size.

scroll up/scroll down   VDT commands that advance a story up or down the screen.

second-day lead   a lead on any version of a story but the first in which the news is originally reported; a second-day lead generally takes a feature angle or highlights a new—but not always important—action in a continuing story.

section flag   similar to a nameplate, except the section flag announces the section of the newspaper. Also called a "logo."

sent del   a VDT command for "sentence delete."

serif   additional strokes on letters which make type easier to read. Type lacking serifs is *sans serif*.

shop   the area of a newspaper building where stories are set in type and pages put together. Also called production.

sidebar   a story related to a major story, but keying on one special point.

sidesaddle headline   used alongside rather than above a story.

sign off   a VDT command telling the computer that the reporter is through using the terminal.

skip to start   a VDT command key that will send the cursor to the beginning of the story, requiring the story to move with it so that the beginning of the story will appear at the top of the screen with the cursor.

slug   identifying information given to a story by a reporter or editor. Usually the slug tells something about the story, such as "hotel/fire."

soft news   the timeless or feature content of a newspaper that usually has some relationship to a recent news event. Also, often a derisive term for stories of mass appeal but not of mass benefit.

split page   any page that begins any section (except the first); also called a "break page."

split screen   a VDT capable of displaying two stories side by side.

stack   a one-column breakdown of a longer story; a story spread evenly over five columns is said to have five stacks of type. Some editors refer to "sticks" or "legs" of type.

standing headline   a headline used unchangingly day in and day out to identify a type of news. Verbotten when used as the main headline on a story. For example, *Weather* as a standing headline lacks the communicative strength of *Hurricane expected.* Standing heads should not be used in place of an original headline.

streamer headline   see **banner headline.**

stet   a printer's term (derived from the Latin *stare*) to advise the person setting type to disregard a correction or to let a word stand as is even if it appears incorrect. The word has no use in a computer system.

style   the prescribed way of processing ambiguous or ambivalent usages in a news stories. Style should always be consistent.

subhead   a subordinate headline appearing within the body of a story.

supplementary wire service   a service that completes rather than competes with the two major wires. Supplementary wires provide opinion columns, analyses and features not common to the AP and UPI.

tabloid   a newspaper format that is half the size of a standard newspaper. Also a phrase used to describe sensationalistic newspapers.

take   a portion of a story, usually one page; for a wire story, 450 words.

time element   usually the day of the week a news story takes place. Yesterday, today, tomorrow, last night, this morning, in addition to the days of the week, are acceptable time elements.

transition   a word or phrase that tips the reader to a change of subject in a story.

typo   a typographical error.

United Press International   a privately owned news-gathering organization.

up style   capitalizing the first letter of each word (except articles and short prepositions) in a headline.

video display terminal   a television screen connected to a typewriter keyboard on which commands made on the keyboard appear on the screen. Also called a VDT.

wicket   similar to a kicker, it appears at the side of a headline.

wire service symbols and codes   see Chapter 9.

wrap   type that extends around a graphic element is said to wrap. Any display of type around a graphic element, whether in the news columns or in advertisements.

zoned edition   an edition of a newspaper that includes a page or section emphasizing news of a small area within the newspaper's larger circulation area.

APPENDIX D

A Budget for Beginners

Journalism students about to seek their first job usually don't know what constitutes a good salary. One major reason for their ignorance is their lack of understanding of what bills they'll have as they begin life on their own.

To help you, I have prepared a checklist of typical items you will have to budget for. If the job is in a strange city, talk to reporters on the staff about typical expenses so you'll have an idea of what figures to put in the blanks. Try to find a reporter similar to yourself. If you're single and just beginning, talk to a single and fairly recent addition to the staff. Other members of the staff will have different perspectives and may unintentionally provide misleading figures. A typical budget:

rent	mad money
food	minor medical
car payments	dental
car registration expenses	life insurance
car insurance	utilities
gasoline	clothing
college loan repayment	professional memberships
hobby	magazine subscriptions
savings	alumni association
furniture payments	Total (take home pay)
credit card payments	

To the take-home figure, add approximately 25 percent to find out your gross salary. The 25 percent covers Social Security payments and tax deductions, both of which are especially heavy and burdensome on low-income and single people. This budget assumes that the company pays for medical insurance and all contributions to the company pension fund. If it does not, adjust accordingly. Be willing to compromise, but not to starve.

—R. Thomas Berner

INDEX